T0351018

THINK LIKE A TERRORIST TO COMBAT TERRORISM AND RADICALIZATION IN PRISON

Think Like a Terrorist to Combat Terrorism and Radicalization in Prison provides guidelines for hardening facilities, training staff, preparing for radicalized-terrorist inmates' incarceration, and monitoring these inmates after their release. The book combines practitioner experience with scholarly insights to offer practical suggestions bolstered by research. The authors offer suggestions for housing, programming, security, and staff training with the ultimate goal of keeping correctional facilities, staff, and other inmates, safe from radicalization and spreading terrorist doctrines and terrorist acts, which requires examining and potentially changing prison and correctional officer policies and procedures, hiring and training suitable staff, and ensuring technology is available.

Correctional facilities can curtail the recruitment and radicalization of inmates by developing staff training, de-radicalization programs, management methods, techniques, and practices that address the recruitment issues associated with this threat. The need for understanding, and the role line correctional officers and first-line supervisors play in preventing radicalization, is critical in this process. It is also vital to connect with and maintain communication with appropriate security and intelligence agencies as needed.

Key Features:

- Outlines common terrorist and extremist activities in prison using relevant real-world examples
- Instructs on how to detect and recognize such efforts as recruitment and radicalization and how to curtail and prevent such activity
- Provides guidance on establishing de-radicalization programs within prison facilities
- Presents recommendations on collecting, analyzing, and disseminating intelligence to correctional, law-enforcement, and intelligence agencies on potential terrorist activities and recruitment efforts

THINK LIKE A TERRORIST TO COMBAT TERRORISM AND RADICALIZATION IN PRISON

William P. Sturgeon and Francesca Spina

CRC Press is an imprint of the
Taylor & Francis Group, an informa business

Cover design by Xavaier Bolton.

First edition published 2023
by CRC Press
6000 Broken Sound Parkway NW, Suite 300, Boca Raton, FL 33487-2742

and by CRC Press
4 Park Square, Milton Park, Abingdon, Oxon, OX14 4RN

CRC Press is an imprint of Taylor & Francis Group, LLC

ISBN: 978-1-032-25980-2 (hbk)
ISBN: 978-1-032-25979-6 (pbk)
ISBN: 978-1-003-28594-6 (ebk)

DOI: 10.4324/9781003285946

Typeset in Palatino
by MPS Limited, Dehradun

This book is dedicated to the men and women of the criminal justice family. Thank you for the professionalism, dedication, and courage that you demonstrate every day in the performance of your duties!

CONTENTS

ABOUT THE AUTHORS

William "Bill" P. Sturgeon has more than fifty years of experience in the criminal justice field as a practitioner and consultant. He is also an author, teacher/trainer, expert witness, and internationally recognized criminal justice consultant, and the recipient of numerous awards and commendations for his criminal justice work.

Sturgeon has held supervisory and managerial positions in both law enforcement and corrections. He has consulted for the U.S. Department of Justice's National Institute of Corrections, Federal Detention Trustees, and the U.S. House of Representatives on counterterrorism, correctional management, operations, training, gangs/subversive groups, youthful offenders, security operations, and supervision.

Based on his extensive background in special operations training and management, he co-authored two books, *No Time to Play* and *Recess Is Over* and he wrote two chapters for the Civic Research Institute's, *Managing Special Inmate Populations in Prisons and Jails* "Managing Violent Youthful Offenders," in Volume one and "Managing Terrorist Inmates" in Volume two.

He has also consulted abroad in the United Kingdom, the Netherlands, Haiti, South Africa, and the Philippines. Mr. Sturgeon wrote several articles on security operations, management, first-line supervision, emergency planning and management, gangs, training, program development, and evaluation methods.

Mr. Sturgeon has a bachelor of science and master of arts degrees in criminal justice administration and received training in mediation and conflict resolution from the Harvard School of Public Health. He is a decorated Vietnam veteran who served with the 101st Airborne Division.

Dr. Francesca Spina has her Ph.D., Criminal Justice and Criminology, from the University of Massachusetts Lowell. And since 2019, she has served as the chair of the Criminal Justice Department at Springfield College where she is an associate professor of criminal justice.

She co-wrote a book: Boyd, L.M., & F. Spina, (2019). *Massachusetts's Criminal Justice System.* Durham, NC: Carolina Academic Press; and has authored numerous book chapters in several books, many professional journal articles, book reviews, and made a host of professional presentations at conferences, plus authored several web-based publications.

She has achieved the Excellence in Teaching award from the Division of Online and Continuing Education, University of Massachusetts Lowell. She is also the recipient of several grants and fellowships. Her specialty areas include corrections, criminology; gender, race, and crime; and violence in America.

She holds memberships in the American Association of University Professors, the Academy of Criminal Justice Sciences, and the American Society of Criminology.

A NOTE TO THE READER

Everyone associated with the field of corrections should use this opportunity to collaborate, on a worldwide basis, to determine how to manage, deradicalize, and rehabilitate the terrorist-inmate populations—both our homegrown terrorists and those radicalized by foreign groups. What may be Europe's problem today could very easily be an American problem tomorrow. It is vital to know what works in other countries and what has worked here in management, security, operations, philosophies, methods, and techniques.

We hope that readers of this book will learn some new methods and procedures that they can employ and implement before there is a need rather than remedying growing problems.

INTRODUCTION

Just as this manuscript was ready to be sent to the editor, President Biden announced that all American military forces would leave Afghanistan by August 31, 2021, changing the counterterrorism landscape! Then, on August 26, 2021, thirteen American Marines, one Army, and one Navy corpsman were killed after a terrorist attack on the Kabul airport in Afghanistan. As a nation and as a world, we will see what these events will mean to the growth of terrorism and the increase in the number of terrorists, including those who end up in our jails and prisons.

Sturgeon originally started to write this book less than a year after September 11, 2001 and later reached out to Dr. Francisca Spina, Ph.D., a person whom he has known for many years. Sturgeon has been a guest lecturer for Dr. Spina's criminal justice class at Springfield College. Sturgeon and Dr. Spina have discussed how to bridge the gap between scholarly research and practical applications, so when the time came to write the book, it only made sense to ask Dr. Spina to be co-author and link their two strengths.

The authors both believed based on Dr. Spina's research and Sturgeon's boots on the ground that correctional agencies would eventually receive extremist terrorists as inmates. As we continued to follow terrorist events worldwide, Europe saw an increase in terror-related crimes. Because Sturgeon's career required him to travel to various foreign countries through 2015, he experienced, first-hand, how other countries attempted to deal with the growth of terrorism and extremists who committed violent terrorist acts.

In the 1980s, Sturgeon worked with an international team on a classified counterterrorism project concentrating on physical security, security policy/procedure development, and security training. The project was intense because of the importance of the areas being assessed, the scope of the project, and the complexity of the counterterrorism plan that had to be developed. One of the many takeaways from this experience was his appreciation that others had more recent, real-life experience dealing with terrorists than the United

States did then. Additionally, he also realized that correctional operations were not keeping up while law enforcement was adapting their policies, procedures, and training initiatives.

The extremist world has continued to morph and grow. New groups arose in the United States and around the world. Various ideologies emerged, including religious/interreligious, political, ethnic, racial, pro-government and anti-government, hate-based groups. Our emphasis on foreign terrorists must now extend to many of those groups monitored by The Southern Poverty Law Center—more than 1,600 domestic hate groups and other extremists—including the Ku Klux Klan, White nationalists, the neo-Nazi movement, anti-government militias, and others on the far-right "Patriot" movement (Extremist Files, Southern Poverty Law Center, accessed September 15, 2021).

This issue is complicated by the "The presence of off-duty officers, firefighters and corrections officers from other agencies around the country in the protest crowd [on January 6, 2021]. [It] was a reminder of how members of a lawless movement have been able to find a place in their ranks" (Wilson, 2021).

> For years, domestic terrorism researchers have warned that there are police departments in every region of America counting white supremacist extremists and neo-Nazi sympathizers among their ranks. To these experts and the activists law enforcement officers have targeted in past years, it was no surprise that police officers were part of the mob that stormed the US Capitol on January 6. The acceptance of far-right beliefs among law enforcement, they say, helped lay the groundwork for the extraordinary attacks in the American capital. (Levin, 2021)

Before this attack, the United States and most industrialized nations were focused on extremist terrorists emanating from the Middle East, with some real justification caused by activities in Syria, Iraq, and the migration into the African continent and Europe. More than 300 people have tried to leave the United States to join al-Qaeda, then the extremely violent ISIS (Myre, 2018).

Simultaneously, as these foreign extremist-terrorist groups were growing in size, expanding their territories, and recruiting, many domestic groups (ranging from far right to far left) were doing the same, as documented on the Southern Poverty Law Center website (Extremist Files, Southern Poverty Law Center). Most of these groups became adept at using the internet for recruiting and maintaining communications. Another advantage of using the internet was to reduce in-person meetings that could arouse authorities' suspicion.

While correctional facilities have well-established processes to classify, house, operate, manage, secure, and rehabilitate inmates, such policies and procedures may not be suitable for violent extremist terrorist inmates because these inmates are not individuals who had just committed crimes; they committed crimes in pursuit of their ideology, their belief system, and their extremist objectives.

The introduction of extremist terrorists into prisons is reminiscent of "prison gangs" formally organizing, gaining positions of power, and introducing youthful offenders (adjudicated juveniles) to adult corrections. There is, however, one exception: "prison gangs" were composed of criminals first and gang members second. Belonging to a "prison gang" was a "situation of convenience" while incarcerated. If a "prison gang" had an ideology, it was not the driving force behind its existence.

This book is intended for audiences across the world, who can modify the suggestions and recommendations in this book to fit the needs of the prison system in their country and the legal and philosophical needs of various ethnic and religiously diverse inmates. The authors recognize that prison regimes and inmate cultures differ, and prison leadership must be aware of these differences and factor them into their plans.

The authors believe in the principles of reform, and realize that both Guantanamo and Abu Ghraib have boosted Muslim resentment, and strongly urge prison leaders to allow prisoners their rights but to be aware of potential problems, and to design systems for dealing with these issues *before* they arise so that there will be no extraordinary renditions or the lack of proper judicial procedures.

If the staff of correctional facilities is not prepared, then extremist-terrorist inmates will initially have the upper hand. Our experience demonstrates that when new inmate populations with unique issues, skills, and ideologies enter a correctional facility, the staff has a learning curve. For example: when inmates with HIV-AIDS began to enter correctional facilities, staff had to receive specialized training on interacting with the population.

If correctional staff can receive specialized training before introducing a significant number of extremist-terrorist inmates, this will assist the staff in interrupting the terrorist inmates' ability to spread their ideology throughout the facility. Adding to this international terrorist threat are the growing realizations of the existence of domestic terrorists, some of whom were present at the January 6, 2021 attack on our nation's capital, which challenged the precepts of our democracy.

Some domestic terrorists belong to the active right-wing and are hostile to traditional laws, customs, races, and religions. We will discuss some of these right-wing groups later in this book. The internet, however, gives access to individuals, referred to as the "Lone Wolf," who foster and harbor right-wing beliefs. The internet is often the sole source for recruiting lone wolves to radicalization and is a way to maintain their anonymity.

Jails and prisons must be prepared for the introduction of extremist terrorists and other extremists. In most cases, initially, they will be booked and detained in local jails, but then they will be housed in state and federal prisons. After serving their sentence, they will be supervised by probation or parole agencies when they leave the facility. All through the various stages, the goal should be to manage extremist-terrorist inmates and other extremist groups under the constraints of proper inmate management, laws, and standards, so that they cannot spread their ideology and recruit others in the facility and later in the outside world. The goal is to serve their sentences peacefully without violence toward other inmates or staff and leave the facility as peaceful individuals without a terrorist agenda.

Those who say radical incidents can't happen here at my facility may become victims of such a terrorist attack. "In 2019, 149 suicide bombings were carried out in 24 countries by 236 suicide bombers, among them 22 women. In these suicide bombings, 1,850 people were killed, and 3,660 were wounded" (Schweitzer, Mendelboim, & Ayalon, 2020). While this number of suicide bombings is down from 469 suicide bombings across the globe in 2016 (Schweitzer, Mendelboim, & Rosner, 2017), the Islamic States of Iraq and Syria (ISIS) are still the leading perpetrators of suicide bombers.

The ultimate horror for correctional staff might be the October 20, 2020, ISIS attack on a Congo jail that allowed 1,300 prisoners to escape (Ives & Kwai, 2020). This book is to help prevent such an attack from coming to your facility.

Even if your facility is spared, you may be housing extremist-terrorist inmates and other extremist groups who can spread their radical agenda to other inmates and the public. We discuss prisons conducive to radicalization conditions, providing some details for prison administrators and other staffers to show them how this process works and discuss how to implement effective strategies combating radicalization and potential terrorist attacks in the facility and after release.

This book's major aim is to demonstrate to lawmakers, politicians, correctional administrators, sheriffs, managers, first-line supervisors, line staff, and the public—how difficult these extremist-terrorist populations can be to manage, but how vitally important it is to do so! This extremist-inmate population brings with them new challenges, requiring new correctional solutions. The authors are confident that this book is only the first step in developing strategies to manage and hopefully deradicalize this unique inmate population.

TOPICS DISCUSSED

Some of the major areas discussed in this book include what the correctional community can do to keep staff, inmates, and the public safe while combating the growth of extremist-terrorist inmates.

- Eliminate, as much as possible, the extremist-terrorist inmates' ability to recruit new members.
- Expand the security-operations paradigm.
- Develop training programs to address the changing inmate populations and the issues associated with these populations.
- Establish deradicalization programs within the facility.
- Ensure that only approved religious materials are permitted within the facility.
- Permit only approved imams and other religious leaders to conduct formal religious services.
- Collect, analyze, and disseminate intelligence to other correctional agencies, law-enforcement agencies, and intelligence agencies.

The authors describe how to evaluate the "problem" of inmate radicalization to stop its escalation, including knowing the following information:

- Knowing if the number of extremist-terrorist inmates and other extremist groups in your facility is increasing, and at what rate and what groups are growing?
- Analyzing whether these increases have a direct effect on housing, security, staffing, and operations?
- Knowing who is in your facility? What groups compose the extremist-terrorist inmates and other extremist groups you

house, such as White supremacists/right-wing groups, Antifa/ left-wing groups, Middle-Eastern-based inmates, and Mexican drug cartels?

- How are the extremist-terrorist inmates in your facility adjusting to prison life? You can get a good read on this by reviewing all incident and disciplinary reports to determine the nature of their offenses and the level of their violence. Are there any injuries to staff or inmate/s, and what provoked the incident/s? What action/s did the staff take?

These answers should also play into the training programs that you have or are developing. Further details are in Chapter 8 on training, which is of utmost importance in keeping a safe facility.

If you are currently working in a facility, examine how extremist-terrorist inmates and other extremist groups influence your correctional facility's management, operations, training, and security, which will require reviewing the incident and disciplinary reports and conducting interviews with staff, including administrators, non-security personnel, first-line supervisors, and frontline staff who interact with the extremist-terrorist inmates.

Be aware of how the extremist-terrorist inmates and other extremist groups influence the other inmates they meet during their day. If you do not currently house any extremist-terrorists or other terrorist group members, use this time to prepare for the eventuality you may, as the number of such terrorists is growing in U.S. prisons (Jones, Doxsee, & Harrington, 2020).

Document or conceptualize what methods and techniques extremist-terrorist inmates and other extremist groups use or could use to attract recruits to their ideology. The importance of intelligence-gathering, analyzing, and disseminating such information will help identify recruiting methods and techniques that extremist-terrorist inmates and other extremist groups use to recruit new brothers and sisters. While the number of women terrorists is far less than male terrorists, don't discount the influence of women terrorists.

Are there any incidents of recruitment or violence from members of these terrorist groups?

- Has the staff become targeted?
- Has the facility become a target?
- Have other challenges surfaced that could be new to the correctional world?

One thing is certain: more research is needed. From that research, correctional experts will develop programs and make operational adjustments to help manage extremist-terrorist inmates and other extremist groups to reduce the number of incarcerated inmates radicalized in correctional facilities. Also, program administrators and government officials will need to develop programs to deradicalize those who have become radicalized, including programs for those leaving the facility on probation or parole. Such programs would be in addition to those developed to enhance operations, security, and staff training.

The authors believe that correctional facilities can curtail the recruitment and radicalization of inmates by developing staff training, deradicalization programs, management methods, techniques, and practices that address the recruitment issues associated with this unique population, and thus, much of this book is devoted to these concerns.

The role of line correctional officers and first-line supervisors is critical. They are the "boots on the ground"—the eyes and ears of every correctional facility. They need to be well trained in intelligence gathering, observation skills, report writing, situational awareness, personal safety, and management techniques for handling extremist-terrorist inmates, which is discussed throughout the book, especially in Chapter 8 and Appendix 2.

Most of this book is a primer to assist correctional agencies worldwide in developing strategies, methods, and techniques for managing the changing face of correctional facilities that house extremist terrorists. While correctional facilities have always had some violent inmates, anecdotal evidence indicates that violence in jails and prisons worldwide is escalating.

Eleven correctional officers were injured this past week from multiple inmate attacks at Rikers Island Davoren Complex in New York, the *New York Daily News* reported. According to an internal incident report, these gang members gave officers broken ribs, concussions, and other injuries (Lonas, 2021).

Academics, judges, law enforcement, and the general public need to be aware of the difficulties associated with incarcerating these groups who will not hesitate to use violence on prison staff, criminal inmates, and rival groups.

Now, correctional practitioners can develop management methods and practices *before* being overrun by an inmate population different from traditional inmates. The number of extremist-terrorist inmates, while growing daily, is still manageable in United States' facilities, but this is not true in Europe and the Middle East. Additionally, there are groups of right-wing White Supremacy members, cartels, and other violent groups already incarcerated in American and other correctional facilities. From prior experience, we believe that White Supremacy Groups have been and will continue to be invigorated by the violence occurring in American cities over the past couple of years.

On January 6, 2021, Americans got a wake-up call when the United States Capitol Building's external and internal security perimeters were breached by a mob of right-wing terrorists mixed in with anarchists. What was supposed to have been one of the most secure buildings in the United States was successfully compromised in a very short period with only one shot being fired. What could they do to your facility or those in your community if they could break into such a secure facility?

1

Extremist-Terrorist Inmates and Others

"Terrorists are those who support or commit ideologically motivated violence to further political, social, or religious goals." (Quershi, 2020)

The extremist-terrorist inmate population has continued to grow and change since September 11, 2001. On that date, the world changed because al-Qaeda, with the blessing of its leader Osama bin Laden, attacked the World Trade Center in New York City, the Pentagon in Washington, D.C., and had plans for a plane headed for Washington, D.C., which crashed in a field in Shanksville, Pennsylvania. From then on, the world of extremist groups, foreign and domestic, has grown, splintered, and aligned around political, religious, ethnic, and radical and right- and left-wing causes.

Extremists of all descriptions are a global concern for correctional agencies and politicians, law enforcement, governments, intelligence agencies, and religious groups. These extremists and terrorist groups look for "soft targets" worldwide. They attack these "soft targets" because their risks are slight, and they can do significant damage to the target, gaining them media coverage. "Soft Targets and Crowded Places (ST-CPs), such as sports venues, shopping venues, schools, and transportation systems, are locations easily accessible to large numbers of people and have limited security or protective measures in place, making them vulnerable to attack" (U.S. Department of Homeland

DOI: 10.4324/9781003285946-1

Security, 2018). The Cybersecurity and Infrastructure Security Agency's *Security of Soft Targets and Crowded Places Resource Guide* (2019) offers concrete suggestions and would be a useful resource for correctional staff.

Many correctional facilities could also be classified as "soft targets" because most correctional security operations are devoted to observing, preventing, controlling, and reacting to situations that arise within the secure perimeter, Sturgeon claims based on his domestic and international experience. The paradigm of the administrations and staff of correctional agencies/facilities must change to a more global-security approach. Correctional facilities, police stations, courthouses, and other areas represent the "established government," making them targets (Gettys, 2021).

Correctional administrators should begin a process to extend the facility's security to incorporate a 360-degree posture and "harden" the facility where needed to dissuade would-be attackers. We discuss 360-degree security and facility hardening later in this book.

The fear of being attacked by extremist terrorists or other extremist groups appears remote to most Americans. As someone remarked to one of the authors, "I am more likely to get hit by lightning than be a victim of an extremist-terrorist attack." Unfortunately, that was the same thinking many Americans had before September 11, 2001. While law enforcement and intelligence agencies have prevented several extremist-terrorist attacks, other attacks have been successful. At least 843 terrorist plots against the United States occurred from 1994 to May 2020 (Jones, Doxsee, & Harrington, 2020). Many of these are homegrown terrorist plots (Bucci, Carafano, & Zuckerman, 2013).

Now, however, extremist-terrorist groups contain both foreign and domestic extremists. These groups riot, assault police, assault other people who do not adhere to their belief system or ideological views, burn down buildings, and attack federal buildings and police stations. We can and should identify the individuals belonging to these groups as domestic-extremist terrorists. The FBI (n.d.) lists the following categories of domestic terrorists: members of the Sovereign nation, White supremacists, animal rights and environmental extremists, anarchists, militia, and abortion extremists.

PROTESTS

Peaceful protest is legal and a guaranteed constitutional right in the United States. After all, where would we be today if American patriots did not dump English tea into the Boston harbor? However, we are not talking about those who protest peacefully but those whose actions lead to illegal acts for which these people are arrested, jailed, and then imprisoned. Note that not all terrorists are foreign-born. As correctional professionals, we have to be aware of the power of terrorists and extremists of all persuasions in our facilities. Not giving domestic or foreign extremist terrorists enough credit may harm staff, other inmates, the physical facility, and lead to the widespread dissemination of their terrorist doctrines.

CONSTITUTIONALITY

Many legal complications arise from managing terrorist-extremist inmates, and prison officials must ensure that they do not infringe upon these inmates' constitutional rights. Prison and jail administrators should check with their legal department to ensure they do not violate extremist terrorists and other extremist groups' rights. Doing so could have repercussions, resulting in costly lawsuits and further enflaming the terrorist agendas. According to the United Nations, efforts to address violent extremism cannot undermine fundamental human rights. Additionally, international human rights law prevents torture and the inhumane or degrading treatment of all prisoners, including terrorists (Bryans, 2016).

Consequently, staff must be taught to treat terrorist-extremist inmates and other extremist groups professionally and respectfully and not violate their human rights (Turner & Wetzel, 2014). If correctional personnel treat these inmates respectfully, they will be less apt to cause disturbances or disorders within prisons (Bryans, 2016). Similarly, it is crucial to avoid situations in which terrorist-extremist inmates claim discrimination, mistreatment, or torture. This type of behavior can result in negative publicity, protests, or hunger strikes (Atherton & Jurisic, 2015). People on the outside take an increased interest in politically motivated prisoners. So, it is imperative to minimize any mistreatment that could lead to grievances, attract negative publicity for the government, or help the terrorists gain momentum for their cause.

Also, people are entitled to adopt the religious beliefs of their choosing. In countries such as the United States, constitutional practices make it harder for prisons to challenge inmates' religious beliefs. Moreover, religion is a way for inmates to cope with their sentences, and most inmates use religion constructively. Faith can help them reflect on the crimes they committed, and it can play a positive role in their adjustment to life behind bars. However, international law restricts religious beliefs that pose a security risk to the public. Also, United Nations' members prohibit the promotion of national or religious hatred that encourages discrimination or violence (Bryans, 2016).

When restricting terrorist-extremist inmates' rights, administrators must indicate *why* they limit these rights (Marchese, 2009). They must stress that restrictions are in place to protect other inmates, staff, and the public. For example, if terrorist-extremist inmates and other groups cannot attend religious services together, the administrator must specify that a greater possibility for disturbances or an increased risk of violence may occur if they attend the same services. Since inmates have a constitutional right to attend services, a solution is to offer separate services. Because these inmates pose a greater security risk, correctional administrators must ensure that they do not threaten others based on religious beliefs and extremist ideologies.

ROLE OF JAILS

An inmate's first introduction to the corrections system is often through a police station lockup or a county jail. County jails are especially vulnerable because, for the first several hours after an arrest, the staff cannot be sure of who they have in custody and are unsure if an inmate has co-conspirators. Given the behavior of individuals who belong to extremist groups in the "free world," correctional officials should be prepared to manage such extremist inmates from the minute they enter correctional facilities.

All facilities that confine such inmates must have policies and procedures to prevent extremist inmates and other extremist groups from assaulting staff, other inmates and damaging the facility. (See Chapter 5 on examining policies and procedures.) The initial contact period with extremist-terrorist detainees may leave correctional officials uncertain and confused, permitting extremist terrorists and other extremist groups to take advantage of untrained jail staff. Post-arraignment, extremist terrorists and other extremist groups can be held in county jails before and during their trials. Of course, when these inmates are transferred to prisons, the same cautions are necessary.

The very presence of extremist-terrorists and detainees should trigger an increase in security precautions and staffing. Correctional administrators and staff must use extreme caution when interacting with extremist detainees. Remember that these inmates have assaulted law enforcement personnel with various weapons and will commit arson and damage to property given the opportunity.

County jails, local sheriffs' departments, and police are the first lines of defense in protecting their local communities from terrorist-extremist attacks. These officers are first on the scene and make the arrest/s. Police will take these suspected extremist terrorists to the county jail for booking. At this point, the law enforcement personnel and the correctional staff may not know who they have in custody. However, the exception: a "lone wolf," who could already be known to local authorities.

Why should correctional personnel, who work in local jails, care if their jail houses extremist-terrorist inmates—either domestic or foreign? The public often thinks that once such terrorists are incarcerated, they have nothing left to worry about. Nothing could be further from the truth. Extremist-terrorist inmates and other extremist groups spend their time spreading their belief systems and recruiting new brothers and sisters to their cause. They spread the doctrines of their ideology to other criminal inmates, and the violence they advocate upsets the places where they are confined, including other inmates and the staff. As these newly influenced inmates become radicalized, they then become spreaders of their ideology. As the Chinese philosopher Lao Tzu told us, "There is no greater danger than underestimating your opponent."

VIOLENCE OF EXTREMISTS

Correctional personnel should be aware that extremist-terrorist inmates and radical groups will use violence during their confinement and may use violence when released unless they have received appropriate deradicalization programming and other rehabilitation programs. Some extremist terrorists, who were ISIS fighters, are very adept and accustomed to using violence and have turned to the Internet to communicate with each other, use technological methods/tactics that sanction the use of violence, to include and recruit lone wolf believers to their ideology.

> Internet use is limited and monitored in federal facilities and may be limited or prohibited in most state or local facilities. The Federal Bureau of Prisons has tried to address the growing problem of cell phones in the hands of incarcerated inmates. In the event you do not know, cell phones and iPads (Microsoft Surface MSFT +0.2%) are illegal in federal prisons. However, they are everywhere in prisons across the country. (Pavlo, 2020)

Inmates' visitors have access to the Internet, and they can inform the inmates about what is happening and links with terrorist groups. For these reasons and many others, visitors' conversations with extremist-terrorist inmates should be monitored/recorded, as we discuss later.

We still have much to learn about how these foreign extremist-terrorist inmates operate. As for domestic extremist groups, correctional officials/intelligence units working in concert with local law enforcement and the local Joint Terrorism Task Force and others can share information beneficial to everyone.

We know that staff training, day-to-day procedures, and emergency operations impact the overall security of correctional facilities worldwide. This book suggests examining such procedures and training to best cope with this new population of inmates. In a few years, we will revisit this topic, examining how the methods of handling the extremist-terrorist inmates and other extremist groups have worked in prisons and jails, especially in dealing with security, management, operations, and training.

The authors' goals for this book are to encourage and assist correctional professionals in taking proactive steps, developing appropriate management methods and techniques, and making operational adjustments to supervise this new, unique inmate population.

Incarcerated extremist terrorists actively recruit new believers/followers/brothers/soldiers and sisters to their groups' religion and ideology. Chapter 12 details the recruiting worldwide in correctional facilities, and it would be naïve to believe that it can't happen in the United States.

The authors hope that readers of this book, whether correctional practitioners, intelligence professionals, judges, prosecutors, scholars, politicians, or the general public, will understand how challenging, dangerous, and widespread the extremist-terrorist inmate population can be to correctional security and operations worldwide. Assuming that these extremist-terrorist inmates, including the right-wing terrorists, are just another group of difficult inmates who cling to an ideology that justifies their actions as acts of their faith is a serious and dangerous error.

The authors believe that extremist-terrorist inmates and other extremist groups will increase as the various extremist groups evolve without and within correctional facilities worldwide. The authors want correctional staff to be prepared and not to be caught without adequate plans and preparation.

One of the authors (William (Bill) Sturgeon), who saw the rise of prison gangs during the seventies and eighties, was assured that "we have everything under control" by several experienced correctional administrators and supervisors. Of course, the reality was otherwise. Similarly, he is again warning that the correctional professionals must be prepared for this new population of inmates. The authors show how to train staff to interrupt the spread of radicalism within and outside the facility, secure the perimeter and the rest of the facility, and prepare terrorist inmates to leave the facility after their sentence is done. As this terrorist population increases, they will present new and difficult challenges for the entire criminal justice community. By paying attention to the problem now, you will have a better handle on it when it comes to your facility.

Extremist-terrorist inmates and other extremist groups demonstrate daily that many traditional correctional methods and practices do not work with them. Methods and practices mentioned in this book will evolve as the field becomes more proficient at managing these inmate populations. The authors employ a phrase when conducting counterterrorism seminars/classes—"We don't know what we don't know." Be alert to the many unknowns of managing this inmate population.

Bill Sturgeon shares his professional knowledge, drawing on his experience in corrections and with gangs and counterterrorism. In contrast, Dr. Francesca Spina's research abilities have helped develop a book that considers research and scholarly endeavors. The two authors believe that there is value in incorporating both the practical and the research.

Because the authors approached this topic from both a practitioner's perspective and a scholar's research, the authors had different opinions. These differences often parallel debates between researchers and practitioners at all levels. They offer readers an opportunity to get ahead of the curve, be ready to handle such inmates, and keep their facility safe. Both the practitioner and the researcher offer dynamic ways to get the best results for handling this difficult population. Such a dual approach means that this book may be suitable for police and correctional academies and college courses in corrections and criminology.

Sturgeon believes that while others conduct the research, develop the statistics, and formulate theories and other ideas—the practitioners must manage, in real-time, these extremist-terrorist inmate populations daily. The authors are very aware that this book is the beginning of volumes to be written about the dynamics of managing terrorist-extremist inmates and other extremist groups.

It Was Inevitable

Sturgeon began collecting information about extremist terrorists shortly after the World Trade Center bombing (February 26, 1993). After spending many years in criminal justice, law enforcement, and corrections, Sturgeon realized that eventually America and other nations' correctional facilities would have to deal with a new type of inmate—the terrorist and this extremist-terrorist inmate population would significantly differ from other inmate classifications. The foreign extremist-terrorist inmates believed in and followed an ideology, a belief system integral to their daily lives. They would follow this ideology even if it meant dying. As a part of this ideology/belief system, the afterlife will be the greatest reward.

"Muslim self-justification of suicide bombing lies in the interpretation of jihad. While Western scholars of late argue that jihad refers primarily to internal struggle, Islamic writings feature jihad as physical warfare" (Bukay, 2006a, 2006b). Historian Bernard Lewis finds that most "classical theologians, jurists, and traditionalists ... understood the obligation of jihad in a military sense" (Bukay, 2006c).

Sturgeon's first experience working on a designated counterterrorism project was in the mid-1980s. His specific tasks were to develop physical security plans, policies, procedures, and protocols for a series of highly vulnerable buildings and training curricula for security personnel to meet the emerging terrorist threat. As the newest member of an international counterterrorism team with significant counterterrorism experience, he brought an extensive background in staff training and physical security.

One of Sturgeon's counterterrorism project leaders was the "Brigadier," who had more than twenty years of experience in counterterrorism and securing high-profile buildings with high-profile people in them. The Brigader had amazing insight into how terrorists thought. He told the team many times: "To defeat a terrorist, you must think like a terrorist, "which is why we named our book: *Think Like a Terrorist to Combat Terrorism and Radicalization in Prison*.

After the eight-month project, the team went their separate ways. Sturgeon continued to work with his American counterparts on other domestic and international projects. What became increasingly obvious was that law enforcement agencies and correctional systems, globally, did not have a real understanding of how committed these extremist-terrorist inmates and other extremist groups were and how their commitment affected their operations.

What Sturgeon learned on the job was invaluable—extremist terrorists view life and death very differently than other people. They are "true believers" in their faith and their causes. Correctional personnel, academics, law enforcement, politicians, and the public must understand how extremist terrorists think. What we consider so brutal and uncalled for, the extremist terrorists accept as fulfilling their faith-inspired mission.

For example, journalist Daniel Pearl was beheaded in 2002 by extremist terrorists:

> Danny is without his glasses in the footage, with a few days' stubble. He professes his Jewish heritage and criticizes the alliance between the United States and Israel—obviously reading from a script—as the sound of exploding mortars blasts in the background. Suddenly Danny is on his back and a hand holding a long knife saws furiously at his throat. The next frame comes quickly—the video has obviously been edited—and shows Danny supine, a bloody swamp in place of his neck. The film cuts to the killer holding Danny's head up high by his hair for a good ten seconds. (Nomani, n.d.)

As an aside, Daniel Pearl worked for Sturgeon's local newspaper, *The Berkshire Eagle*. While Sturgeon didn't know him personally, he enjoyed reading his articles.

These terrorist groups think much differently than most of us do about life, death, and devotion to their religion/cause. Extremist terrorists, both foreign and domestic, are at the extreme fringe of their religions, and extremist-terrorist criminal activities are the outward manifestations of their ideology and beliefs. The extremist terrorists do not view these criminal activities as crimes. They believe that their criminal activities are part of a holy war. If you do not believe in what they believe in, it is permissible for them to kill you.

In a publication for the Department of Justice, de Armond (1999) said that,

> Domestic terrorists of the American far right are driven by zeal for heretical distortions of Christian theology. These include millenialism, which envisions the imminent end of the age and the advent of a new dispensation; post-millenialism, which holds that Christ's return will not come until after the battle of Armageddon ushers in a 1,000-year global dominion by victorious 'true Christians'; and antinomianism, under which believers follow a 'higher law' and intentionally violate societal norms. These zealots view themselves as actors in God's plan for a cataclysmic overturning of the current order.
>
> At the deepest level, these are actors who deploy weapons of mass destruction in a sacrificial ritual of mass murder and suicide, a magical act intended to alter the relationship between God and mankind. These groups include Klan/neo-Nazi groups, anti-abortion groups, the 'Patriot' group, and the 'Wise Use' sect. These terrorist actors are well-informed about policy initiatives, responsive to new policy, organized as flexible decentralized networks, able to respond faster than institutions, and creative and effective propagandists. The most likely forms of WMD threats from these groups are conventional explosives, toxins, industrial chemicals, nuclear materials as radiation sources and toxins, and crude biological weapons. (de Armond, 1999)

"Much like al-Qaeda and the Islamic State, violent right-wing extremists—who refer to themselves as 'Soldiers of Odin,' 'Phineas Priests,' or 'Holy Warriors'—are also inspired by religious concepts and scriptural interpretations to lash out and kill in the name of religion" (Johnson, 2018).

On September 11, 2001, deadly extremist-terrorism came to the United States, and thousands died. This attack validated everything Sturgeon had learned from the Brigadier and other members of the team. The 9/11 attacks reinforced Sturgeon's belief that extremist-terrorist inmates and other extremist groups would constitute a new inmate population with different operational, management, security, religious, and programming needs. The authors believe that it is a serious mistake not to understand the ideology of this new breed of inmates. Knowing the extremist-terrorist inmates' mindsets and adherence to religious beliefs will assist correctional personnel in program development for this inmate population, including their housing, classification, and security interactions.

The radicals' Islamic ideology is a belief system based on an extreme interpretation of Islam. Their belief system is so strong that many who accept it are willing to die for it and anyone who does not accept and adhere to it is the enemy, and it is permissible to kill them.

Further, in this book (Appendix 1 and in other places), we share information from an *al-Qaeda Training Manual* seized during a raid in Manchester, the U.K., that instructs extremist-terrorist inmates and other extremist groups in how to conduct themselves while incarcerated or while they are transported, or in a courtroom. This information is valuable because it demonstrates that the extremist-terrorist inmate population has been prepared to be incarcerated and use the system while confined within it. Because the field of corrections is so regimented and routines are predictable, it gives the extremist-terrorist inmates and other extremist groups a heads-up on how correctional facilities operate. With this knowledge, they can do considerable harm.

In Sturgeon's many years of working in the criminal justice system, he rarely interacted with criminals whose belief system was so strong that they would die for their crimes. As police arrest more people who adhere to extreme ideologies for crimes that fall under the categories of terrorism or terrorism-related offenses, we must focus intensely on how this unique inmate population will affect the training, operations (security/programs), and intelligence gathering in police programs and correctional agencies worldwide.

Sturgeon and Spina have worked in the field of criminal justice for most of their lives. They and their colleagues experienced the HIV/AIDS epidemic, bird flu, swine flu, increasing numbers of youthful offenders (adjudicated juveniles sentenced as adults to adult correctional facilities), COVID-19, and prison growth and gang dominance.

Sturgeon recalled the most dramatic evolution of organized prison gangs. Before the field fully comprehended the threat of prison gangs, they gained a foothold and became a dominant force within correctional facilities. Throughout his career, Sturgeon has seen prison gangs evolve from a few inmates who were bullies or belonged to street gangs or knew each other "from the neighborhood" before being incarcerated. Once incarcerated, these prison gangs attracted criminal inmates.

When Sturgeon started in corrections many years ago, the correctional operational paradigm was rigid and inflexible with the false belief that "everything is under control." Sturgeon's personal belief is that this rigidity, inflexibility, and the false belief that "everything was under control—when it was not under control" contributed to the riots of the seventies and eighties and the expansion of prison gangs.

Staff training became stagnant and ineffective, and complacency became more widespread. The old rigidity, inflexibility, and the belief that "everything was under control" were outpaced by the dynamics of the new breed of inmates coming through the gates. These new inmates included the youths protesting the Vietnam War.

Sturgeon refers to "convicts" as those who knew how to play the correctional game and get along while incarcerated. This new breed, referred to as "inmate," did not play the game; rather, they questioned everything. "WHY" was their favorite word. Sturgeon mentioned to a shift captain that he thought a group of inmates was forming a gang. The captain's response was, "Don't worry about it; we've got everything under control." Everything wasn't under control.

Both practitioners and researchers realize that any correctional facility's overall conditions will directly influence the entire inmate population. "Prisons may also provide a unique opportunity for authorities, drawing on global best practice, to counter the efforts of violent extremists to radicalize and recruit new members" (Commonwealth, n.d.). Moreover, "over-crowding and under-staffing amplify the conditions that lend themselves to radicalization" (Neumann, 2010). As such, "the first and most important recommendation is to improve general conditions, avoid overcrowding, train staff, and provide meaningful programming that allows prisoners to develop stable inmate identities" (Wilson, 2011).

While some academicians believe that the degree of radicalization in American prisons is minimal, Sturgeon cautions them not to underestimate what a few dedicated inmates with a strong leader can accomplish. Sturgeon recalls the explosion of prison gangs in the seventies and points out that many researchers doubted these gangs' influence, much to their chagrin. Correctional facilities have long been breeding grounds for all types of criminals and other forms of antisocial behaviors.

> Jihadist and criminal groups are recruiting from the same pool of people, while their social networks are also converging, the International Centre for the Study of Radicalisation and Political Violence (ICSR) found what it dubbed a 'new crime-terror nexus.' (Basra, Neumann, & Brunner, 2016)

Adding to the concern of how these extremist-terrorist inmates and other extremist groups will manifest themselves while incarcerated is whether they will add to the increased incidents of violence against staff and other inmates. "The twenty-seven-year-old inmate, considered a 'radicalized' Islamist, attacked prison staff while shouting 'Allahu Akhbar' (God is Greatest), prison staff representative Alassanne Sall told AFP" (Radicalised Prisoner, 2019).

In another incident,

> Unconfirmed reports say the woman [a co-conspirator] called for help from two guards, and then the pair launched their attack, described by Ms. Bellobet as a 'terrorist' incident. Both guards were seriously wounded, one with injuries to the thorax, the other to his face, colleagues said. (BBC News, 2019)

Like any other organization, correctional facilities can succumb to voids in management, organizational structure, training, security, and operations. Of all the phrases, excuses, and reasons for not making a change that Sturgeon hears at the facilities he has visited, the most common is "Because we have always done it that way." Throughout this book, the authors continually reinforce the need to ensure no managerial voids exist in correctional facilities. Correctional personnel have experienced managerial voids in the past, and once formed, they are difficult to eliminate.

Practitioners and researchers know that radicalization is occurring in correctional facilities around the world. "Numerous violent extremists and terrorists have been radicalized in prisons" (Speckhard, 2019).

The correctional staff faces various subgroups: White supremacists, prison gangs, political extremists, and extremist religious groups. Now, inmate recruiters are recruiting criminal inmates into radical-extremist ideological groups.

> The United States faces a growing terrorism problem that will likely worsen over the next year. Based on the Center for Strategic and International Studies (CSIS) data set of terrorist incidents, the most significant threat likely comes from White supremacists, though anarchists and religious extremists inspired by the Islamic State and al-Qaeda could present a potential threat as well. Over the rest of 2020, the terrorist threat in the United States will likely rise based on several factors. (Jones, Doxsee, & Harrington, 2020)

Based on this reality of radicalization, the correctional staff and their leaders (including politicians in charge of funding allocations for corrections) must address many issues that include the following:

1. Determine how prevalent radicalization is within specific correctional facilities.
2. Control the potential for radicalization to metastasize within correctional facilities.
3. Learn what correctional administrators can do to *curtail* radicalization within their facilities and then do it—even with budget limits and staff shortages.
4. Develop training programs for staff on how to recognize when radicalization is occurring and how to react when it occurs.
5. Establish deradicalization programs—even before there is a need for them.

Sturgeon intentionally uses the word "curtail" rather than "stop" because he is a realist who believes, because of his "real-world" experience, that someone always will be trying to recruit inmates for nefarious reasons.

The question remains: how many of these radicalized inmates who leave correctional facilities will remain extremist terrorists who commit terrorist acts or domestic extremists who will return to their groups' illegal activities? Several documented cases of radicalized inmates committing acts of terrorism upon their release from correctional facilities exist here and worldwide. The question for corrections is: What can be done to prevent this?

> 'Lots of my clients were radicalized in prison,' said Dominique May, a defense lawyer involved in the 2005 case in which Kouachi and others were convicted of attempting to go to Iraq to wage jihad. (Birnbaum, 2015)

Correctional operations worldwide are developing and implementing new management, operations, security, training, and programming strategies. Correctional agencies should determine the best methods and techniques to use in their day-to-day interactions with extremist-terrorist inmates. The authors believe that correctional facilities will have to develop new policies or adapt policies, methods, practices, procedures, staffing patterns, intelligence gathering techniques, and staff training initiatives to manage extremist-terrorist inmates and other extremist groups securely. This book offers guidance on doing that.

Some may criticize the authors for overstating the potential numbers and impact of foreign extremist-terrorist inmates. Correctional administrators need to pay close attention to the domestic extremists who appear to gain power and followers. The day will come when they will influence prison operations. As a practitioner, Sturgeon has experienced how one inmate can change the chemistry of an inmate's living area and gain followers.

RIGHT-WING EXTREMISTS VERSUS TERRORISTS

Some believe that with the defeat of ISIS and the loss of the caliphate, terrorism will be less of a problem than White supremacist extremists. Evidence shows that extreme right-wing White supremacists and neo-Nazi groups and incidents are increasing worldwide (Farley, 2019). What separates extreme right-wing White supremacists and extremist-terrorist inmates, and other extremist groups are the following:

1. Extremist-terrorist inmates and other extremist groups believe in extreme faith-based ideologies and adhere to an all-encompassing belief system. Extremist-terrorist inmates and other extremist groups are willing to die for their ideology.
2. Correctional professionals have been dealing with White supremacists and associated right-wing groups for several decades. Experience suggests that White supremacists do not embrace the deep-seated ideology and religious belief system, even if many have tattoo crosses on their bodies. However, they do manifest hatred for certain minorities groups, religious groups, and governmental issues. They strongly uphold the Second Amendment, "the right to bear arms." They also concern themselves with drug dealing, prison gangbanging, protection,

movement and smuggling of contraband, and other illicit criminal activities.
3. Splinter extremist-terrorist groups are emerging and morphing, a topic the authors discuss later in this book.

Correctional professionals can learn from what other countries are experiencing and doing about their extremist-terrorist inmates and other extremist groups and build their plans around them. Currently, Europe is dealing with many more extremist-terrorist inmates and other extremist groups than the United States.

CONCLUSIONS

Now, correctional professionals have an opportunity to get ahead of the issues associated with extremist-terrorist inmates and other extremist groups and be *proactive* by implementing strategies, methods, and techniques to manage this extremist-terrorist inmate population rather than being reactive and playing catch-up. Those who care about the welfare of staff in corrections and those who love democracy across the world must not let this opportunity to be prepared slip away.

The authors believe that many of the new challenges this extremist-terrorist inmate population will bring to correctional agencies/facilities will be non-traditional correctional challenges. Non-traditional issues will include the following: confrontations with staff, refusals to perform traditional inmates' jobs, employing religious beliefs to justify doing or not doing something, the possibility of a suicide bomber in the visiting rooms, or a direct attack on a correctional facility, along with other potential problems. "A suicide bomber driving a tractor blew himself up Monday close to the infamous Iraqi Abu Ghraib prison, wounding four civilians in the second insurgent attack around the prison in two days" (Worth, 2005). The norm since September 11, 2001 has changed and will never be the same.

Before implementing any of the recommendations in this book, obtain approval from the agency's legal department. Get buy-in from those in charge of operations, security, and training because these three elements are integral to managing correctional facilities.

2

The Scope of Terrorism

> The assault started when a car bomb targeting the prison's main gate detonated just after 6:30 p.m. Sunday, killing three policemen. But as Afghan security forces rushed to the scene, one group of gunmen took over a high-rise building abutting the complex. In contrast, a second group launched another attack from the back of the prison, using rocket-propelled grenades to blast through a perimeter wall bordering a residential neighborhood. (George, Tassal, and Hassan, 2020)

THE SCOPE OF THE PROBLEM

Prisons across the world not only are incubators for radicalizing jihadists, but they may be the sites of terrorism, as given in the quote above about the attack on an Afghan prison. Such attacks on prisons have also occurred in the United States and not infrequently worldwide to get fellow terrorists out of jail. Thus, prisons and jails holding terrorists have to be hardened, their staff trained, and all aspects of their operations examined. Such attacks could happen at your facility. The purpose of this book is to help you prevent such occurrences and to stem the tide of inmates who are radicalized in your facility.

Some extremist terrorists radicalized in prison include Abu Musab al-Zarqawi, the founder of the group that became the Islamic State of Iraq and Syria (ISIS). Historically, Islamist extremists recruited followers in Arabic prisons, but evidence indicates that Western prisons are now

DOI: 10.4324/9781003285946-2

fertile grounds for radicalization. Several extremists radicalized in European prisons are Richard Reid, the 2001 "shoe-bomber"; Muktar Ibrahim, the 2005 London bomb plot leader; and Safe Bourada, the 1995 Paris metro bomber (Brandon, 2009). Anis Amri, now deceased, who was connected to the 2016 Berlin Christmas market attack, was radicalized in an Italian prison (Faiola, Kottoor, & Pitrelli, 2016).

Examples of radicalization in U.S. prisons are also notable. One example is Kevin Lamar James, a convert to Islam in the California state prison system. While incarcerated, James founded the Jam'iyyat Ul-Islam Is-Saheeh (JIS), or the "Authentic Assembly of Islam," a terrorist group targeting enemies of Islam (Ballas, 2017). In 2004, James recruited another inmate, Levar Washington, to join JIS, and they began plotting to target the U.S. government and supporters of Israel (Abrams, 2009).

Upon his release from prison, Washington recruited Gregory Patterson, who worked at Los Angeles International (LAX) Airport and Hammad Riaz Samana, a Pakistani citizen, to serve as Muslim warriors promoting jihad. To kill as many people as possible, they plotted to attack Jewish institutions in the Los Angeles area, including synagogues, the Israeli Consulate, and U.S. military bases. In 2005, police arrested Washington for robbing gas stations throughout the Los Angeles area to finance JIS's goals (Ballas, 2010). James was sentenced to sixteen years in prison. Washington received twenty-two years for their attempted terrorist plots (Federal Bureau of Investigation, 2009).

Another example of radicalization within a U.S. prison was Jose Padilla, a Chicago Latin Kings' gang member who converted to Islam while incarcerated. Padilla, arrested in 2002, planned to explode a dirty bomb and is currently serving a twenty-one-year prison sentence (*The Guardian*, 2014). Also, Michael Finton, another American, converted to Islam while incarcerated. Finton attempted to bomb the Paul Findley Federal Building in Springfield, Illinois, in 2009 (Johnson, 2009). In 2011, Finton received a prison sentence of twenty-eight years (Detro, 2011).

THE EXTENT OF PRISONER RADICALIZATION

These are examples of individuals who converted to radical Islam while behind bars. *Prisoner radicalization* is the process by which prisoners adopt extremist views that promote violence to achieve religious, political, or social objectives. Extremist views, including White supremacism and Black nationalism, historically existed in American prisons. However, terrorism and extremism, especially Muslim extremism, have become a growing concern in our nation's prisons (Silke, 2014). The number of Muslim prisoners in Western prisons is increasing, and Islam is becoming the fastest-growing religion in Western prisons since 9/11 (Hamm, 2009). While the exact nature and extent of the radicalization problem are unclear, the possibility for radicalization is greater in European prisons than in the United States.

For example, Spain's foreign prison population has grown from 18 percent of the total convict population at the beginning of 2000 to 33 percent by the end of 2007. In 2007, prisoners from countries with a Muslim majority constituted approximately 10 percent of Spain's prison population. Furthermore, 142 of these convicts were considered *violent jihadists* (Gutierrez, Jordan, & Trujillo, 2008), or "radicalized individuals using Islam as an ideological and religious justification for their belief in the establishment of a caliphate—a jurisdiction governed by a Muslim civil and religious leader known as a caliph—via violent means" (Bjelopera, 2015).

Muslims also comprise nearly 70 percent of inmates in the French penitentiary system. The French government estimates that approximately 1,400 prisoners were radicalized (Bryant, 2016). The number of people incarcerated for terrorism-related offenses has also increased 63 percent since 2011 in Britain. In 2016, 152 people in Britain were behind bars for a terrorism-related offense (*Express*, 2016).

The number of people incarcerated for terrorism-related offenses in the United States increased from approximately 275 in 2007 to 443 in 2015 (Fairfield & Wallace, 2016). This statistic is especially alarming because the United States has the highest incarceration rate in the world. With 2.2 million people behind bars (Kaeble & Glaze, 2016), many of these individuals are angry young men susceptible to radicalization by terrorist organizations. Sturgeon cautions correctional officials to also prepare for female extremist terrorists.

While prisons in the United States do not have official statistics on inmates' religious affiliation, many inmates have an existing religious affiliation, and other inmates adopt their faith while incarcerated (Hamm, 2009). A fifty-state survey of prison chaplains indicated that 73 percent of chaplains thought that conversion efforts were common. Finally, 41 percent of prison chaplains thought religious extremism was common, especially among Muslim inmates (Liu, 2012).

This perception varies, often by the security level of the institution and the faith of the chaplain. Chaplains working in higher-security facilities are more likely to think religious extremism was common; Catholic chaplains were more apt to think religious extremism was more common among Muslim inmates (Liu, 2012).

CONCERNS ABOUT RADICALIZATION IN PRISONS

Since 9/11, the spotlight has been on Muslim inmates. Some people think that the Muslim faith gives inmates an opportunity for rehabilitation. Others believe that Islamic prisoners threaten U.S. security. The greatest danger to security is in mutating forms of "Prison Islam." American versions of Islam use cut-and-paste versions of the *Koran* to recruit new members. These inmates have gang values, but they know little about the actual Islamic faith. Furthermore, al-Qaeda training manuals identify American prisoners as candidates for conversion because they may harbor hostility toward their government. Specifically, African-American offenders may support terrorist goals as payback for their injustices—real and perceived—in America (Hamm, 2007).

When terrorist-extremist inmates and traditional inmates unite, they network and transfer criminal skills. Traditional inmates are often knowledgeable about the limits of police powers, have easy access to weapons, and are familiar and comfortable with violence (Basra, Neumann, & Brunner, 2016). Terrorist-extremist inmates recognize the importance of radicalizing vulnerable individuals possessing said skills because people with these skills help promote their extremist agendas.

Radicalization in prison often results from prison conditions (for example, the need for protection, the search for meaning, or the desire to defy the system). Consequently, terrorist-extremist inmates pose challenges for correctional staff, including recognizing radicalization, monitoring terrorist inmates, and controlling external sources of radicalization (Neumann, 2010). Research indicates that maximum security facilities are the most prone to produce radicalized prisoners because they have fewer rehabilitation programs, higher crowding levels, and more serious gang problems (Hamm, 2007).

When terrorist-extremist inmates recruit other inmates in prison, the radicalization may extend into the community when released (Ballas, 2010; Silke, 2014). Once these inmates are back in society, they could engage in acts of violent jihad, as evidenced by Amri and the attempted plots of Reid, James, and Washington. Given the increasing number of prisoners incarcerated for terrorism-related offenses and the growing number of inmates converting to Islam, Western prisons must be prepared to release more violent jihadists, a topic discussed in Chapter 15. The following chapters discuss the recruitment process, radicalized inmates, how terrorist-extremist inmates differ from traditional inmates, the challenges these inmates pose for correctional staff, and best practices to effectively manage these populations.

CONCLUSIONS

At present, the extent of radicalization is higher in European prisons than in American prisons. "An increasing right-wing terrorist threat complicates the fight against terror as it stretches the resources and personnel employed to counter terrorism" (Pauwelis, 2021). Still, American correctional leaders cannot rest on their laurels but must use this time to harden their facilities and prepare for an onslaught of radical-terrorist inmates and right-wing terrorists. Many radical terrorist extremists have subscribed to a form of Islam based on proselytizing, not an in-depth study. The vulnerable inmates use their new faith to network and transfer their criminal skills. In becoming radicalized, they often seek protection, meaning, and engage in defiant behavior.

3

Characteristics of Radicals

RADICAL BASE—WHO ARE THEY?

Some experts believe that 71,000 people in North America, Europe, and Australia are ready to radicalize. Western recruits' average age is twenty-six years old; 86 percent are male, and 73 percent come from middle- or upper-class backgrounds (Long, 2015). A database containing more than 4,000 ISIS recruits from approximately seventy countries indicated that jihadists who joined ISIS were more educated than expected. One-quarter had a college education, and some recruits had PhDs, master's degrees, or MBAs. This database indicated that two-thirds of the jihadists were in the twenty-one through thirty age groups, but they ranged from under fifteen years old to seventy years old. Most fighters were single, 30 percent were married, and many had children (Smith, Connor, & Engel, 2016).

others?Given these estimates, it appears that extremist recruits in the free world could come from all walks of life. However, they are primarily males in their twenties. Unfortunately, being a young male could describe many incarcerated people, especially in the United States. If terrorist-extremist inmates are not all the same, how can we identify a profile? Why are some inmates more susceptible to radicalization than

US TERRORISTS: RISK FACTORS

- Having a history of violent criminal behavior
- Being involved with a gang or delinquent peers or having a terrorist friend

DOI: 10.4324/9781003285946-3

- Being a member of an extremist group for an extended period and having a deep commitment to an extremist ideology
- Having psychological issues
- Being unemployed
- Having a sporadic work history
- Having less education
- Having a lower social economic status
- Failing to achieve one's aspirations
- Having trouble in romantic relationships
- Having trouble in platonic relationships
- Having been abused as an adult
- Being distant from one's family

(Smith, 2018)

However, Borum (2014) contends that mental illness and other personal traits are not generally associated with terrorist behaviors. Consequently, there is no profile for a terrorist.

The radicalization of inmates takes place every day. One of the first was Richard Reid, "The Shoe Bomber" (Jager, 2018). Since then, those inmates converting others to radicalization are not doing it in a vacuum. They are being kept up to date and are very familiar and continuously aware of what is happening in the free world.

Unfortunately, minimal empirical research exists on radicalization within prisons, and it is unclear which factors are a catalyst to radicalization. However, it is important to know which inmates are at risk for radicalization so they do not hatch terrorist plots or execute these plots once they are released from prison. However, by examining patterns in individuals who have already been radicalized, we can better target people who could be prone to radicalization before it happens.

We have several examples of inmates who converted to Islam while in prison and several inmates who radicalized in prison. We will examine what we know about individual factors and factors related to the prison experience to determine if there are any patterns related to a person's susceptibility to radicalization while incarcerated.

WHY DOES RIGHT-WING EXTREMISM APPEAL?

Right-wing extremist rhetoric does many things. It often pits elites against the ordinary people in ways that place blame for economic

> troubles squarely on the shoulders of governments. When people experience economic precariousness, they can be more vulnerable to that kind of rhetoric. But even more importantly, we are seeing extraordinary levels of isolation, loneliness, depression, and anxiety among young people. This is a generation that spends more time alone than any previous cohort. They are eager for connection and meaning, and are vulnerable to rhetoric that promises them a sense of belonging, purpose, and a way to contribute to a cause bigger and better than themselves. This is the same dynamic that motivates foreign fighters to join Islamist extremist groups—the idea that they can be a part of something and that their lives will have meaning and purpose, whether that is to restore a sacred geography like the Caliphate or rescue white people from dying out as a race. The language of 'white genocide' and 'ethnic replacement' (as cited by the New Zealand terrorist, for example) captures this quite clearly, because it is paired with a call to action. This is not to say that all young people are vulnerable to extremist rhetoric. But more young people than ever today are lonely, anxious and want a sense of connection. That increases the number who will be vulnerable to extremist promises of meaning and purpose. (Miller-Idriss, 2019)

CONCLUSIONS

Based on the existing research, we can determine some patterns among inmates susceptible to radicalization. These characteristics include the following:

- Being a male in his twenties
- Coming from an impoverished background
- Having a criminal history: often a history of violence, prior gang involvement, previous incarcerations, and violence toward staff or other inmates
- Turning to religion to find meaning in their lives and fill a need for belonging and protection
- Feeling like of victim of a governmental injustice
- Having a father who converted to Islam in prison

As previous research has mentioned (Borum, 2014; Basra, Neumann, & Brunner, 2016), while it is possible to find common threads among radicalized inmates, it is hard to determine a concrete profile primarily because most of these characteristics could apply to the vast majority of inmates in American prisons. However, more research is needed to continue pinpointing common threads among radicalized inmates to prevent future terrorist plots. With more than 70,000 people ready to radicalize in the West (Long, 2015), we will likely see more people convicted of terrorism-related offenses in the coming years. Add to these numbers the radical domestic terrorists, and the numbers grow increasingly dramatically. Also, these individuals will be looking to recruit new inmates to help promote their extremist agendas.

We will build upon this topic in the next chapter. Specifically, we will examine how terrorist-extremist inmates are different from traditional inmates and the means used to assess these inmates.

4

Terrorist-Extremists versus Criminal Inmates

In the past three years, more than fifty jihadist attacks occurred in the West, and nearly 75 percent of the terrorists attacked the country in which they were citizens. Of these attacks, seventeen occurred in France, and sixteen happened in the United States. As senior members of ISIS are killed and the Islamic State shrinks, many militants return to the Western countries where they originated. These militants *want* to be sent to Western prisons to create a new jihadist movement in prison (Davies, 2017). They welcome their incarceration because other inmates make a captive audience for recruitment.

Historically, most Western countries have had few terrorists within their prisons, but these prisoners can be very problematic when they are in prison. Not only do they create heightened safety concerns for correctional staff, but there is also the possibility of them recruiting criminal inmates. This chapter will discuss how terrorist-extremist inmates and other extremist organizations differ from criminal inmates and some assessment tools used for people convicted of terrorism-related crimes.

CHARACTERISTICS OF CRIMINAL INMATES

The typical prisoner in the United States is impoverished and earned less than $20,000 per year before incarceration (Rabuy & Kopf, 2015). Fifty-three percent of inmates housed within the state correctional systems are

DOI: 10.4324/9781003285946-4

incarcerated for violent crimes, such as homicide, forcible rape, robbery, or aggravated assault. Nineteen percent are incarcerated for property crimes, including burglary, larceny-theft, or motor vehicle theft. Sixteen percent are incarcerated for drug crimes, while the remaining 12 percent are imprisoned for public order crimes, such as driving under the influence or possessing illegal firearms (Carson, 2016). Moreover, approximately 60 percent of inmates in state prisons and county jails meet the criteria for substance abuse or drug dependence (Bronson, Stroop, Zimmer, & Berzofsky, 2017). Approximately 40 percent have a history of mental health problems (Bronson & Berzofsky, 2017).

Criminal inmates pose challenges for correctional administrators and staff, who have to manage gangs, and handle substance abuse issues, contagious diseases, aging, terminally ill inmates, and mentally ill inmates, among other special populations of prisoners. Our purpose is to paint a brief picture of a typical inmate in the United States. Essentially, most offenders in American prisons are impoverished. They likely committed a crime because they were poor, were involved in a gang, had a substance abuse problem, or had mental health issues. In the sections below, we will discuss some of the differences between international terrorist-extremist inmates and criminal inmates.

A report of the National Institute of Justice (2020) sheds some light on the differences between domestic terrorists and gang members that administrators, programmers, and other correctional staff can use to plan safer facilities and de-radicalize these inmates. According to the authors' research, the international extremist-terrorist inmates (as opposed to the domestic terrorists) often are foreign-born with some level of military experience with Muslim-extremist organizations.

Table 4.1 compares common attributes and profiles of gang members versus domestic extremists. It also shows the importance of media in influencing radicalism—something very important for extremist terrorists from all backgrounds. Because of media reach, it is important to restrict Internet access and screen visitors and materials coming into the facility that transports such radical ideas.

This table offers correctional staff some clues about what may work in deprogramming extremists. The extremists generally were not seeking to get rich but to get personal standing and resilience from their principles. Thus, substituting enriching activities that buttressed their identities as significant individuals might help them form a less dissident identity. Some of this work should be undertaken by counseling and chaplaincy staff.

Table 4.1 The Strikingly Different Profiles of Gang Members and Domestic Extremists

	Domestic Extremists	**Gang Members**
Gender	10% were female.	33% were female.
Race/Ethnicity	Domestic terrorists more closely approximated the overall racial and ethnic composition of the United States.	Gang members more closely reflected the composition of millennials. They were more likely to be Black or Hispanic.
Generational Presence in the United States	Gang and nongang extremists were overwhelmingly third or more generation citizens, but nongang extremists were more likely to be first-generation residents than gang extremists.	79% of all adult gang members were third or more generation U.S. residents, but there was a much greater second-generation presence in gangs.
Religion	Survey data from extremists revealed that, before they radicalized, they were less likely than gang members to be associated with no religion or Catholic or Protestant; they were more likely to be Muslim or Jewish.	Gang members were more likely to be Catholic or Protestant.
Perceived Rewards of Involvement in Gangs Versus Extremist Organizations	Extremism was associated with *emotional* rewards.	Gang membership was associated with *material* rewards.
Different Strains Field by Extremists and Gang Members	• For extremists, strains caused by cultural disillusionment and socially based loss of significance were stronger. • Extremists were more frequently exposed to threats to their cultural or social identities.	• For gang members, *economic strains* were stronger. • Gang members rarely experienced strains that extended to their cultural identity.

(*Continued*)

TABLE 4.1 (Continued)

	Domestic Extremists	Gang Members
Sense of Community and Family Relations	Extremists were likely to experience a tragic loss of a parent or partner, but social bonds were weak for both organizations.	Gang members experienced a higher rate of loose community relations and low-income family connections than extremists. Gang members' relationships with parents or guardians were more often fraught, distant, or abusive.
Media Use	Nearly exclusive to extremist organizations was the use of message boards, forums, or other forms of media, a fact that may relate to the political nature of extremism.	Pathways into gangs were largely local. Gang recruitment is often the product of neighborhood-based ties and friendships.

This table is adapted from Gary LaFree's "A Comparative Study of Violent Extremism and Gangs," (2020). Emphasis by the authors.

Before discussing terrorist-extremist inmates, it is important to define *terrorism*. Although there is no universal definition of terrorism, the following two definitions are widely accepted.

WHAT IS TERRORISM?

Title 22 of U.S. Code Section 2656f defines terrorism as "premeditated, politically motivated violence perpetrated against noncombatant targets by subnational organizations or clandestine agents." However, the Department of Justice defines terrorism as "the unlawful use of force or violence against persons or property to intimidate or coerce a government, the civilian population, or any segment thereof, in furtherance of political or social objectives" (Legal Information Institute, n.d.).

Although these definitions differ, they both consider the offender's use of *violence* in achieving political goals. Terrorist organizations have political, religious, or social objectives that they pursue through violence (Rapoport, 2008). Their use of violence is intended to send a message to the public and gain attention for their cause.

Not all extremist-terrorists are the same, so it is also important to consider a group's *ideology*. An ideology is a set of beliefs and ideas and the group's strategy to address issues through violence. Terrorist group ideologies attempt to justify violence so they can achieve their objectives. Many terrorist organizations are often organized into categories based on their ideology. For example, "Left-Wing" terrorist organizations include the Red Brigades or the Red Army Faction, "Ethno-Nationalist" terrorist organizations include the Irish Republican Army or the Tamil Tigers, and "Right-Wing" terrorist organizations include Neo-Fascist Skinheads and Neo-Nazis (Gonderme, Kayt, Safya, Kayet, & Yorunia, 2008). As we emphasize later, it is important to know who you have in your facility because this will provide some idea of both what to expect from them and to begin to find ways to de-program or educate them in democratic principles.

There are also religious-related terrorist organizations, such as al-Qaeda and ISIS, involved in the jihadi movement. These individuals hold extreme political or religious views, promoting violence to further their agenda (Silke, 2014). Specifically, these organizations believe that violence is necessary to defend the Muslim community against their enemies. Thus, people incarcerated for engaging in (or attempting to engage in) terrorist attacks and who hold these extremist religious views are the individuals we refer to as "terrorist-extremist inmates" throughout this text.

After 9/11, former President George W. Bush established a detention camp at the Guantanamo Bay Naval Base in Cuba to hold people convicted of terrorism-related crimes. The United States maintained that because Guantanamo Bay is not on U.S. soil, the U.S. Constitution does not cover it. Prisoners at Guantanamo were not the same protections as those housed within the United States. Given the controversial nature of and alleged abuses sustained by inmates at this camp, former President Barack Obama signed an executive order to close the prison at Guantanamo Bay in 2009. However, the detention center did not close because of challenges in relocating the prisoners, and many of them eventually were sent back to their home countries (Guantanamo Bay Naval Station Fast Facts, 2017).

> In the 17 long years since the naval base was used to detain prisoners merely suspected of having something to do with anti-American terrorism, 780 men have passed through its walls. Today, 40 men remain. (Swain, 2019)

TERRORIST-EXTREMISTS DIFFER FROM OTHER INMATES

Both criminal inmates and terrorist-extremist inmates can engage in violence, but politically motivated violence separates the two. Respectively, many terrorist-extremist inmates do not view themselves as criminals but rather crusaders or freedom fighters. Many, including right-wing terrorists, believe that they are on a mission from God, and they engage in violence to complete their mission (Sturgeon, 2010).

Moreover, the intentions of criminal inmates and politically motivated ones differ. Criminal inmates often commit crimes because they lack the financial resources to reach their goals legitimately or commit crimes to feed their addictions. Their motivation to commit crimes is to achieve material or personal goals.

In contrast, politically motivated criminals act on behalf of a group or society as a whole. These offenders claim that breaking the law is justified if a political or religious system is illegitimate and motivated to change the existing system. For example, extreme religious organizations believe that acts of terrorism are justified by commands found in religious texts, such as the *Koran* (Hill, 2016).

Also, because of their beliefs, terrorist-extremist inmates are willing to sacrifice their lives for what they believe to be a religious cause (Sturgeon, 2010). There were 469 suicide bombings worldwide in 2016, and ISIS claimed responsibility for 70 percent of these attacks (Schweitzer, Mendelboim, & Rosner, 2017). If the perpetrators of these attacks survived, we would have many more terrorist-extremist inmates in Western prisons. However, when this terrorist attack does not go as planned, the perpetrator ends up in prison rather than deceased. Recall that Richard Reid, the "shoe bomber," attempted to detonate explosives in his shoes on a flight from Paris to Miami. Fortunately, passengers subdued him, and his attempt failed. Although Reid is currently serving a life sentence for eight counts of terrorism, he is an example of someone willing to risk his life for his religious beliefs.

Besides, many terrorist-extremist inmates have received some level of military training in Iraq, Afghanistan, or America (Sturgeon, 2010), giving them knowledge and experience using machine guns, explosives, and other military weapons. The right-wing is also strongly entwined with guns (Fuchs, 2019). The authors believe that it is relevant to mention that right-wing organizations also receive some military-type training. White supremacy organizations have past and current military members as members of their organization. Moreover, both groups are familiar with military strategies, tactics, and recruitment techniques. For instance, Richard Reid and Jose Padilla both received militant training run by al-Qaeda while in Afghanistan (Elliot, 2002).

Also, terrorist-extremist inmates can continue their work while they are incarcerated. They can develop the movement's strategy and mobilize supporters on the outside. Terrorist-extremist inmates are more likely than criminal inmates to have supporters outside who do not accept their incarceration's legitimacy. These supporters may be apt to publicize the prison's actions and gain additional supporters for the cause (Neumann, 2010).

Like gang members, terrorist organizations will have their supporters. They will settle near the prison(s) where their colleagues are being held. Their supporters will settle near the correctional facility where their colleagues are being held. These supporters will visit and accept telephone calls from the inmates, write letters, if permitted, contribute to their canteen fund, and so forth. These supporters are morale builders and transmitters of information of all types.

Intelligence transmission is a two-way street. Intelligence gathered by the inmates is passed to the outside supporters through visitors, mail, telephone calls, and on some occasions correctional personnel. Intelligence gathered by outside sources is passed to the inmates through the same methods.

> Take advantage of visits to communicate with brothers outside prison and exchange information that may be helpful to them in their work outside prison [according to what occurred during the investigations]. The importance of mastering the art of hiding messages is self-evident here. (*al-Qaeda Training Manual*, Lesson 3 Prison and Detention Centers, see Appendix 1)

Staff intimidation, either at work or outside the facility, is another tactic used by prison gangs, White supremacists, and other extremist organizations. For example, if terrorist-extremist inmates claim discrimination, mistreatment, or violations of their freedom of speech or religion, this could result in negative media attention or protests in the free world. People outside could then organize additional support for these politically motivated prisoners, contributing to their cause (Atherton & Jurisic, 2015).

Similarly, terrorist-extremist inmates can also continue their agenda through recruitment efforts. Prisoners angry about their incarceration make a captive audience for radical Islam (Silke, 2014). Once terrorist-extremist inmates have identified which inmates are suitable candidates for radicalization, they establish relationships and preach their extremist ideologies.

Finally, before their incarceration, violent extremists often pursue attention from the general public, while criminals strive to avoid it (Skillicorn, Leuprecht, Stys, & Gobeil, 2015). Terrorists commit acts of violence to cause fear among the general public to promote their cause. The media perpetuates this attention by reporting acts of terror to the masses which become panicked by the violence. Sturgeon notes that most successful criminal inmates kept the knowledge of their exploits to a very select group not to get caught for other crimes in addition to the ones for which they were currently imprisoned! However, extremist terrorists want publicity to promote their cause/s.

CONCLUSIONS

With the fall of Afghanistan, ISIS and al-Qaeda may experience a resurgence. Before this event, many of these militants plan acts of terrorism in their home countries, using any weapon available, including homemade explosives and vehicles. Alarmingly, they hope to be sent to prison because they view prisons as fertile grounds for radicalization. With millions of angry young men and women behind bars, these militants believe that many criminal inmates are suitable candidates to be recruited into the jihadi movement.

Consequently, it is more important than ever to understand the differences between terrorist-extremist inmates and criminal inmates. They are vastly different in their ideologies, motivations, intentions, personal characteristics, and backgrounds. Furthermore, it is imperative to use the proper risk and needs assessments to classify these inmates and provide suitable interventions while incarcerated. Researchers need to conduct further research on foreign and domestic terrorist-extremist inmate organizations and the effectiveness of assessing these inmates' risk and needs. In the next chapter, we discuss practices currently used for managing terrorist-extremist inmates.

5

Planning and Implementing Change

Throughout this book, the authors accentuate the difference between incarcerating foreign and domestic extremist-terrorist inmates and criminal inmates.

Whether a facility has one, ten, or more individuals sentenced for terrorist-related crimes, they should classify them as extremist-terrorist inmates. The facility should take immediate action to either create or adapt its policies/procedures, operations, staff training, and staff selection to work with this inmate population. Any facility incarcerating extremist-terrorist inmates and other extremist organizations should also enhance its physical security.

Meeting the challenges of today's post-9/11 and January 6, 2021 world and the ever-increasing number of foreign and domestic extremist-terrorist inmate organizations will require serious efforts from everyone with interaction or management responsibility for these extremist-terrorist inmates. In the past, security personnel and occasionally program staff received specialized training. With extremist-terrorist inmates, everyone (medical, kitchen, maintenance, and others) should receive specialized training. Agencies may need to develop individualized, specialized training for specific disciplines. Please see further details on training in Chapter 8.

DOI: 10.4324/9781003285946-5

POLICIES AND PROCEDURES

Correctional agencies should develop a multidisciplinary team to review and assess current policies and procedures. The team should examine policies to ensure that the current policies have the following characteristics:

- "Operationally Functional"—defined for this document as policies, procedures, and protocols that can be enacted in the field by staff, as they are written, 95 percent of the time. There will be situations where correctional personnel must adjust their actions to manage the specific situation.
- Providing up-to-date and relevant training during basic and annual training sessions.

The team should also do the following:

- Review and assess policies and procedures to ensure that its policies and procedures are "Operationally Functional"! If a policy/procedure is not functioning as desired or written, the facility must correct its operational deficiencies.
- Promptly transmit the update to the training staff for inclusion in the facility's training initiatives.
- An efficient method to get up-to-date training is using roll calls and short online training sessions.

Correctional agencies/facilities must comprehensively review every component of their operations, security policies/procedures, post orders, and religious policies and procedures. As anyone who has prepared for an American Correctional Association audit knows, conducting a comprehensive review of an agency's or facility's policies and procedures and operations is a massive undertaking. An organizing instrument may help correctional personnel focus while conducting their comprehensive review of policies, procedures, post orders, operations, and other areas.

Correctional agencies should have policies and procedures that address the following areas dealing with recruiting:

1. The agency should have a policy stating that the recruiting efforts by any individuals identified by correctional administrators and security-threat-group personnel as being part of an extremist-terrorist organization will be considered a disciplinary violation.
2. The first offense of an extremist-terrorist inmate or any other inmate identified as an extremist convicted, by a disciplinary board, of recruiting shall receive a sentence to be determined (TBD).

The development and implementation of new techniques and methods of prison security, operations, management, and staff training will require everyone at every level of the correctional chain of command to have an open mind—to realize that radical inmates could be housed in their facility.

The "Paper" section of this matrix requires an analysis of policies, procedures, and other written documents that guide what happens in the facility.

PAPER

Paper, the first element of the matrix, is the sole subject of this chapter. The next chapter discusses the other elements of the matrix—people and the places that need special attention, and the following chapter is on the equipment and physical actions required. The paper element instructs people on what to do, how and when to do it, how to report and evaluate it, and how to record what occurred and learn what training is needed.

The paper component comprises all written documents that direct people on every facet of operations, security, administration, and any subdivisions under these major categories. The paper component includes the paperwork necessary to "harden" the facility and enhance the security for managing terrorist inmates and other extremist organizations. Foremost, the paper element is a comprehensive review of all the facility's existing policies and procedures, with special attention given to security issues.

"Security issues" should be more than just be a term. When reviewing security issues, add reality to them. For instance, define exactly and specifically the elements and duties associated with perimeter patrol. Explain what makes perimeter patrol a viable element of the overall security program of the facility. Operationally functional policies, procedures, protocols, and other documents are the foundations for a comprehensive security program that is continually operationally functional. Its followers should also be vigilant, flexible, and responsive in evaluating the security program at least twice a month to ensure that all security program operations are updated.

Complacency is the Achilles' heel of correctional operations! Paper documentation enables the staff to reduce the opportunity for those (extremist-terrorist inmates/White supremacists, cartels, other subversive organizations, and prison gangs) to exploit any lapse in the security operations.

POLICY IMPLICATIONS

The practice of managing terrorist-extremist inmates and other extremist organizations is still in its infancy (Sturgeon, 2010). As we discussed, Western prisons are striving to manage this unique population of inmates effectively. They have created policies to classify, properly house, and monitor terrorists in prison. They have also taken steps to minimize radicalization from outside sources by strictly monitoring terrorist inmates' mail, visits, and telephone calls. However, as we move forward, prison administrators should continue to focus on certain areas, which we discuss, to ensure they are doing their best to prevent the spread of violent extremism.

Emergency and medical transports and other transports of terrorist-extremist inmates and other extremist organizations require special precautions during transport to and from a medical facility, courts, or other venues. Exercise caution when conducting emergency transports. The correctional officers conducting these types of transport should receive specialized training and be constantly vigilant for inmate-escape attempts or an ambush by outsiders to free the inmate/s being transported.

Recreation. Initially, recreation periods for extremist-terrorist inmates and other extremist organizations should be solitary, according to local laws and agency policies and procedures. Correctional officers' constant supervision is required during recreation for extremist-terrorist inmates, other extremist organizations, and others identified as extremist by the security-threat-group division.

When/if extremist-terrorist inmates and other extremists are put together, the correctional officer on duty must check that video surveillance and recording devices are operational before permitting extremist-terrorist inmates and other extremist organizations in the recreation areas. Security-threat-group personnel should review the video/s after recreation periods for intelligence purposes.

- Install warning and instructional signs in appropriate languages, informing the extremist-terrorist inmates, other extremist organizations, and other inmates that audio and video surveillance/recording is being used.
- Inform extremist-terrorist inmates, other extremists, and others of the rules and regulations during their orientation. Informing any new inmates, including extremist-terrorist inmates, of the rules and regulations is a proactive way to avoid future problems. It may be necessary for the facility to hire a person fluent

in whatever languages the inmates speak to instruct the them in their languages. Remember, some extremist-terrorist inmates and other extremists may not read at a sufficient level to understand the rules and regulations, so provide the orientation verbally and in written form.

- Pay special attention during religious services, especially if the facility does not vet the imam preaching. Note the interaction among inmates during the service. Prison gang members have used religious services to communicate with one another.
- All religious volunteers should have comprehensive background investigations before being permitted within the facilities.

Contents of Emergency Plans

- ***Hostage Situations***. Much can be learned and shared among agencies worldwide about hostage-taking. In one staff-hostage incident in the UK, officers were injured but freed.

> A male guard was recovering yesterday from a broken cheekbone after he was held hostage by three prisoners at Full Sutton prison, near York, on Sunday, while a female warder suffered wounds to her arms as she tried to prevent her colleague from being attacked. During the siege, the attackers reportedly threatened to kill the officer while making "extremist demands." The three inmates demanded the release of radicalized student Roshonara Choudhry, who was convicted of the attempted murder of Labour MP Stephen Timms in 2010. It has been reported that the attack was triggered by an imam at the prison, asking Muslim inmates to pray for murdered soldier Lee Rigby. (Meredith, 2019)

SUGGESTIONS

Solicit input from the Federal Bureau of Investigation or military hostage rescue units to develop hostage-incident scenarios involving extremist terrorists. Remember, once again, "We Don't Know, What We Don't Know!" **Language-transcription software** was developed by the military (Eggen, 2007).

Again, there must be policies and procedures in place to deal with extremist-terrorist inmate hostage incidents.

- *Attack from External Armed Forces.* While armed attacks are not prevalent in the United States or most of the European Union, they are still possible. Few people thought that individuals would fly planes into the World Trade Center and the Pentagon or run down people on a bridge with a truck, yet these incidents happened. The goal is for correctional agencies and facilities to have policies, procedures, and a reaction plan if the facility comes under attack and to conduct training and exercises on the plan. The Boy Scout motto, "Be prepared," is appropriate.
- *Hunger Strikes.* Extremist-terrorist inmates, other extremist inmates, and other inmates have used hunger strikes for years. Most correctional facilities have policies and procedures on managing hunger strikes, but this policy must be reviewed and updated if necessary.
- *Incoming and Outgoing Mail.* Personnel responsible for inspecting incoming and outgoing inmate mail should wear protective gloves and other protective clothing, as needed. The agency/facility must develop protocols and training for handling suspicious packages and letters. It would be advisable to establish and arrange with the local bomb squad and hazmat team to identify and depose possible explosive and chemical-biological-radiological (CBR) substances. (A real-life experience: Contraband such as cigarettes, razor blades, and messages were getting into the facility. An observant mailroom officer noticed a box of leather dye weighed more than was written on the box. The officer opened the box, and every container of leather dye had contraband of some sort in it. Further investigation uncovered that an inmate's girlfriend had just gotten a job working for the manufacturer of the leather dye and was responsible for packing the boxes. The inmate was selling the items to other inmates.) Nothing is beyond the ingenuity and imagination of individuals who are working to beat the system.
  - **Mail Inspectors.** Personnel inspecting incoming and outgoing mail should receive training in hidden codes. If these personnel find something suspicious, they should immediately report their suspicions to the security chief and the security-threat-group supervisor. They should also seek help

from the Federal Bureau of Investigation in deciphering the possible codes.

The following is advice for those reviewing, updating, revising, or developing new policies and procedures.

- **Think Like a Terrorist**. To be sure, "there is much truth to the 9/11 Commission's finding that a "lack of imagination was our biggest failing before the terrible attacks of three years ago. We allowed ourselves a certain degree of complacency since past terrorist attacks had not killed huge numbers of people, and since past airplane hijackings had typically [sic not] been conducted to bargain for the release of prisoners" (O'Hanlon, 2004).
- **Complacency is the number one enemy** to the safe and secure operation of correctional facilities. People with inadequate staffing and training are especially vulnerable because staying vigilant every hour of every working day is difficult because so much of what correctional personnel do is repetitive and mundane.
- **Weak link.** Inmates, as a rule, will always be on the lookout for the officer who is the weak link—the officer/s who do not follow the policies and procedures, take shortcuts while conducting official counts, overlook violations, and cut corners. The inmates have 24/7/365 to observe correctional personnel doing their jobs and devising ways to beat the system.

Ways of beating complacency

- **Stagger routines** such as counts, group sessions, and other activities.
- **Rotate assignments** that also allow correctional personnel to learn other posts and work assignments. It also keeps officers from becoming too friendly with the inmates.
- **Use imagination**. If the review team can think of something, so can the terrorist-extremist inmates and, for that matter, any inmate. Correctional administrators should take input from their review team very seriously. The days of "We've always done it that way" disappeared on September 11, 2001 and on January 6, 2021.
- **Solicit input**. The line-level security, food service, maintenance, education, health care, and other staff know their facility's vulnerabilities, and the review team should solicit their input.

Many of these extremist-terrorist inmates and others from extremist organizations have received military-style training in areas such as self-defense, escape and evasion, weapons construction, and making "homemade" explosives and incendiary devices. Staff should solicit help from law-enforcement bomb squads or military-explosive-ordnance-disposal personnel and conduct a review of the facility to identify potential bomb-making material.

The extremist terrorists have received instruction in recruiting staff members and volunteers to become brothers and sisters and engage in intelligence gathering, analysis, and sharing.

OPERATIONALLY FUNCTIONAL POLICIES

If a policy or procedure is inadequate or impractical to follow as written, the line staff will make real-life adaptations to perform their duties. The team responsible for revising or developing new policies and procedures should solicit information on why policies and procedures are not working and revise the policy to make it "operationally functional." Sturgeon suggests that the more the first-line supervisors and line staff are included in the policy and procedure development and implementation, the better the policies and procedures will be. The staff will follow them more closely because they helped write them.

People who have worked in corrections for any time know that some policies and procedures are not "operationally functional" (Sturgeon, 2014) because of their ambiguity and vagueness. Policies and procedures should be clear and straightforward. Write them in plain English, not legalese.

Here is an example of a poorly written policy that Sturgeon came upon while conducting a security audit years ago: "Deadly force shall not be used until the escaping inmate has breached the last bastion to freedom and has shown a clear intent to escape." Example of an "Operationally Functional" policy is: Deadly Force should only be used as a last resort to stop an escaping inmate (s). Verbal commands, alarms, radio communications, and perimeter patrol alerts should initially be used to stop escaping inmate/s, time and circumstances permitting. Instead, it should have read something like the following: Do not use deadly force until there is no other option to stop an escaping inmate.

Post orders must be reviewed carefully, updated, or completely rewritten, if necessary, twice a year or sooner if the post requirements change. When conducting security audits and teaching classes on security, Sturgeon found that class participants told him that post orders are often not followed as written because they are outdated or do not relate to the "real-life" operations/situations. Post orders are placed in a drawer or on a shelf somewhere and are rarely read in many instances. During security audits that Sturgeon conducted or participated in, the officers and first-line supervisors could not locate most of the post orders for several of the posts. The ones that they found were out of date and irrelevant to the current operations!

The authors suggest implementing new policies, procedures, post orders, and other paper documents for a trial period of thirty to forty-five days to ascertain if the facility can successfully implement the new version as written in real time. Basically, is the document "Operationally Functional?" Schedule meetings with the staff who must work with policies and procedures as part of their daily duties. Share with the staff how the team determined the changes and why the changes were necessary. Solicit feedback, with suggestions from the field, about the applicability of the document(s). What may look good on paper does not always work in practice. The goal of policies, procedures, post orders, protocols, memorandums, and other documents is to give "real world" direction to the employees, inmates, volunteers, inmate families, and other concerned parties.

SECURITY POLICIES AND PROCEDURES

Focus on the idea: It is always better to be proactive rather than reactive! The terrorist-extremist inmate classification initially should be at the highest security level available. One of the first-line supervisors' and managers' responsibilities is to ensure that staff follows all security policies, procedures, and post orders. The first-line supervisor should document any exceptions as to the time, individual (s) involved, the reason for the variation (be specific), and the supervisor's name approving the variation.

First-line supervisors and line staff must work as a team with the extremist-terrorist inmate population and White supremacists, prison gangs, and all inmate classifications. Prison gangs and other organizations have used the divide and conquer strategy for years. They try to compromise an officer, nurses, teachers, and maintenance personnel into believing that they, the inmate(s), are better friends than their fellow staff members.

As previously mentioned, some of these extremist-terrorist inmates, and other extremist organizations, such as White supremacist-extremists, have received military training while in the service. They may use this training given the opportunity. American military troops who responded to a poll cited White nationalists as a greater national security threat than domestic terrorism connected to Islam or immigration (Shane, 2020).

"Situational awareness" takes on entirely new importance when managing extremist-terrorist inmates and other extremists. First-line supervisors should be alert to what is currently happening and aware of things around them while reminding line staff always to maintain situational awareness, predict what might come next, and be prepared for that next step or stage.

"ISIS suspects shout 'hail Islamic State' before attacking Kolkata jail warder. A suspect Islamic State terrorist lodged in a Kolkata jail on Sunday tried to slit the throat of a warder after hitting him with a brick, grievously injuring him" (*Hindustan Times*, 2017).

Newspaper reports and Internet searches indicate that staff assaults and overall violence in correctional facilities are on the rise.

> Thinking of starting a career as a prison guard? Before taking this step, make sure you're aware of the risks involved. Life as a correctional officer isn't easy. In fact, it has nothing to do with what you see in movies and TV series. Prison guards have the second-highest mortality rates of any profession; extreme stress, substance abuse, depression, workplace injuries, and suicidal thoughts, are just a few of their daily struggles. (Picinu, 2019)

According to accepted policies and procedures, the **internal movement of extremist-terrorist inmates** and others designed as extremists should be conducted with diligence and caution. Ensuring that there is always adequately trained staff on duty should be a top priority for correctional administrators.

Too often today, staffing is inadequate for correctional facilities in general and special management specifically. Staffing patterns should be determined whenever possible by the "internal classification" of the extremist-terrorist inmate and other extremist offenders. If it is deemed necessary or the agency's policy and procedure, the extremist-terrorist inmate should be in full restraints with an appropriate number of escort officers. Closed-circuit TV (CCTV) should monitor the extremist-terrorist inmate's movements. When moving high-security inmates such as extremist-terrorist inmates and other extremists or any other high-security inmates, use additional precautions such as those mentioned in this chapter.

TRANSPORTING INMATES

Whenever possible, avoid the external movement of extremist-terrorist inmates and other extremist inmates. If external movement is necessary, use every precaution, and develop a comprehensive plan before leaving the facility's security. Employ the following steps:

1. Predetermine how many extremist-terrorist inmates and other extremists will be transported in one vehicle. The authors do not recommend transporting extremist inmates for various groups together. Ideally, if possible, transporting one extremist inmate at a time is best.
2. Predetermine if there is a need for escort vehicles.
3. Predetermine what weapons escort officers should carry, what additional weapons will be in the vehicles, and how these will be secured.
4. Select the appropriate vehicle/s. Thoroughly check out vehicle/s before leaving the secure facility. Ensure that radio communication is operable and that there is a spare tire, lug-nut wrench, and other tools in case of problems.
5. Stagger the travel routes, both for leaving and returning to the facility. Avoid routes and times of the day where you could get caught up in a traffic "bottleneck" that could lead to being ambushed. "Armed gangs crashed car into prison van to free two men …" ("Salford prison van escape," 2014).
6. Stagger departure times, arrival times, and return times.
7. Ensure that an armed staff member/s always remains with the vehicle/s.
8. Thoroughly search all returning vehicles *before* they enter the secure perimeter. This search should include, but not be limited to, the vehicle's roof, engine compartment, and undercarriage of the vehicle.

9. Know how to react to an ambush incident. Combine Situational Awareness and Think Like a Terrorist! Do not panic. "REACT." First and foremost, GET OUT OF THE "KILL ZONE!" Depending on the type of ambush, this will determine where the "Kill Zone" is.
10. If the ambush is "fixed," in one location, the driver must make all types of diversionary moves—speed, swerve, and reverse course if that way is clearer than driving straight ahead, and other methods to get out of the "Kill Zone." Inform dispatch that the vehicle is under attack and to send help. Give the exact location and direction of travel.
    - In a fixed, stationary ambush, the "Kill Zone" is also fixed.
    - If the ambush is a "rolling ambush," where vehicles are chasing the transport vehicle and possibly shooting at the vehicle or trying to force the transport vehicle off the road, the driver should take evasive actions—speeding, swerving, and so forth. Inform dispatch of the situation, the direction of travel, and request assistance.
11. Correctional agencies/governments should seriously consider establishing a special classification for extremist-terrorist inmates and other extremists. This classification should be a separate and distinct classification for the extremist-terrorist inmates, with varying degrees of security levels, after assessing the risk each extremist-terrorist inmate poses to the staff, other inmates, and the overall security of the facility. Justification for temporarily establishing a separate classification system determines how the extremist-terrorist inmates and other extremists may affect the facility's operations and security and how the facility will manage any possible situation/s. Additionally, you should assess whether there is a need for new training and new policies and procedures.

Deradicalization. If an extremist-terrorist inmate and other extremist inmates appear to be accepting the de-radicalization program, and correctional personnel verify this with staff members of the de-radicalization program, the facility should have a protocol to move the inmate into another housing unit. While extremist-terrorist inmates and other extremists are in this new location, staff members of the unit should assess the extremist-terrorist inmates and other extremists in the step-down unit to ensure that they are sincere about being de-radicalized.

If the step-down unit staff believes that the extremist-terrorist inmate is not accepting the program, confront that inmate and, if deemed appropriate, return the inmate to the prior special housing unit or other housing to ensure the inmate's safety. The people in the new unit should monitor the inmate to be sure he or she was not posing to gain a transfer but is still radical and possibly disseminating radical ideas to other inmates.

CLASSIFICATION

Developing a special internal classification for extremist-terrorist inmates, other extremist, and others who should be classified as extremists could be especially useful in managing this population. Use this internal classification to identify the hardcore extremists from those inmates who could be de-radicalized.

The internal classification should make the appropriate designation.

1. Initial security level should be determined by crime, duration of the sentence, pre-trial behavior, and internal and external intelligence.
2. The initial security classification should be used to determine housing assignments.
3. Work assignments and eligibility for them should be determined by behavior. There should be a rotation of work assignments.
4. The inmate's behavior should determine eligibility for recreation times and other privileges. The inmate's behavior should determine the availability frequency and duration of visits.
5. Program activities—The eligibility for programs should be determined by the inmate's behavior and how well the inmate performs in the activities.
6. Deradicalization—The inmate's eligibility should be determined by the terrorist-extremist inmate's desire, behavior, and conduct. The inmate's progress should be carefully monitored.

CONCLUSIONS

Whenever an agency/facility takes on a comprehensive audit/review of its management, operations, security and training policies, procedure, curricula, protocols, and other paper documents, it should have a detailed plan, such as the Matrix with its three-pronged approach, that will be more fully discussed in the next two chapters.

Operating correctional agencies and facilities is complex and demanding, with a tremendous number of moving parts. While developing the Youthful Offender Program in South Carolina, Sturgeon used his Matrix to help keep the team focused on all that had to be accomplished. Correctional staff should use the Matrix to prepare for the influx of extremist-terrorist inmates so that they can be handled safely and with care for staff and other inmates' safety.

6

People in the Matrix

The *people* element of the matrix takes into consideration every person with anything to do with the operations, security, and administration of the facility, including all the staff, inmates, extremist-terrorist inmates, criminal-inmates, volunteers, visitors, delivery personnel, law enforcement, the Joint Counterterrorism Taskforce, and emergency medical and firefighters who are part of the facility's emergency/contingency plans.

Additionally, consider other organizations of people when drafting new policies and procedures or adapting old ones. These include the foreign extremist-terrorist inmates, White supremacists, inmates' families, the media, politicians, diplomats from foreign countries, and the local civilian population. All these people and organizations could be considered "stakeholders," people with a vested interest in what is occurring. The agency's legal department must review all new and revised policies and procedures.

As the old saying goes, "We are only as strong as our weakest link." Correctional administration, security, and security-threat-group personnel must become an integral part of the approval process for all new and adapted policies, procedures, post orders, protocols, and other documents. Some extremist-terrorist inmates and other extremist organizations have been trained to locate weak links within the staff (Appendix 1).

While Chapter 8 discusses training, it is important to be aware that sworn correctional officers and civilian employees who will have any contact with extremist-terrorist inmates, other extremist organizations, and other extremists should receive specialized training in the following subjects:

DOI: 10.4324/9781003285946-6

- The importance of following security policies, procedures, post orders, and memoranda.
- How to recognize, gather, and report intelligence.
- Self-defense.
- How to recognize when inmates show signs of radicalization.
- How to identify the recruiters.
- The procedure for reporting that an extremist-terrorist inmate has threatened them. The report must include what the extremist-terrorist inmate exactly said or gestured. Staff should receive training on writing and following clearly defined methods of reporting personal threats against officers and other staff by extremist-terrorist inmates. (Trying to intimidate/threaten correctional staff is a tactic that prison gangs and others have used for years.)
- How to report extremist-terrorist inmates' attempts to recruit staff, volunteers, and others.
- How to identify the hierarchy of the organization (Who are the leaders?).
- The importance of understanding "situational awareness."
- Learn about the cultural and religious issues of various religions.

First-line supervisors have a tremendous responsibility for ensuring that line staff follows all policies, procedures, post orders, and so forth. Additionally, they need to provide oversight of the extremist-terrorist inmates and other extremist organizations and their activities. First-line supervisors should know who is associating with whom within the inmate population, who appears to be the leaders, teachers, recruiters, followers, and how they occupy their days. Staff should be trained to report any changes in the extremist-terrorist inmates and other extremists' daily routines and new inmate associates to the first-line supervisor.

First-line supervisors have these added responsibilities because they can move more freely through the living areas where extremist-terrorist inmates and other extremists are incarcerated. First-line supervisors must also observe staff and ensure that the staff is adhering to all policies and procedures and are not becoming too close to the extremist-terrorist inmates. Extremist-terrorist inmates and other extremists must not intimidate them. First-line supervisors must be looking for signs of "burned-out" staff.

With their day-to-day contact and interactions with this extremist-terrorist inmate population, line staff provides a vital link. The bulk of the intelligence will come from them, and their arena is where there is potential for security policies and procedures to be compromised.

Continuous, relevant, up-to-date, and comprehensive training will have to become the norm rather than the exception. Some extremist-terrorist inmates and other extremist organizations received training on manipulating and compromising daily correctional management and security methods. "Violent extremist prisoners may attempt to undermine the professionalism of the staff and seek to exploit staff to obtain illicit goods, to assist with escape attempts, or to act as a conduit to criminal groups outside of the prison" (Bryans, 2016). Correctional administrators are responsible for ensuring that staff receives training in the current management and security techniques that work with this extremist-terrorist inmate population.

Staff rotation will reduce staff "burnout" that can happen to staff assigned to high-stress situations for long periods. One example of staff rotation is rotating staff on a staggered basis, so the specialized housing unit(s) do not lose the continuity of operations and the unit's history and inmates. The staff could be rotated out of the specialized housing unit bimonthly on a staggered basis. Working with extremist-terrorist inmates and other extremists requires correctional staff to maintain a high degree of vigilance under stressful conditions. Initially, the administration should over-train the required number of staff for the specialized unit/s. The rationale for this overtraining is to ensure a sufficiently trained staff to accomplish rotation and prevent staff burnout.

> We found that the BOP has not effectively monitored the mail of terrorist and other high-risk inmates. Our review determined that the BOP's monitoring of inmate mail is deficient in several respects: The BOP does not read all the mail for terrorist and other high-risk inmates on its mail monitoring lists, does not have enough proficient translators to translate inmate mail written in foreign languages, and does not have sufficient staff trained in intelligence techniques to evaluate whether terrorists' communications contain suspicious content. Similarly, we found that the BOP is unable to effectively monitor high-risk inmates' verbal communications, which include telephone calls, visits with family and friends, and cellblock conversations. Besides, the Department does not require a review of all international terrorist inmates to identify those who should be subjected to

> Special Administrative Measures (SAMs), the most restrictive conditions that can be placed on an inmate's communications. (U.S. Department of Justice, Office of the Inspector General, Evaluation and Inspections Division, 2006)

> Top officials at the Bureau of Prisons acknowledged that three men imprisoned for the bombing of the World Trade Center in 1993 wrote about ninety letters to a Spanish terror cell and other Islamic extremists. Part of the reason this occurred was due to a lack of staff knowledgeable in the language. Arabic experts say prison officials underestimated the potential recruiting power of the letters from convicted terrorists. (Myers, 2005)

OVERCOMING LANGUAGE DISADVANTAGES

Today's correctional officials must be constantly vigilant not to become complacent, underestimate, or lack imagination when managing extremist-terrorist inmates and other extremist populations. Persons willing to die for their cause can do anything and pose a constant threat to the institution's security, staff, and criminal inmates.

Specialized staff who can speak and read the extremist-terrorist inmates' language/s and that of other extremist organizations are needed. These language speakers can review incoming and outgoing mail and identify and explain the mail's nuances to security personnel. Another added skill would be identifying codes in all terrorist mail (incoming and outgoing). European prison officials find that the codes may also be in right-wing terrorist material (Fielitz, 2020).

When monitoring inmates' mail, phone, and in-cell conversations, it is important to understand what they are saying. If no one in the administration can speak or understand the language, it will be necessary to get a translator or record conversations and transcribe them quickly. Assign staff knowledgeable in the inmate's respective language where their services may be most effective. Other solutions include using some of the language-transcription software developed for the military or limiting communications.

It is always advantageous to have correctional staff of the same ethnic background, speak the languages, and know the customs. "Every effort should be made to recruit staff from ethnic organizations and religious and racial minorities, indigenous people, represented among the violent extremist prisoner population" (Bryans, 2016).

However, prison administrations should be aware that "in some cases, staff from the same ethnic, religious or cultural background as their violent extremist prisoners may be seen as traitors by those prisoners, which, in itself, might generate conflict" (Bryans, 2016).

Gender-sensitive staffing is yet another concern when it comes to managing extremist-terrorist inmates and other extremists. "Women staff should be recruited and trained to work with female-violent-extremist prisoners and design and deliver gender-appropriate interventions" (Bryans, 2016). In some countries with strict adherence to Sharia law, staffing is by gender; males supervise males and females supervise females, but all security precautions and practices should still be followed. There are special sensitivities among many males with Islamic backgrounds about being seen by women while naked, which is a troubling area in the United States because it creates conflict with work opportunities for women, union agreements, and equal rights laws, both federal and state. The nation's laws and the agency's policies, procedures, and court decisions should decide these gender-sensitive issues.

CONCLUSIONS

The staff must be made aware of the differences in managing extremist-terrorist inmates and other extremists and criminal inmates. The staff must understand some important issues that extremist-terrorist inmates believe in and adhere to religious/political ideologies that justify their criminal activities. They try to recruit new criminal inmates to become members who accept their ideology. These extremist terrorists could present new criminal/correctional emergencies. However, if staff are prepared, they should be able to cope with these extremist-terrorist inmates and not allow them to disrupt the facility's operation or engage in radicalization efforts.

7

Places and Technology in the Matrix

Places, in the matrix, has taken on entirely new importance since the summer of 2020, when federal buildings and police buildings came under attack from various extremist groups. What became glaringly apparent was that the perimeters of these buildings were left unsecured, thereby allowing the attacker to access some of the buildings. Additionally, similar issues permitted the attack on the U.S. Capitol on January 6, 2021; the perimeter collapsed. Similarly, correctional perimeters' security can be a facility's Achilles' heel when attention is mainly focused on the prison's interior.

The authors suggest that when assessing the vulnerability of the facility's perimeter start at the perimeter and work inward.

1. Parking lots (How close are they to the perimeter?)
2. All roads approaching the facility (Are they a straight shot to the perimeter?)
3. The overall condition of the perimeter fence or wall (If the perimeter consists of fence, ensure that all the anchor bolts are secure.)
4. Determine the times when the pedestrian and sally ports are in use (Whenever there is an increase in traffic through the pedestrian or vehicle sally ports, the perimeter is compromised and vulnerable.)
5. Determine the speed of the sally port for vehicles (Check with the manufacturer to determine if the speed can be increased.)

DOI: 10.4324/9781003285946-7

When conducting security audits of facilities, we recommended that officers start with cells that house extremist-terrorist inmates. A good procedure for searching a cell is to visually inspect the ceilings left to right, walls to floors. The searcher looks for any type of destruction or anomalies to any of those areas within the cell, especially for any distortions, scratch marks, missing paint, different/discoloration of paint on *any* surface, which could indicate that an inmate or inmates were using those surfaces to sharpen shanks and tools for digging or other purposes.

As an aside, toothpaste mixed with scrapings has been used to cover up scratch marks on floors and walls. Older correctional facilities have an area behind the back wall of every cell called a "Pipe Chase." If inmates can gain entry to the "Pipe Chase," they have free access to move about areas behind the cells and to escape.

Another troublesome area is the commode/sink apparatus. A sound way to thoroughly check the commode/sink apparatus is to see if it is secured to the wall and that no parts are missing. Lastly, check to ensure that nothing is stored in the bowl or down the sink or toilet drainpipe.

> On the night of June 5, a little after 11 p.m., they climbed through holes they had cut—over months, with tools smuggled in by a prison guard—in the cell walls. They snaked through tunnels and between walls and through a steam pipe, which took them underneath the prison. They popped out of a manhole in the village. (Kirby, 2016)

Thoroughly inspect all furniture in the cell to ensure that it is completely intact. Anything can become a weapon if that is one's intent. For example,

> A Washington state Muslim prisoner screamed 'Allah Akbar' and repeatedly hit a guard on the head with a metal stool. The inmate pried a round metal seat off a stool in a cell and hit the officer over the head until other inmates stopped the attack. (Spencer, 2016)

While officers are inspecting/searching the cell, they should check for excess bedding, clothing, or magazines. Another important area to observe is what, if anything, is inmate writing or reading. Remember, in the United States, all "legal mail" is protected and cannot be read without legal advice. If the officers searching believe that contraband is within the "legal mail," the searching officer/s should treat the materials as evidence in a criminal case. They should "Bag and Tag" it but must not read it!

Any unauthorized religious mail, reading materials, and audio-video materials that are not on an approved list should be considered contraband and removed from the inmate's cell. Consider these materials evidence to be used in a disciplinary hearing. Therefore, they should be bagged and tagged, and officers must follow the chain of custody of their organization. Correctional staff and outside religious and legal consultants should develop an approved reading materials and audio-video materials list.

The inspection/search should move from the cell search to the general/common areas to which extremist-terrorist inmates and other extremist inmates would have access. Once again, the searching officers should stand still and let their eyes conduct a visual search and "Think Like a Terrorist." Some officers may ask themselves why they are being instructed to "standstill" and visually search the area.

Many years ago, when Sturgeon was a new correctional officer, he and three other correctional officers were assigned to search a four-person cell. Instructions were to look for a 357 revolver. Four of them approached the cell like a swarm of bees, rolling up mattresses, searching drawers and other areas, but they found no gun. At this point, Sturgeon saw the inmate, known to be the leader of this four-person cell, look to the wall. The gun was a picture of a 357 Magnum revolver cut out of an outdoors/sports magazine and glued to a 1-inch-thick piece of cardboard that gave the picture depth. When these inmates would shakedown other inmates in the exercise yard, one of them would stick the picture of the gun in his belt, then flash his coat open, exposing the gun or what the inmates thought was a gun. Three teaching points:

1. Perhaps if the team had conducted a visual search first, someone would have noticed the picture of the gun hanging on the wall.
2. The team's paradigm was that they knew the shape, weight, and size of a 357 Magnum revolver, which precluded them from accepting other facts.
3. When conducting a cell search or area search where inmates are present, have one of the searching officers observe where the inmate/s is looking. An old inmate once said that if an inmate is hiding something, "He will almost always look where he hid his stash." This advice has proven to be true. Perhaps it is human nature.

Search general/common areas where extremist-terrorist inmates and other extremist inmates will have access. These include the following areas and rooms, both before and after the inmates' use.

- Recreation areas (indoor and outdoor)
- Prayer rooms
- Program/education rooms
- Dayrooms
- Showers and shower drains
- Mop closets and slop sinks
- Work areas (kitchen, shops, etc.)
- Library
- Classrooms
- Visiting rooms and any restrooms for visitors

Thoroughly search these areas before the extremist-terrorist inmates and other extremists enter them and again when they leave. The first-line supervisor should rotate the officers conducting these cell and area searches. The rationale for rotating search officers is as follows:

1. If the same correctional officers conduct searches of the same common areas, again and again, complacency could set in, and they could miss something. These extremist-terrorist inmates and other extremists observe correctional officers performing their duties, looking for the weakest link—the officer who takes shortcuts or is slack.
2. The extremist-terrorist inmates and other extremists may try to befriend officers who appear vulnerable or afraid.

Addressing corrupt correctional officers is always a sensitive and difficult subject, which must be discussed by the facility-security administrator, the security-threat-group managers, internal affairs, the legal advisor, and the human resource managers. They all should be involved in any investigations involving suspected officer/staff corruption. "The tragic events that transpired on June 6, 2015, at the maximum-security Dannemora State Prison in New York State were a startling reminder that correctional officers are human beings and subject to corruption" (McKinley, 2015).

There are several reasons why correctional officers become compromised and corrupted:

1. Financial gain
2. Sexual favors
3. Intimidation (fear for themselves and their families)
4. Become enthralled with the organization
5. Belong to something
6. They can be "somebody"
7. Addictions

Whatever the reason for a correctional officer being compromised or corrupted, there is a danger to the staff, other inmates, and the facility's overall security when this occurs!

HARDENING SECURITY THROUGHOUT

Immediate actions are necessary to "harden" all aspects of a facility to manage extremist-foreign and domestic terrorist inmates, and other extremist organizations. The staff must analyze the entire physical plant, management, and operations to assess its security. "Harden" means to make the facility more secure. During his presidency, Abraham Lincoln described a situation still applicable today to demonstrate how correctional agencies and facilities must approach the management of terrorist-extremist inmates and other inmates: "The dogmas of the quiet past are inadequate to the stormy present. The occasion is piled high with difficulty, and we must rise with the occasion. As our case is new, so we must think anew and act anew ..." (Lincoln, 1862).

TECHNOLOGY, EQUIPMENT, AND MATERIALS (TEM)

When addressing technology, equipment, and materials (TEM), remember that TEM augments the human and structural elements of correctional operations; it does not replace them. Over the years, some believed that technology could replace the human element, and the results were disastrous for several reasons:

1. Staff became overly reliant on the TEM and did not perform their duties properly.
2. The technology (TEM) did not perform as described.
3. Inmates found ways to beat the technology (inmates started making shanks [homemade knives] out of plastic, thereby beating the metal detectors).
4. The facility installed cameras throughout every inmate living area to reduce the number of officers walking through the cellblocks. While they were able to see certain areas of the cellblock, they could not see other areas. The inmates quickly found out that by turning on the showers or turning up the volume on their

TVs and radios, they could negate the listening devices' ability to operate properly. The facility should have left the officer/s in the cellblock and installed the cameras and listening devices to augment the officers' presence.

When designating the TEM for areas where extremist-terrorist inmates and other extremists are or will be incarcerated, consider the following:

1. What is the purpose of the TEM?
   Detail exactly what each technology, piece of equipment, and specific materials will contribute to its security program. TEM will see, hear, detect, lock, unlock, or control. Here are more specifics:
   - **See**: This, for example, includes cameras that can pan, tilt, zoom, use night-vision/infrared monitors, riflescopes, or other capabilities. They might include monitors watched by humans or technology that will alert humans if activated.
   - **Hear**: This category includes listening devices, recording machines, and other devices.
   - **Detect**: These devices include officer body alarms, smoke alarms, carbon monoxide monitors, motion-interior and exterior sensors, water pressure gauges (for fire suppression), freezer temperature settings, and other devices.
   - **Unlock** doors, gates, and other areas.
   - **Control** water pressure and access to areas.
     How specifically will the TEM augment the human and structural elements? The best way to determine this is to describe how the human will interface with the TEM. An example of how technology and human interface work: The perimeter-security cameras record a facility's external perimeter activities. This activity is transmitted to monitors watched by a human. The human then reacts to whatever is happening on the perimeter. In the foreseeable future, technology could replace the human observing the monitors, which can be accomplished by programming the monitors for an alert when the cameras observe an anomaly to the program.
2. How will the area/facility continue to operate if it should lose any or all the TEM? What immediate measures will the administration take to ensure the facility's security should the TEM become inoperable? For example, what if there is an extended loss of power due to weather issues, electrical grid blackouts, and sabotage? It is crucial to know what *specific* technology and other electrical equipment will be dependent on the emergency generator/s.

3. How long will the facility's emergency generators operate on their existing fuel? What is the "burn rate" per hour? How are the emergency generators powered (gasoline, propane, natural gas)? Are there sufficient reserves to keep them going over an extended period? How long will they last? The authors recommend connecting emergency generator/s to natural gas as a source of fuel.
4. How long will it take for each of the TEMs to come back online (reboot)?
5. What is the average "downtime" for each piece of the TEM? The downtime is an important concern because in any correctional facility [especially those that incarcerate extremist-terrorist inmates, other extremists, and other high-security inmates], any part of the security operations that fail could cause dangerous situations.
6. Can in-house maintenance personnel perform repairs? Ascertain this information *before* purchasing any TEM. Some agencies have built into the Request for Proposal the cost of training programs for their in-house maintenance personnel.
7. How long will it take for off-site repair personnel to respond? Consider this carefully because the longer the TEM is nonoperational, the more vulnerable the facility will be. Today, many high-tech security companies have 24/7/365 personnel on call, and their response time is acceptable. However, some facilities are in remote areas. These facilities should have policies and procedures to use the human element to replace the technology element until the technology is up and running, which will require staff training in manual-operation procedures!
8. For years, airlines have strategically placed spare parts that commonly wear out at locations along their flight route. Correctional facilities could employ the same practice. Before purchasing any TEM, solicit a list of the parts that break down most often from the vendor. If possible, have in-house maintenance personnel trained to repair these most common breakdowns. Correctional facilities can take a lesson from major airlines and keep spare parts on hand for those that fail most often.
9. If the TEM functions as an alarm, before purchasing, ascertain what the false-alarm rate is. Knowing the false-alarm rate is very important because if a piece of equipment or technology has continuous false alarms, the staff will become complacent about their response. The extremist-terrorist inmates and other extremist organizations will observe this slow reaction by staff, and they could use the slow response time to their advantage.

10. As mentioned previously, correctional facilities should run drills on how to operate the facility manually. Conduct these drills during every shift, and submit detailed reports describing what went well and where additional training and practice is needed. Two key areas are the following:
    - How quickly did the staff respond to converting to manual operations?
    - What additional training, practice, and policies and procedures are needed for personnel? Once you know this answer, be sure to implement additional training or practice quickly.

When incarcerating extremist-terrorist inmates, all correctional personnel need to be super vigilant and aware when it comes to the following areas:

A. Their personal safety and security must become paramount!
B. The security of the unit/facility and the safety of the inmates are vital.
C. Each person must display situational awareness. Situational awareness means that while it is difficult to remain vigilant constantly, it is tremendously important that personnel assigned to these special living units know what is going on within the unit with the inmate/s and what roles individual inmates are playing. It is worth repeating the following things that staff must know:
   1. Who are the leaders?
   2. Who are the recruiters?
   3. Who are the soldiers?
   4. Who are the spiritual leaders?
   5. Identify foreign- and domestic-extremist-terrorist inmates with special skills:
      - Writing
      - Preaching
      - IT
      - Prior military training (military occupational specialty)
      - Prior jobs
        - Be aware of when something is different among extremist-terrorist inmates. Always have a plan for what to do if "X" happens.

DAY-TO-DAY OPERATIONS

Staff should never forget that they deal with extremist-terrorist inmates and other extremists, first and foremost, and criminal inmates, second. Each inmate population presents its concerns and challenges. The increase in violence within correctional facilities worldwide, but especially in the United States and the United Kingdom, is of utmost concern. Correctional professionals must consider how the introduction of foreign and domestic extremist-terrorist inmates into a correctional facility will influence:

1. The criminal inmates
2. The other extremist organizations, such as prison gangs, other extremist-terrorist inmates.

For example, there has been a horrendous increase in violence at Rikers Island (Durkin, 2019). Violence between inmates surged to 69.5 incidents a month for every 1,000 people in the jail population during the 2019 fiscal year, up from 55.8 incidents the year before. Serious injuries and attacks also jumped from 2 to 22.5. Inmate assaults against staff jumped to 12.6 for every 1,000 detainees, up from 9.2 in 2018 (Durkin, 2019). While it has not been stated whether some of these inmates mentioned in this article were foreign or domestic extremist terrorists, these are significant issues such as the escalation of violence. As the authors have said, "Whatever happens in the 'Free world' will eventually manifest itself in the correctional world."

EMERGENCY OPERATIONS: ASSESS-RESPONSE-ENGAGE/ CONTROL-REPEL/CONTAIN/RECOVER

Assess

Should a terrorist event occur, the on-site correctional staff must act as quickly as possible to assess the situation, report up the chain of command what is happening, and what type of response is required.

Response

Responding to terrorist events will entail training staff to respond efficiently and effectively. If an agency/institution cannot *prevent* a terrorist event, it must immediately respond to a terrorist event. As agencies/institutions develop the response to these events, they should realize that terrorists initially will have the element of surprise, and terrorists will be using lethal weapons and explosives (Sturgeon, 2005).

Terrorist attacks will be well planned, hard-hitting, swift, and lethal. Also, there is a strong possibility that multiple events will occur simultaneously, a common tactic terrorists use. The on-duty manager/supervisor quickly will have to determine whether there is a terrorist attack. There will not be time to call an on-duty administrator.

Some preliminary indicators of a possible terrorist attack could be the following:

- An explosion anywhere within the institution, anywhere along the perimeter, sally port, or parking lots.
- Any penetration of the external perimeter from the outside by persons or vehicles.
- Multiple violent, disruptive events happening simultaneously.
- A direct attack on any part of the institution where the attackers use firearms and explosives.

A crucial element of the response plan should include predetermined assignments for all staff. Some of the predetermined assignments should be for managing the inmates, while other personnel's primary assignments should be to respond to the possible terrorist event. The individual selected to be the institution's primary responder to possible terrorist events should receive additional training in the agency's observation, countermeasures, and techniques. These individuals should also be given additional equipment to always keep on their person or at their workstations.

Engage/Control

As correctional agencies/institutions develop the engage/control element, they must determine where they will attack terrorists using various scenarios. For example, if the attack is through the front lobby and in the sally port simultaneously, or if there is a suicide bomber in the visitor reception area and a vehicle penetrates the perimeter, the staff should be prepared to respond to multiple events.

As part of this planning effort, agencies/institutions must also identify what methods, tactics, techniques, weapons, and strategies they will use to engage/control events. Correctional institutions are built to keep people incarcerated using the physical building, electronic devices, personnel, lighting, and firearms. Firearms are nonexistent for all practical purposes within the secure perimeter. Firearms are located along the external perimeter and with the external roving patrol. Should a correctional facility come under armed assault the facility's emergency plan must have plan to engage armed intruders who have penetrated the external perimeter. They should identify ways to use these attributes as part of their defensive strategies. Former Mayor Rudolph Giuliani allegedly said, "I tried to expect the unexpected from what was clearly a shrewd enemy." Consider the following:

- Lighting can be disruptive to night vision equipment and used as a weapon.
- Use the personal sally ports to trap people.
- Use captured terrorist weapons to defend life and property.
- Use fire hoses as weapons.
- Use fire extinguishers as weapons.
- If chemical agents are used, this could prolong the incident because everyone involved has to be decontaminated.

Recovery

Recovering from a terrorist attack on a correctional institution will depend on a variety of factors. These include the number of staff and inmates killed or injured, damage to the institution, contamination concerns, and outside utilities such as water, wastewater, heat, light, and cooling. Additional concerns will be relieving or replacing staff involved in the attack, preserving the scene, getting reports written, ensuring that the institution is re-supplied, recharging/replacing batteries, transferring inmates should the institution be unsafe or lack sufficient security capabilities, and the ability to quarantine the institution should that be necessary. Other factors that should be part of the recovery plan include the following (Atherton & Phillips, 2007):

- Remaining on lockdown until the security of the facility is determined
- Securing the crime scene
- Securing, identifying, and properly storing dead bodies
- Keeping the families of staff and inmates informed
- Coordinating numerous official and volunteer agencies

- Securing the perimeter (possibly portions of the perimeter, which were destroyed)
- Sweeping of the institution by explosive-ordnance-disposal personnel
- Conducting a comprehensive search of the entire facility by security personnel
- Providing post-trauma screening and treatment for all staff
- Maintaining continuous 360-degree situational awareness of the external areas of the facility. This awareness is crucial to being proactive in preventing attacks on the facility by an external force. More than one attack may be in the works

Most extremist-terrorist attacks are well planned. There should be special surveillance of external areas of the facility, to include the following:

- The perimeter (by employing video-surveillance cameras to record external perimeter activities).
- Security personnel should review the recordings at least daily, looking for the following:
    - Anyone taking photographs of the facility, anyone taking photographs of agency personnel entering and leaving the facilities and what vehicles they are driving.
    - Any visitor/s acting suspiciously before and during visiting periods. Suspicious activity could be questioning rules and regulations, fidgety behavior, overly nervous behavior, excessive perspiring, being inappropriately dressed for existing weather conditions, acting out of sorts, and other "out of joint" activities.
    - Vehicles that drive by the facility at a slow rate of speed on several occasions, possibly to take pictures.
    - Security personnel should work with other agencies (Joint Counterterrorism Taskforce, local and state police, the FBI, and other federal agencies) to identify suspicious people.
    - Inmates ask correctional officers about operational and security protocols.

Correctional security operations must always maintain a proactive approach by being overt with external security to discourage potential extremist terrorists and/other extremists from viewing correctional facilities as possible "soft" targets.

Historically, correctional personnel focused solely on what was going on *inside* the facility's four walls or fences. With the advent of extremist-terrorist inmates and other extremists directly attacking correctional facilities, digging tunnels, flying drones, and engaging in other unique tactics, it is crucial that correctional personnel take on a 360-degree and "sky to sub-ground awareness" of the exterior perimeter and beyond so that they will be fully aware of what is going on within the facility as well as in the surrounding area.

TUNNELS

> Inmates reportedly used plates and pan handles to burrow an escape path; dumped excavated dirt in the sewer system, garbage cans, and hollow shafts they found in their wing … The six fugitives—two of whom are still at large—escaped by digging through the concrete and metal rebar flooring in their bathroom and removing a slab that led to a series of cavities in the prison's structure. They used these to leave the compound underground and then tunneled their way up to a road on the south side of the facility (*Times* of Israel Staff, 2021). "An Israel Prison Service official described the escape as 'a major security and intelligence failure.' Palestinian militant groups hailed it as 'heroic.'" (BBC News, 2021)

> In 2013, almost 2,000 inmates, including hundreds of terrorists, have escaped prisons in Iraq, Libya, and Pakistan. The series of ultra-violent, highly organized attacks has the US scared, and al Qaeda celebrating in Iraq. (Chitty, 2013)

> The militants report that they spent more than five months digging a tunnel more than 1,000 feet long to the main prison in southern Afghanistan, bypassing checkpoints, watchtowers, and concrete barriers topped with razor wire. The diggers finally broke through a concrete floor at Sarposa prison in Kandahar city on Sunday. They spent 4 ½ hours ferrying away nearly 500 inmates without a shot being fired, according to Taliban and Afghan officials. Most of the prisoners were Taliban militants. (National Public Radio Staff, 2011)

When Sturgeon originally wrote the article "Checking for Tunnels" in 2012, some colleagues thought that the article was interesting but not relevant to modern-day corrections with its high-tech equipment and systems of checks and balances. However, several events prove that "Tunneling Out of Prisons" is more fashionable than his colleagues thought. Escapes from two major maximum-security prisons—Dannemora (New York State DOC) and Altiplano (Mexico) prison occurred in 2015 (Mann, 2016) as well as the dramatic foreign escapes noted earlier. Therefore, once again, Sturgeon advises his correctional colleagues to search for tunnels. He cautions that staff must ensure that the search extends beyond the facility's external perimeter. Maintenance hole covers should be tack-welded down.

The Dannemora escape amazed Sturgeon when he realized that the pipe-chases were not part of the regular security inspections. Anyone who has worked in an older facility knows that pipe-chases are a security concern and should be regularly checked by security and maintenance personnel. When was the last time you checked for tunnels leading to and from your facility? This question may appear extreme to people in many industrialized nations, and it may well be. Yet, Sturgeon says that if he were still involved in a correctional facility's day-to-day security operations, he would certainly conduct security checks using ground-penetrating radar for tunnels, and here is why.

> Throughout the world, from the Middle East to the Mexican border, tunnels have become a method of moving guns, drugs, explosives, and people. Today's tunnels run the gamut from crude and dangerous to highly sophisticated. Some tunnels have airflow systems and electricity, and they are large enough to enable the operation of a small-motorized vehicle. (Sturgeon, 2014)

> Joaquin Guzman, the convicted Mexican drug lord known as El Chapo, has escaped twice from maximum-security prisons in Mexico, once by digging a mile-long tunnel from his cell. (Stempel, 2019)

It is a safe bet that in certain areas within the United States and throughout the world, some offenders have experience constructing tunnels. However, many Americans lack understanding and experience in uncovering tunnels, some because they believe, "That will never happen here!" Experts are available to teach correctional personnel how to search for tunnels. Many of these experts are in the U.S. military and the U.S. Border Patrol. The U.S. Border Patrol has uncovered tunnels for many years and has experience with every type of tunnel imaginable.

Those in the criminal justice field must continue to adapt our tactics to the changing world around us. The methods and techniques terrorists and criminals used in the Middle East, Europe, China, Africa, and other areas will eventually be used in the United States (Sturgeon, 2012).

CLASSIFICATION OF TERRORIST-EXTREMIST INMATES

These extremist-terrorist inmates, other extremists should be considered for more than one of the current correctional inmate classifications. They are a new breed of inmates, requiring novel and additional security, revised operations, and management. Training for all levels of staff is especially crucial.

The overall classification of extremist-terrorist inmates and other extremists should be broken down into sub-classifications of their own to be determined by the following:

- Initial charges (level of violence)
- Background intelligence
    - Criminal background
    - Number of arrests and charges
    - Returning overseas fighter/s (document from where)
    - No background information (undocumented)
    - Limited background information (for example, the extremist-terrorist inmate is a U.S. citizen, was a college student studying in Europe, and was unaccounted for three years before returning to the United States in 2019, via South America)
    - "Lone wolf" with a criminal record/extremist [more about lone-wolf terrorists in subsequent chapters]
    - Prior military experience
- Position within the group (leader/follower/assassin/recruiter/recruit)
- How long has the inmate been a member with this ideology? The longer the individuals have been brothers/sisters in extremist organizations, the more profound their indoctrination is and the stronger their belief in their group. Additionally, some brothers/sisters have moved up the organization's hierarchy because of

their length of service. They are more entrenched in the ideology and less willing to change, and they may be in more of a leadership position.
- Other acquaintances (non-extremist-terrorist inmates) within the facility
- Age (documented)
- Education (documented)
- Work experience (documented)
- Behavior while incarcerated
- Willingness to participate in de-radicalized programming (Clutterback, 2015)
- Exhibit hardcore Jihadist beliefs or extremist right-wing beliefs
- Converted while incarcerated.

The authors believe there is justification for housing extremist-terrorist inmates and other extremist organizations together. It would be too costly to train staff and harden several facilities or several areas within a prison to the extent necessary to house this inmate population and control their living conditions within the facility if they were housed in separate areas.

> Professor Peter Neumann, a counterterrorism expert at the International Centre for the Study of Radicalisation and Political Violence, King's College London, said that holding them [terrorists] in one place could inadvertently enable to them to form a command structure in a way that they could not when dispersed. 'You don't want to create a focal point for public protests—a 'British Guantanamo,' however much of a misrepresentation that might be—or provide an opportunity for terrorist prisoners to create operational command structures inside the prison that might not have existed outside,' he said. (McSmith, 2016)

While Professor Neumann's points are well taken, Sturgeon believes that he may have missed a couple of points:

- Correctional personnel are very skilled and have a lot of "real life" experience identifying and disrupting leaders of subversive organizations, such as prison gangs.
- The reference to Guantanamo Bay is more of a political issue than a disciplinary or security issue. Correctional administrators

are tasked with the institutional security and safety of the staff, the inmates, and the general public.

While these arguments for dispersing extremist-terrorist inmates and other extremist organizations have some valid points, Sturgeon believes that some correctional administrators and politicians have not fully comprehended that they cannot manage this classification of extremist-terrorist inmates and other extremists the same way as other categories of inmates are managed.

Make no mistake that foreign and domestic extremist-terrorist inmates are ideologues first and criminals second. White supremacists can be as ideological as any other extremist organization. They adhere to the belief that the government does not have control of them—their God does. They need to belong to something they consider to be more important than themselves.

On occasion, correctional administrators can underestimate, and politicians understate the potential for violence, which occurs when discussing extremist-terrorist inmates' possible impact on correctional operations and security. Be aware of and respect this inmate population's capabilities, experiences, and deeply religious, political, and ideological beliefs.

Appearing before the House of Commons Justice Select Committee, Mr. Acheson, a former prison governor, warned:

> There are a small number of people whose behaviour is so egregious in relation to proselytising this pernicious ideology, this lethal nihilistic death cult ideology, which gets magnified inside prison particularly when you have a supply of young, impulsive and often highly violent men, that they need to be completely incapacitated from being able to proselytise to the rest of the prison population. (McSmith, 2016)

While your authors believe that separate housing units are prudent, for the time being, they will keep an open mind as more experience and research becomes available. Some proponents for dispersing extremist-terrorist inmates and other extremist organizations do not credit correctional administrators, supervisors, and line staff. These experienced correctional professionals have encountered and overcome challenging issues in the past. With proper appreciation of and training for this unique inmate population, they will rise to the situation time and time again.

The authors have adopted the belief that it is not sound practice to speak in absolutes when discussing anything associated with criminal justice. In the field of criminal justice, there are few absolutes about predicting human behavior!

As more experience and research become available, administrators will need new and additional security, operations, staffing patterns, and staff training. They will develop these new methods and techniques through real-world experience and research. Once the staff receives new training, they will acquire the necessary skills to manage this extremist-terrorist inmate population.

The special commission investigating the attacks of September 11, 2001 concluded twenty months of investigation and hearings with a report that said,

> The U.S. government failed to protect the American people. The panel says the blame lies not with either U.S. President George W. Bush or his predecessor, Bill Clinton, but with the nation's security apparatus, which it said did not adapt to new threats in a changing world. (Tully, 2004)

Hindsight is always 20/20. Finding fault after an event is much easier than seeing into the future to prevent an event. Correctional administrators have an opportunity to prepare for the challenges of extremist-terrorist inmates. This opportunity will not last forever. Almost daily, extremist terrorists are being arrested, convicted, and sentenced to prison.

CONCLUSIONS

In reality, "we simply don't know what we don't know" how these extremist-terrorist inmates and other extremists will spread and increase their numbers or the events that will lead to arrests and incarceration. Another unknown is how extremist terrorists and other extremists will manifest themselves once incarcerated. The authors are endeavoring to be proactive, encouraging correctional agencies worldwide to prepare methods and strategies for this unique inmate population, in other words, to use their imagination—something not exercised during 9/11. Some of our European counterparts are already struggling with extremist-terrorist inmate populations. We can learn a great deal from their experiences.

As more facilities incarcerate additional extremist-terrorist inmates, the field of corrections will be required to make adjustments to security, operations, management, programming, and training needs. When these new issues arise, correctional professionals and agencies must take immediate action to address these situations. Many of the adjustments and adaptations necessary for incarcerating extremist-terrorist inmates and other extremists will also enhance any correctional facility's overall operations and security.

Whether an agency/facility uses the suggested matrix or develops its method for conducting a comprehensive review of this magnitude, its policies and procedures must be carefully examined to ensure that they are "operationally functional" and assist in hardening the facility, both internally and externally.

8

Staff Recruitment and Training

RECRUITMENT FOR STAFF DIVERSITY

Increased efforts are necessary to recruit correctional staff possessing the racial, ethnic, and religious characteristics of people represented among extremist populations, which is important for many reasons. First, it will ensure that staff understand the inmates' culture better and will be less apt to discriminate against them. Second, it will help to build a sense of trust between terrorist inmates and line officers. Finally, it will help address language barriers, making it challenging for staff to interpret conversations or written material (Bryans, 2016; Williams, 2016).

Staff selection is crucial to managing these various inmate populations. Only the most conscientious, skilled, and resourceful staff members should be considered to work with those in "specialized units." Line staff are obligated to protect the security of correctional institutions and uphold the dignity of offenders within correctional facilities (including terrorist-extremist inmates). Consequently, correctional officers should be selected based on their professionalism and integrity (Bryans, 2016), and they should receive specialized training to manage terrorist-extremist inmates adequately (Sturgeon, 2010).

Careful selection of the staff assigned to work in special inmate housing units is vital. An old saying in the criminal justice field that the authors have seen borne out is that "The best staff get the worst assignments!" Correctional staff selected to work with extremist-terrorist

DOI: 10.4324/9781003285946-8

inmates and other extremist organizations should be required to pass comprehensive background investigations, according to the United Nations Office on Drugs and Crime (2016).

> Staff working with violent extremist prisoners requires a combination of personal qualities and technical skills. They need personal qualities that enable them to deal with all prisoners, including the difficult, dangerous, and manipulative, in an even-handed and in a just manner … . Violent extremist prisoners may attempt to undermine the professionalism of staff and seek to exploit staff to obtain illicit goods, to assist with an escape attempt, or to act as a conduit to criminal organizations outside of the prison. Prison staff, therefore, need to meet the highest standard of professionalism and personal conduct at all times. (Bryans, 2016)

Since Sturgeon began his criminal justice career, insufficient staffing has been an issue and has gotten worse in recent years. In specialized inmate living areas, very much as in other high-security areas, proper staffing always is imperative. The correct number of staff with the proper training must follow policies and procedures relevant and written in a way that applies to this extremist-terrorist inmate population. Thus, line staff and line supervisors can effectively manage this population, given proper staffing. Staffing shortages continue to be a significant problem in many of the industrialized nations.

Staff training is one of the most crucial aspects of keeping a well-run facility and preventing radicalization.

> The European Commission stressed again the need to enhance the exchange of good practices for training prison staff in the prevention of radicalization in prison and the development of de-radicalization programs. Educating workers and interventions in prisons became key features of these initiatives. (ICF Consulting, 2019)

Correctional officers should be familiar with the policies and procedures established by their particular agency and facility, including classification, surveillance, and emergency protocols for terrorists. Prison staff should know the basics of terrorism and counter-terrorism strategies, recognize radicalization, and understand how the radicalization process works. Additionally, they should be familiar with the dangers that terrorist-extremist inmates pose to other inmates, staff, and the community.

WHY TRAINING IS CRUCIAL

Insufficient or out-of-date training can lead to disastrous outcomes for individual officers, inmates, facilities, and agencies. High-quality staff training can solve many of the problems facing today's correctional operations, management, security, and programming.

The staff must receive specialized training before initiating work within the extremist-terrorist inmate population. Many of these extremist-terrorist inmates and other extremist organizations and right-wing extremists have more sophistication than many organizations and agencies think. Extremist-terrorist inmates and other extremist organizations of every persuasion bring with them the skills, abilities, and desires that can create challenges to the operations, management, and security of correctional facilities worldwide.

Moreover, line staff cannot always understand the languages spoken by inmates, and there are not always translators on-site. Therefore, experts recommend that someone within the prison (in other words, a correctional officer, imam, or a translator) is on-site to understand what terrorist-extremist inmates are saying at all times. Finally, staff-awareness training is necessary to ensure that prisons treat all inmates fairly and do not violate their constitutional rights. If staff are educated about legal issues, terrorists will find it harder to obtain outside support for their grievances and mistreatments.

Use intelligence obtained by line staff to develop training initiatives to teach staff what actions they can take to curtail recruiting efforts within the correctional facility. Managers, supervisors, wardens, and sheriffs should determine what additional management, security, and operational adjustments should be instituted to ensure the facility's security and protect other inmates and the public. Some of the following questions should be examined by the head of the facility and that person's top advisers.

1. What additional staff training is needed to ensure the safety of the staff, visitors, inmates, and the security of the correctional facilities?

2. What new policies, procedures, and post orders will you need to create and implement?
3. Determine if the housing arrangements that the facility is using are working. These housing arrangements may include special inmate housing where extremist-terrorist inmates and other extremist organizations are housed, thereby isolating them from the criminal inmate population or interspersing extremist-terrorist inmates and other extremist organizations throughout the facility.

VARIETY OF TRAINING

Training is crucial for retooling prison operations to manage extremist-terrorist inmates and other extremist organizations and other potential extremist organizations. By the number of times training is referred to in this guide, the reader will see the importance that the authors place on training.

In a conversation Sturgeon had with the late Raymond K. Procunier, former Director of Corrections for Texas, Procunier noted that changing prison culture could not be done by edicts and commands but by training the staff in how to change. Throughout his career, Sturgeon found Director Procunier's philosophy to be spot-on. People/staff will adapt to change if they are trained/taught how to change.

While it is clear that staff training is crucial for effectively managing terrorist-extremist inmates, considerable variation exists in training staff on these matters. For example, the United States has fifty different state prison systems, a federal system, various local jail systems for initial detention, and private prison systems, with variations in implementing staff training within each system (Neumann, 2010).

Prison administrators must also continue to invest in staff training to manage terrorists in prison effectively. Considerable variation exists in implementing staff training within the federal and state prison systems throughout the nation (Neumann, 2010). Although there is limited research on this subject, all correctional facilities—federal, state, local, and private—should make greater efforts to train staff on issues related to radicalization and managing terrorists in prison.

Although limited research is available on this subject, Merola and Vovak (2012) found that 27 percent of wardens in maximum-security state prisons in the United States indicated that they did not provide their staff with any training to identify inmates posing a threat of extremism.

Furthermore, 65 percent did not offer training to manage the routine interactions with inmates holding extremist beliefs. Consequently, there needs to be greater emphasis on training staff on radicalization in prisons and more research on this topic.

ROLE OF THE CORRECTIONAL OFFICER

The role of the correctional officer in minimizing radicalization is vital. Correctional officers interact with prisoners daily and have the ability to detect trouble. However, most correctional officers do not have the training to recognize and manage the radicalization process. Moreover, correctional officers are often on rotation, so it may be hard for them to familiarize themselves with and supervise the activities of terrorist-extremist inmates (Gutierrez, Jordan, & Trujillo, 2008).

Get Ready Now

Often, when extremist-terrorist inmates and other extremist organizations arrive at the facility or are identified by the security-threat-group personnel, none of the staff have been trained to manage them. To counteract this problem, ahead of need, select staff for assignment to the "special management unit."

Before the need arises, develop training protocols to permit the agency to staff up a new or large facility quickly. Initially, if the unit were overstaffed, permit half of the staff to be trained in the morning and the other half of the staff in the afternoon. This model also allows trained staff to be available, if needed, to replace staff calling in sick, unable to work in the unit, or staff burnout. New policies and procedures also allow for new information/intelligence obtained by correctional personnel working in the "Specialized Unit/s to be reported to training personnel for incorporation into the training curriculum and to the security-threat-group officials to be analyzed for intelligence purposes."

Training programs for staff working with extremist-terrorist inmates and other extremist organizations must remain dynamic. In the past, some prisons' training became stagnant for three reasons: funding shortfalls, staffing shortages, and insufficient feedback and input from the field. The training departments did not stay up to date with the facility's changes, especially gang training. Not until correctional agencies realized that gangs were dynamic and constantly evolving did some correctional agencies initiate a monthly review of what gang activity transpired over the previous month.

CONTENT OF TRAINING PROGRAMS

> Training programs for dealing with extremist-terrorists should "include the specialized training of prison staff and the involvement of a diversity of experts and professionals, including psychologists, family members, religious scholars, victims of terrorism, prominent community members, and even 'formers.' (Rosand, 2017)

The training department should review and incorporate the extremist-terrorist review committee's monthly report into basic and annual training and additional courses or updates to existing topics.

A couple of other methods that have worked in the past are the following:

- Schedule mini-training sessions for staff working directly with the extremist-terrorist inmates, should the need arise.
- "Quick Briefings" should occur at the beginning and end of each shift. The outgoing shift supervisor should brief the incoming shift supervisor of any incidents or management/operational issues that arose during the shift. This briefing should include the basic who, what, when, where, how (if known), and what action(s) was taken to manage the situation. Sturgeon states: recording what action/s took place proves to be very important in any report, but especially in use-of-force reports because this information can reduce the possibility of future incidents.

From top administrators to line correctional officers, staff need specialized training in the management of extremist-terrorist inmates.

> Prisons incarcerating violent extremist prisoners in their presence will also require training and political intelligence. They need to be able to manage prisoners who have a high profile with politicians, media, and the public, which brings greater scrutiny and sensitivity to any operational decision made concerning those prisoners. It is important, therefore, that prison directors understand the broader landscape and be able to navigate through additional pressures. (Bryans, 2016)

Sample Training Curriculum for Correctional Personnel with Direct Contact with Extremist-Terrorist Inmates

> If you know the enemy and know yourself, you need not fear the result of a hundred battles. If you know yourself but not the enemy, for every victory gained, you will also suffer a defeat. If you know neither the enemy nor yourself, you will succumb in every battle. (Tzu, 2012)

"Training, which is crucial to any environment, is especially important for people working with violent-extremist prisoners" (Bryans, 2016).

As part of preparing correctional personnel to manage extremist-terrorist inmates, teach them the basic tenets of Islam and recognize right-wing terrorism. See, for example, Appendix 4, which Sturgeon intercepted at one prison. Instruct correctional personnel that not all the people who practice Islam follow the extreme version.

Extremist-terrorist inmates differ from criminal inmates in the following ways: they believe that they answer to a higher authority. Some are willing to die or become martyrs for their beliefs. They believe that people who do not believe the way they believe are infidels or are wrong thinkers. As we discussed, many of them were trained in military tactics. Some could be returning from fighting with ISIL in Syria, Africa, Iraq, or other areas, and they may have killed in the past.

Correctional personnel should use the following management techniques and methods to deal with this extremist-terrorist inmate population.

Correctional personnel must adhere to agency policies and procedures in response to a verbal assault by an extremist-terrorist inmate. They must maintain composure and status as correctional professionals and not get trapped into a verbal confrontation with extremist-terrorist inmates. All correctional personnel should receive instruction on how to treat extremist-terrorist inmates in a respectful but firm way. Instruct correctional personnel always to maintain their professionalism and integrity. Often, extremist-terrorist inmates use verbal confrontations as either a power play or they are performing for potential recruits.

Correctional staff must understand clear instructions on policies and procedures for reporting extremist-terrorist inmate threats to the proper correctional authorities. Correctional staff should never feel that the administration is not backing them up. The training should reinforce the importance of following the chain of command.

Situational awareness is crucial when assigned to the extremist-terrorist inmates' housing unit. Staff should always know where they are in the unit and where other officers assigned to the unit are. They must know where there is a "safe" area to get to if something should happen. Similarly, they should know where in the housing unit there are "dangerous places." "Dangerous places" are those areas where other staff personnel cannot see them, and they cannot see you. In these places, video/audio surveillance cannot observe their movements and actions. In these places, they could be trapped, assaulted, or taken hostage.

Intelligence gathering and reporting. Staff need to learn what they should look for when gathering correctional intelligence? Some of the things include the following:

- Know who the leaders are.
- Know who the members are.
- Learn how to identify the recruiters.
- Are there inmates who distance themselves from identified radical/extremists?
- Know who is associating with whom and for what purpose.
- Know where the radical-extremist inmates congregate during mealtimes, recreation, and out-of-cell time.
- Know what languages they speak and, if possible, learn a few key phrases.
- Determine if they understand English.
- Learn what they talk about (if they do not speak English, get translations of their conversation).
- Observe what types of relationships they have with the correctional staff.
- Observe if there are changes in the demeanor and relationship with other inmates and correctional staff.
- Know how to recognize information that might be valuable and gather this information and report it quickly to intelligence.
- Learn how to identify the hierarchy within the terrorist-extremist inmate organization.

Describe the contents needed in an intelligence report: <u>who</u> must include every person, staff, and inmates who witnessed anything or were participants. <u>What</u> exactly describes what transpired: an incident, verbal threat on staff/another inmate (s), an attempt to coerce staff/inmates to break the rules.

When means the day, date, time the incident occurred. Where describes the location of the incident. Be specific as to the exact location! How did the incident progress from the beginning to the end? Knowing the details provides important information for security, intelligence, and training because it brings to light their "modus operandi" of approaching and targeting.

Self-Defense Techniques

Correctional staff assigned to work with terrorist-extremist inmates should receive "specialized" self-defense techniques on how to:

- Repel an unarmed attacker.
- Repel an armed attacker.
- Get off the ground.
- Break holds if attacked from behind and other moves.

Training on Customs/Religion

Staff should receive instruction on religious and cultural customs, which includes:

- Cross-gender issues.
- Respect for religious items.
- Respect for religious practices.
- Knowledge of religious holy days and how the inmates observe them.

Emergency Procedures

Staff should receive instruction on *emergency procedures*:

- Their response should be measured—do not initially overcommit. Always be mindful of a trap!
- Reaction—quickly assess the situation—know and report to Control what is going on.
  - If it is a disturbance, how many inmates are involved? How many staff members are involved?
  - Are there any injuries, and how serious are they?
  - Is there more than one situation occurring simultaneously? If so, call for additional help. It's always better to have too many than too few.

- Can the on-duty staff manage the situation(s)?
- Repel any attack, assault, or attempt to take hostages.
- Contain the incident—stop it from spreading.
- Control and re-establish normal operations as quickly as possible.

Personal safety should be *a high priority* at all times. Staff should be encouraged to inform their supervisors when they no longer feel that they can perform their duties and responsibilities safely and securely. They may be approaching or are at the burnout stage and need to be rotated out of the unit.

CONCLUSIONS

The authors have not prescribed a specific time for any actions or responses but left that up to the individual agency/facility, believing they know their employees' needs. A drill sergeant once said, "How you train will be how you'll fight!" Train your staff, and the rewards will be forthcoming!

The military exemplifies what well-developed and expert instruction, implementation, and practice can accomplish. One major job of the administration is to ensure that their people/staff are trained to perform their duties and responsibilities properly. An untrained, or poorly trained staff is not fair to the staff and the inmates. Such training is especially crucial when dealing with extremist-terrorist inmates.

9

Classification, and Other Essentials

CLASSIFICATION

Agencies should consider creating a new classification (a tiered approach) for extremist-terrorist inmates. The authors recommend giving correctional agencies time to gain experience in dealing with this inmate population—both right-wing and other extremist terrorists. The elements to consider in this classification include the following:

1. Is the conviction because of a crime of violence; if so, what is the level of violence?
2. Have you confirmed that the inmate is a known member of a terrorist group?
3. Has the inmate exhibited threatening, violent, assaultive, disruptive, or insubordinate behavior while incarcerated or awaiting trial?
4. How long has the inmate been a member of a terrorist group?
5. Has the inmate held any leadership positions, imam, recruiter, enforcer, executioner, and so forth, within the group?
6. Has the inmate been incarcerated before? If so, how many times, where, what for, and for how long?
7. What is the duration of the current sentence?
8. Does the inmate demonstrate any remorse?

DOI: 10.4324/9781003285946-9

9. Do the inmates demonstrate any desire to disassociate themselves from terrorist activities?
10. Would the team assess the inmate as a threat risk? If yes, what is the inmate's level of threat risk?

THREAT RISK SCALE

1. Severe-threat risk
2. Medium-threat risk
3. Minimal-threat risk
4. Low-threat risk

Once the team determines an inmate's threat level, assign the inmate to a housing unit. As previously discussed, Sturgeon believes that terrorist inmates should be housed together. Inmate classification can be changed, either up or down, based on the inmate's behavior and how the inmate performs in various programs or job assignments.

INMATE MOVEMENT—INTERNAL AND EXTERNAL

Conduct as many court proceedings, medical appointments, and other meetings as possible within the facility's security. Depending on the classification, past experiences, and purpose for the movement of the inmate/s, use special precautions.

Officers should use caution when initially approaching extremist-terrorist inmates and other extremist inmates (or, for that matter, any inmates) before extracting them from their cell. If possible, officers should try to talk to the inmates to determine what mood the inmates are in, and explain to the inmates what is about to happen and what they expect to do (for example, cuffing and shackling) and what the officers expect from the inmate (back-up to the cell door, put your hands behind your back, and so forth), and then follow the agency's existing policies and procedures.

Before opening the cell door, the officers should be prepared for anything that could transpire. For example, the inmate could bolt out of the cell and assault the officer/s or retreat to the back of the cell and refuse to cooperate with the officer's commands. At this juncture, the officer should secure the cell. Follow agency policies and procedures.

> Opening the cells on Thursday morning, an officer was set upon by men wearing a fake suicide belt and wielding a bladed weapon slashing him in the face and shouting Allahu Akbar; one of the attackers had been jailed for plotting to behead an army cadet. (Foges, 2020)

RISK ASSESSMENT

Risk and need assessments are an important part of criminal-justice decision-making to predict an offender's risk of reoffending and provide intervention strategies that target the offender's criminogenic needs. These assessments influence the level of supervision an offender needs, and they target appropriate risk factors to reduce an offender's likelihood of reoffending. Although risk and need assessments cannot predict with 100 percent accuracy if an offender will recidivate, they help correctional administrators and staff make the most accurate decisions to manage offenders safely (Thompson, 2017).

As discussed earlier, it is important to assess terrorists differently from typical criminals because they are different in several ways. First, criminals are primarily motivated by personal gain or addictions, while ideologies drive terrorists and social, religious, or political causes. Second, criminals try to avoid detection, while terrorists often advertise their acts. Third, traditional criminals often have mental health problems, which is not necessarily true of terrorists (Farrell, 2013). Finally, unlike criminals, terrorists do not usually come from an impoverished home or lack education or vocational skills (Silke, 2014).

There are many risk and need assessments instruments available for criminal offenders, and these instruments typically focus on an offender's dynamic (changeable) and static (unchangeable) criminogenic risk factors. Dynamic risk factors include a history of antisocial behavior and personality patterns (in other words, low self-control), pro-criminal attitudes and beliefs, criminal associates, substance abuse issues, weak family or marital relationships, school or work failures, and a lack of prosocial leisure activities (Andrews, Bonta, & Wormith, 2006). While dynamic criminogenic risk factors are influenced through appropriate interventions, static factors cannot be. Static factors are fixed, and they include factors such as an offender's number of prior convictions and age at first arrest. Once practitioners identify an offender's dynamic criminogenic needs, they can match the offender with the appropriate interventions in hopes of reducing the risk of recidivism.

Risk-Assessment Tools

Because terrorist-extremist inmates follow ideologies, they are not the same as criminal inmates; it is important to use different risk-assessment tools. At least one measure, the Violent Extremist Risk Assessment (VERA 2R), shows some promise for assessing an offender's risk of radicalization to violent extremism. Elaine Pressman developed this instrument in 2009 and revised it in 2010 and 2015. Several European countries, as well as Australia, currently use the VERA 2R to assess the risks and needs of a wide range of violent extremists, including right-wing organizations, left-wing organizations, ISIS, al-Qaeda, and other offenders motivated by political, religious, or social ideologies (VERA 2R, 2017).

The purpose of the VERA 2R is to evaluate an individual's risk of future violence and determine appropriate programming during their incarceration. VERA 2R is different from criminal offenders' tools, as it assesses thirty-one factors related to violent extremism. These factors include items related to *beliefs and attitudes* (for example, commitment to an ideology justifying violence, being the victim of perceived injustice, or exhibiting feelings of alienation). Other items include *context and intent* (for example, possessing extremist materials, contacting other extremists, or being willing to die for a cause). It also includes items related to an offender's *history and capability* (for example, exposure to violent militant ideology, prior paramilitary training, or access to resources), as well as *commitment and motivation* (for example, commitment to a political group or glorification of violence) (Silke, 2014).

Although no risk-need assessment can predict future offending accurately, assessment measures are useful for correctional personnel. Most importantly, it is crucial to use different measures to assess violent extremists than those used for criminal offenders because they have different risks and needs. While there is limited research on the effectiveness of

VERA 2R, it appears to be a promising tool to help with the case management of terrorist-extremist inmates.

Because terrorist-extremist inmates and other extremist inmates are not the same as their criminal counterparts, different instruments should assess these distinct groups. The VERA 2R appears to be a promising tool to help with the case management of terrorist-extremist inmates. It identifies inmates associated with radical organizations and assesses the offenders' risk of radicalization to violent extremism and their risk of engaging in future acts of extremism. VERA 2R assesses terrorists on thirty-one factors, including items related to beliefs and attitudes, history and capability, and commitment and motivation (Silke, 2014). Moreover, this instrument can also help practitioners establish appropriate programs and interventions for these inmates (Bryans, 2016; VERA 2R, 2017).

VERA 2R is currently used in Australia and several European countries. However, there is limited research on the effectiveness of VERA 2R and similar instruments. Accordingly, researchers are strongly encouraged to examine whether these tools effectively help correctional professionals manage terrorist inmates. If additional research indicates that these instruments have value, the federal and state governments incarcerating inmates in the United States should consider using terrorist-specific assessment tools, such as the VERA-2R.

PERIMETER SECURITY (INTERNAL AND EXTERNAL)

Ensure that perimeter security is always maintained at the highest level. Use technology to augment the human element and "harden" the perimeter. Today's correctional-perimeter security is all-encompassing. It includes internal and external surveillance, 360 degrees at ground level, above and below the facility's perimeter. As previously indicated, due to drones, the issue of air space takes on new importance.

- *Vehicle sally ports and pedestrian security gates.* If these are not properly secured, they may be vulnerable areas of the facility. Do not use vehicle sally ports for pedestrian traffic. In many facilities, sally ports open and close slowly. When a sally port is open, there is, for all practical purposes, a hole in the facility's perimeter.

SUGGESTION FOR SALLY PORT

Time the vehicle sally port/s gate speed—specifically how long it takes the gate to open and close. Contact the manufacturer to see if the speed can be increased to enable it to open and close faster. Additionally, the policy and procedure review team should ensure that policies and procedures are in place should an attacking force strike through a sally port.

Sturgeon believes that the vehicle sally port presents a significant vulnerable point in the perimeter. Therefore, it should be open and closed as little as possible. If possible, the speed of the gate should be increased so that it is open for the shortest amount of time possible.

MONITORING TERRORIST-EXTREMIST INMATES

While terrorist-extremist inmates are a relatively new phenomenon in U.S. prisons, prison administrators are familiar with managing gangs and other security threat organizations (STGs). STGs engage in much criminal activity within a correctional setting, including drugs, intimidation, assaults, and contraband smuggling. Consequently, STGs require additional resources because they pose an increased threat to the security and operations of correctional institutions. Terrorist-extremist inmates and other extremist inmates are a new type of STG, but correctional administrators and staff can follow similar management protocols as they would for other STGs. Specifically, administrators should consider classification, intelligence, and staff training (Marchese, 2009) when managing terrorists in prison.

INTELLIGENCE

Experience has demonstrated that prisons should also have a robust intelligence-gathering system to collect security-related information regarding terrorist-extremist inmates and other extremist inmates. Collecting, analyzing, and disseminating information about this population is crucial for the safety and security of correctional facilities and preventing radicalization. Based on his experience, Sturgeon contends that intelligence systems help prison administrators make decisions about inmate placement, programming, and the allocation of human resources such as staffing.

Intelligence gathering also allows correctional personnel to access information about terrorist-extremist inmates and other extremist organizations housed within their units (Sturgeon, 2010). Intelligence should also be shared with other criminal justice and governmental agencies to manage these individuals most effectively (Bryans, 2016).

In the United States, the Bureau of Prisons (BOP) and the FBI have developed a Correctional Intelligence Initiative (CII) to prevent and detect radicalization efforts in U.S. prisons. The CII improves coordination on terrorism issues between the Joint Terrorism Task Force (JTTF) and correctional agencies across the country (Bryans, 2016).

The CII aims to improve intelligence collection, provide training, and disrupt terrorist efforts in federal, state, local, and private prisons. Furthermore, they have established a more stringent vetting process for all staff, including contract and volunteer persons entering the prison. They have also improved surveillance, coordinated inmate transfers, and information sharing between criminal justice and governmental agencies (Van Duyn, 2006).

VISITING

Most correctional professionals know that visiting times are always a security concern when recruiting criminal inmates to become extremist-terrorist inmates and other extremist inmates to join their brotherhood. The following quote comes from an al-Qaeda training manual discovered during a raid in Manchester, U.K.

> Take advantage of visits to communicate with brothers outside prison and exchange information that may be helpful to them and their work outside prison (according to what occurred during the investigations). The importance of mastering the art of hiding messages is self-evident here. (al-Qaeda Manual, n.d.)

Visitation. Depending on the agency's policies and procedures for permitting visiting privileges to extremist-terrorist inmates, correctional personnel and the local JTTF must conduct comprehensive background investigations of all potential visitors.

The authors believe that visiting should be part of an incentive program to encourage good behavior and reintegration and deradicalization programs. Studies show that maintaining family ties can be an important method in deradicalization. Consider the complexity of the prison environment and the unavoidable restrictions that directly affect an inmate's liberty. Then, provide the inmate opportunities to maintain positive social interactions with family or significant others.

As with all visiting times, staff must be extremely attentive to what transpires between inmates and visitors. If the visitors appear to be breaking the rules or upsetting the extremist inmate, staff should remove them from the facility and suspend their visiting privileges until the incident is investigated. Additionally, make the housing unit supervisor of the extremist-terrorist inmate who has been in a distressful/emotional situation involving a visitor aware of the situation's details.

Inspecting Outside Visitors

Everyone visiting inmates in the general prison population must be screened for smuggling in contraband, including drugs, weapons, cell phones, and anything else that could threaten the facility's security. However, in the case of terrorist-extremist inmates and other extremists, prison staff must also prevent visitors from bringing extremist messages into the prison.

Consequently, there are more stringent restrictions for people visiting terrorists in federal prisons in the United States. In the Communication Management Units (CMUs) in Terre Haute and Marion, visits are limited to immediate family members, and inmates are limited to eight one-hour non-contact visits each month. According to the Center for Constitutional Rights (2010), "The CMUs house between 60 and 70 prisoners in total, and approximately 60 percent of the CMU population is Muslim, even though Muslims represent only 6 percent of the general federal prison population."

Moreover, inmates at ADX Florence are only allowed five visits per month (Federal Bureau of Prisons, 2014). Correctional officers search all visitors thoroughly for contraband, and all visits are monitored and recorded. Furthermore, visits must be conducted in English or translated by an approved interpreter (Federal Bureau of Prisons, 2015).

Visitor's Parking Area. The visitor's parking areas should be under surveillance during visiting times. The Security Threat Group should receive a video recording of the visiting areas for review, and if deemed necessary, referred to the Joint Terrorism Taskforce. Inmates take advantage of visits to communicate with brothers and sisters outside prison and exchange information that may help them in their work outside of the prison. Inmates are masters of the art of hiding messages (Stojkovic, 2010).

REVIEWING MATERIALS ENTERING PRISONS

As a result of the shortage of religious providers in prisons, there are not enough qualified people to examine the content of material that enters prisons in the United States, much of which is in foreign languages. Also, there is no standard procedure to determine if the material prisoners are receiving is appropriate. Furthermore, staff cannot always distinguish between legitimate religious information and extremist materials (Neumann, 2010). So, it is likely that material promoting extremist ideologies is entering prisons, and without individuals knowledgeable in Islam and other religions, and inmates could easily obtain this information.

However, steps are being taken to prevent this from happening. For example, there are limits on written correspondence for inmates housed in the CMUs in Terre Haute and Marion. At the warden's discretion, correspondence for each inmate is limited to six pieces of paper once a week to and from a single recipient. Moreover, all correspondence is reviewed by the Counter-Terrorism Unit (CTU) before being delivered to the inmate or going out to the public. All correspondence written in another language is translated before being delivered to the inmate or mailed out to the public (Federal Bureau of Prisons, 2015). Sturgeon (2010) also suggested that staff opening incoming mail be in an area away from the facility's ventilation system.

Finally, telephone communication within CMUs is limited to immediate family members. Inmates are allowed three phone calls per month of fifteen minutes for each call. Furthermore, calls are only conducted using the facility's phone lines and are monitored and recorded by CTU staff. All communication must be in English or translated by an approved interpreter (Federal Bureau of Prisons, 2015).

CONCLUSIONS

Monitoring, intelligence operations, and reviewing materials take on a greater role in the overall management, operations, and security of any facility incarcerating extremist-terrorist inmates. Even in the face of staff shortages, these activities are crucial and should not be neglected.

10

Inmate Programs to Limit Radicalization

Aside from assessments for terrorists, prisons in the United States must also consider specific programming for terrorists. As noted in Chapter 5, de-radicalization plays a negligible role in managing terrorist-extremist inmates in U.S. prisons (Dugas & Kruglanski, 2014), and there are no terrorist disengagement programs in the Federal Bureau of Prisons (BOP; Rosand, 2017).

This abstract about radicalization in custody clearly outlines why the United States lags behind other countries to establish deradicalization programming.

> This policy paper explores radicalization and violent extremism in the United States federal correctional system. Federal correctional facilities currently host diverse populations of incarcerated extremists, and dozens of extremist inmates are scheduled for release within the next five years. While problems related to extremism in the U.S. correctional system may seem small, especially in comparison to other issues, the threat of in-custody radicalization and extremist recidivism are growing concerns for U.S. counterterrorism authorities. Despite this increased attention, there is a lack of data regarding the scope and nature of radicalization in custody in the U.S., and a concomitant lack of terrorism prevention programming in American prisons and jails. These two interrelated features

DOI: 10.4324/9781003285946-10

> create a feedback loop—practitioners are loath to implement programs without data, and researchers and analysts cannot generate data without programs. To break this cycle, U.S. federal correctional authorities should consider the implementation of a pilot intervention program for recently-incarcerated extremists, the adoption of a risk and needs assessment model, and the initiation of a long-term study exploring recidivism outcomes of released extremist offenders. These programs should draw from a reconceptualization of how policy makers approach "prison radicalization" to account for the complexity of the U.S. correctional system and individual inmates' experiences with radicalization and extremism. (Clifford, 2018)

Historically, the United States has taken a "security-first" approach when managing terrorist-extremist inmates. Although it is crucial to maintain the security of prisons, it does not mean that the approach has to be "security-only" (Neumann, 2010). If a prison only focuses on security, it will miss out on opportunities for reform. While a formal de-radicalization program in the United States is not necessary, measures must be in place to reform and rehabilitate terrorist-extremist inmates because imprisonment alone will not solve violent extremism (Bryans, 2016).

Throughout Sturgeon's career, he has experienced successful programs for criminal inmates, including educational, vocational, and rehabilitation. Many criminal inmates do commit crimes because they do not have the means to earn their living legitimately. In contrast, others served a sentence related to their substance abuse problems. Consequently, education, vocational programming, and substance abuse treatment should address criminal inmates' needs. A meta-analytic study found that, on average, inmates who participated in correctional education programs were 43 percent less likely to recidivate than those who did not participate in educational programming (Davis, Bozick, Steele, Saunders, and Miles, 2013). Other research shows that offenders who participate in prison-based substance abuse treatment are less likely to relapse or re-offend than those who did not receive this treatment (National Institute of Drug Abuse, 2011).

Similarly, when considering terrorist-extremist inmates, programming must address their specific risks and needs, different from those of criminal inmates. Interventions should address the beliefs and attitudes that drive their extremist ideologies and factors that could make them disengage from terrorism, such as gainful employment or the importance of family. Neumann (2010) recommends various programming to address the unique needs of terrorist offenders, including counseling, religious re-education, vocational training, and proper aftercare.

Programming and interventions should be designed to change terrorists' priorities to see the benefits of leading a normal life rather than reverting to extremism once released (Silke, 2014). By providing various programs to target the inmates' specific needs, many inmates will be less apt to return to their terrorist networks upon release because they will have different priorities and want to be productive members of a civilized society (Rome Memorandum, n.d.).

> ***Radicalization*** is how people adopt extremist views that promote violence to achieve religious, political, or social objectives. Conversely, *de-radicalization* is the psychological process in which psychological experts replace a terrorist's ideology with beliefs of toleration and coexistence. De-radicalization programs introduce terrorists to alternatives to violence so they can undergo an ideological transformation to live a productive life and pose a lesser threat to society. (Silke, 2014)

Aside from de-radicalization, terrorist-extremist inmates must also *disengage* or voluntarily agree to stop fighting (Gunaratna, 2012). While de-radicalization attempts to change the individuals' ideology and attitudes, disengagement aims to facilitate behavioral changes (Hill, 2016). The goal of de-radicalization and disengagement programs is to rehabilitate and reintegrate offenders into society and steer them away from terrorism and violence.

Many countries have used de-radicalization and disengagement programs, including Afghanistan, Iraq, Israel, Pakistan, the Philippines, and Saudi Arabia. These programs differ in delivery, but they typically use theological debates and counseling to promote de-radicalization (Silke, 2014). Moreover, most programs aim to challenge the inmate's violent ideology, provide vocational opportunities, and reintegrate the offender back into society.

For example, Saudi Arabia has a de-radicalization program that uses counseling and education to combat violent extremism's ideological justifications. This program uses religious debates and psychological counseling to correct the inmate's misconceptions about the Islamic faith. The idea is that people recruited by terrorist organizations usually have minimal religious education, and they learn to interpret Islam through discussion and dialogue while in prison. Furthermore, the instructors teach them that acting on radical beliefs with violence is unacceptable (Hill, 2016).

De-radicalization and disengagement programs are also taking place in the Philippines, a country known for its militant organizations, corruption, and political instability. The Philippines' government does not want terrorist inmates recruiting new members to join their militant cause, so it has implemented a de-radicalization program. This program's components include educating correctional staff on terrorism and prisoner radicalization, reducing corruption in prisons, and improving rehabilitation programs (Jones & Morales, 2012).

MAN SENTENCED TO READ FINE LITERATURE

A judge in England had an unusual approach to a right-wing terrorist; a twenty-one-year-old man was sentenced to read fine literature such as Dickens, Austen, and others and be tested on it in place of prison.

The man had become part of the extreme right wing (XRW) online—a term for activists who commit criminal activity motivated by a political or cultural view, such as racism or extreme nationalism. He amassed 67,788 documents in bulk downloads on hard drives, which contained a wealth of white supremacist and antisemitic material.

The judge said: "It is repellent, this content, to any right-thinking person. This material is largely relating to Nazi, fascist and Adolf Hitler-inspired ideology. But there was also a substantial quantity of more contemporary material espousing extreme rightwing, white-supremacist material." However, he noted that the man lacked friends and was susceptible to following others in this way of thinking but he thought he could be turned around (Davies, 2021).

Perhaps there are some elements of bibliotherapy that may be useful for other terrorists as part of rehabilitation programs that might be accompanied by mentorship programs so that the prisoners and their mentors could discuss alternatives to violence and crazed thinking.

Family Involvement. Efforts to involve the inmates' families in the rehabilitation process are important. Because families often share the same values and beliefs as inmates, family rehabilitation is an important part of the de-radicalization process (Jones & Morales, 2012).

While some of these programs claim to be successful, there is minimal research on their effectiveness. Tracking these inmates once they are released is difficult (Jones & Morales, 2012), so the authors lack proper data to aid in this research.

However, one report examined fifteen programs in different countries worldwide, and it determined that de-radicalization programs were vastly different. The more sophisticated programs included various programming, including education, counseling, religious re-education, vocational training, and proper aftercare. In some cases, however, the problems stemmed deeper than the prison system itself. For example, the Philippines has corrupt political systems and structural problems within its government, creating additional barriers to de-radicalization efforts. Consequently, there is no "one size fits all" approach, and programs need to be adapted to fit each country's specific conditions (Neumann, 2010).

Most Western nations, including France, the Netherlands, Spain, the United Kingdom, and the United States, do not have formal de-radicalization programs. Still, they have policies and practices in place to deal with terrorist inmates. As noted earlier, these practices primarily deal with housing inmates (for example, concentration versus separation). The facilities' safety and security are most important in these countries, and there are fewer attempts at rehabilitating terrorists (Neumann, 2010).

Likewise, de-radicalization also plays a minimal role in managing terrorist-extremist inmates in domestic prisons (Dugas & Kruglanski, 2014). As previously noted, there are no terrorist disengagement programs in the BOP (Rosand, 2017). The BOP uses the same programs for people convicted of terrorism-related offenses and the general population. Participation in most of these programs is voluntary, and none of them address extremist beliefs. Furthermore, none of these programs address these prisoners' release back into society or how they will be monitored once they have completed their sentences.

CONCLUSION

Even in the face of budget and staff shortages, it is critical that staff conduct programs that stop "radicalization" while people are incarcerated. Correctional agencies must continue to identify and create deradicalization programs for their extremist-terrorist inmate population. We all must remember that many of these extremist-terrorist inmates will be re-entering society at some point. We have too many examples of people who became radicalized while in prison and then acted on their extremist-terrorist ideology when on the outside.

11

Islam, Conversions, Chaplains, and Imams

Researchers must continue examining the relationship between religious conversion and radicalization. Researchers must also explore the connection between adequate programming and education and derailing radicalism for both right-wing and other radicalized terrorists.

ISLAM

Islam is the fastest-growing religion in Western prisons, and estimates indicate that 80 percent of inmates looking to convert are turning to Islam (Hamm, 2009). We know that the vast majority of inmates who convert are doing so to seek meaning in their lives or deal with their experiences of being incarcerated. But, what about the inmates whose conversion turns to radicalization? Researchers must continue examining prisoners' motivations for religious conversions through interviews with prison chaplains and inmates themselves. These narratives will help researchers determine which factors are the catalyst for radicalization, explaining the relationship between religious conversion and radicalization.

Similarly, researchers must also continue examining inmates who were convicted of terrorism-related offenses. Researchers can uncover patterns in individuals already radicalized by analyzing administrative data and conducting interviews with these inmates. These patterns will help correctional personnel develop appropriate interventions for radicalized individuals, and they could also help target inmates prone to radicalization.

DOI: 10.4324/9781003285946-11

RELIGIOUS POLICIES

Recognized imams and other ordained rabbis, priests, ministers, or recognized religious scholars should review all religious policies and procedures before their implementation.

It is vital to thoroughly vet all religious leaders who provide religious services to the terrorist-extremist inmates and other extremist inmates before they are permitted into the facility. The policy and procedure should require that religious providers and volunteers pass a background investigation, *regardless of their faith*, before being permitted into the facility. Enforcement of this requirement must be strict. However, be aware, some individuals and offshoot organizations from every religion have extreme views.

All written and electronic recorded religious materials must be reviewed and approved to ensure that they contain religious information that adheres to the basic tenets of the individual religions and is not inflammatory. Correctional agencies should have a review committee that approves religious materials before this material is permitted in the facility. This committee should be made up of religious leaders, security personnel, and representatives of the administration.

Any religious materials not approved shall be considered contraband, removed from the facility's secure area (bagged and tagged), and considered evidence. Staff must adhere to the agency's policies and procedures for handling evidence and maintaining the "chain of custody."

Examples of Prison Converts

Most prisoners in the United States undergoing the radicalization process have little religious or ideological affiliation before their incarceration (Silke, 2014). However, they often need to find ways to deal with their prison experience, so many inmates turn to religion or religious organizations to cope with their imprisonment (Hamm, 2009).

Inmate Belief Systems

One of the most significant differences between criminal inmates, extremist-terrorist inmates, and other extremist inmates and other extremists is their ideology and the belief system that drives them. We have divided them into three categories for convenience, though there may be many more applicable groups.

- *Ideological violence.* Groups in this category include those with political ideologies such as nationalist or neo-Nazi groups, White supremacy or hate groups that advocate the use of violence; those that use extreme interpretations of religious ideologies and beliefs that advocate the use of violence; or advocate violent anarchist, or extreme left-wing or right-wing ideologies.
- *Issue-based violence.* In this category, groups include violent animal liberation and animal rights movements; environmental or eco-related violent extremism; or anti-government, anti-globalization, or anti-capitalist movements that advocate violence.
- *Ethno-nationalist or separatist violence.* In this category, groups include violent political or independence struggles based on race, culture, geography, or ethnicity (Lefebvre, 2003).

Extremist-terrorist inmates and other extremist inmates think differently than most Americans, Europeans, and criminal inmates. Different objectives motivate the two organizations. Extremist-terrorist inmates and other extremist inmates follow a formal ideology and hold deep-seated religious and political beliefs. In contrast, criminal inmates do not follow any ideology and are politically indifferent for the most part.

There are five types of converts in prison: *searching, protection-seeking, crisis, manipulating,* and *free-world recruited* converts. Although there is little research on this subject, one study found that the most prevalent type of convert was the *searching* convert, followed by the *protection-seeking* convert. In this study, chaplains also reported few *crisis* converts, and there were no *manipulating* or *free-world recruited* converts (Hamm, 2007). Because protection-seeking converts are the most prevalent types, we will take a closer look at *protection-seeking* and *searching* converts later.

Searching converts are on a mission to find meaning and identity in their lives due to their incarceration. This type of convert is typically better educated and more knowledgeable about current events than other converts. Many of these inmates are dissatisfied with the government, and they often seek out religions that reinforce their opposition to authority. Consequently, *searching* converts could be susceptible to radicalization. Chaplains also noted that *searching* converts consist of different races (Hamm, 2007).

An example of a *searching* convert cited in this report was Mario, born to Catholic parents in Columbia but grew up in a poor area of Brooklyn, NY. Mario began selling crack at ten years old and joined a gang when he was fifteen years old. Although Mario was Latino, he was fascinated by hip-hop music, Black culture, and attaining social justice. He even joined the Zulu Nation, a hip-hop awareness group, which introduced him to Islam. When Mario was eighteen years old, he was convicted of armed robbery and sentenced to twenty-five years in prison. During his incarceration, he converted to Sunni Islam, which helped him settle down and learn about the world. Mario also embraced Black Hebrew Israelism and deified Black male role models in prison, even though he was a Latino. Mario is the textbook example of a *searching* convert because he sought meaning in the world by exploring different religions. Like many other *searching* converts, Mario blended ideas and roles from various faiths (Hamm, 2007).

Another example of a *searching* convert cited in the report was Jemahl, a half-Black, half-White inmate. As a youth, Jemahl went to juvenile hall for robbery, where he became a born-again Christian. However, it was not long before Jemahl viewed Christianity as "brainwashing." He decided to read books to search for his truth. In another stint in juvenile hall, Jemahl's absentee father, a convert to the Nation of Islam, visited him. Once released from juvenile hall, he moved in with his father. Shortly after, he began using drugs and joined the Bloods. When he was seventeen, he was arrested for a triple homicide and sentenced to life without parole. In prison, Jemahl joined the Nation of Islam and began to embrace the Black power movement. He then converted to Sunni Islam within the California state prison system. He was recruited into Jam'iyyat Ul-Islam Is-Saheed (JIS), where he taught inmates radical Islam (Hamm, 2007). Like other *searching* converts, Jemahl jumped from religion to religion, trying to find his place in the world, and he was eventually drawn to the radical views of JIS.

We shift our focus now to *protection-seeking* converts, inmates who join a religious group for protection from violent and property crimes in prison. Similar to a prison gang, religious organizations often provide inmates with protection, as well as a sense of identity. Prison chaplains mentioned that many African-American inmates join religious organizations for protection (Hamm, 2007).

An example of a *protection-seeking* convert was Marcus, a Black inmate from South Central Los Angeles. Marcus was raised in a Christian family, but he lost interest in religion as a child. He joined the Bloods and had several run-ins with the law and several prison stays. Marcus did not grow up with his father; however, a Muslim convert, his father visited him in prison. Marcus' father said that he needed discipline in prison, which attracted Marcus to Islam during his incarceration. Marcus was paroled but returned to prison on a firearms' violation. Marcus became a Sunni Muslim during this imprisonment, and his group came together under the JIS, led by Kevin James. Marcus was in and out of prison but continued to turn to JIS for protection during his incarcerations. Although Marcus was not interested in Islam's religious aspect, he found JIS to be a positive force in his life because it gave him a place to belong and a sense of protection (Hamm, 2007).

These are several examples of individuals and their conversion stories, arguably with potential ties to radical Islam. Many people will convert in prison, while only a few adopt extremist beliefs and fewer act on these beliefs. For most prisoners, religion is a way to do their time. The typical prison convert is a poor, uneducated Black male concerned with surviving the prison experience rather than terrorism. However, how do we explain those inmates who radicalize in prison and act on those extremist beliefs? In the next section, we discuss several examples.

INMATES RADICALIZED IN PRISON

Looking at these anecdotal accounts, we cannot predict who will radicalize in prison. Still, these accounts provide some patterns of these individuals—their backgrounds and traits—that may have contributed to their radicalization. Examining these inmates' lives can help us understand who might be more susceptible to radicalization and may prevent future terrorist plots from happening. This section looks at brief accounts of five individuals who radicalized in prison and were convicted of attempted terrorist plots.

Kevin James, an African-American, grew up in South Central Los Angeles. James was in and out of trouble as a youth, and he eventually became a member of the Crips. At twenty-one years old, he began serving a ten-year sentence for robbery. His father was a former Black Panther, which may have piqued his interest in radical beliefs (Hamm, 2007). While incarcerated, James followed the Nation of Islam but soon followed a group of Sunni Muslims, known as JIS. James began preaching throughout the California state prison system that Muslims should attack Islam's enemies, including the U.S. government (Hamm, 2007). He is currently serving a sentence for his attempted terrorist plots to attack Jewish facilities and U.S. military bases in the Los Angeles area.

Lavar Washington is also an African-American from South Central Los Angeles. He spent time in the California state prison system for robbery when Kevin James recruited him into JIS. Washington had served several stints in prison, and like James, he was also a member of the Crips (Hamm, 2007). Besides, Lavar had recently converted to Islam before James recruited him into JIS. Washington was an ideal candidate to conspire with James because he wanted to get revenge on the United States through extremist measures. He thought that the Muslim world was oppressed and that his mission was to fight for jihad. Washington is currently serving a twenty-two-year sentence for the terrorist plots that he attempted with James.

Jose Padilla, born in Brooklyn, is of Puerto Rican descent. As a child, his family moved to Chicago; he joined the Latin Kings as a teenager. Padilla has a history of juvenile delinquency and violence as an adult, including robbery, aggravated assault, and manslaughter (Saunders, 2004). Padilla converted to Islam in prison, and he began associating with radical Islamists once he was released. After traveling to Saudi Arabia, Iraq, and Afghanistan, the police arrested him for planning to explode a dirty bomb at Chicago's O'Hare Airport in 2002 (Ballas, 2010). Padilla is currently serving a twenty-one-year prison sentence for this terrorist plot.

Michael Finton, a White American, was born in California but later moved to Illinois. Finton had a troubled childhood, and he was in and out of the foster care system. Finton was imprisoned for aggravated assault and robbery, at which time he converted to Islam. Upon his release, Michael worked as a fry cook outside of Springfield, Illinois. One of his co-workers mentioned that "he didn't like America very much" (Johnson, 2009). Finton also told an undercover FBI informant that he wanted to go abroad to fight for jihad. In 2009, he was charged with the attempted use of a weapon of mass destruction and the attempted murder of federal employees for his efforts to bomb the Paul Findley Federal Building in Illinois. In 2011, Finton was sentenced to twenty-eight years in prison.

Richard Reid, the "shoe bomber," was born in London. His mother was White, and his father was Jamaican (Jager, 2018). Reid was in and out of British prisons, and he converted to Islam while incarcerated at the suggestion of his father, a career criminal, who also converted to Islam in prison. After release, Reid received training from al-Qaeda in Pakistan and Afghanistan. In 2001, Reid tried to use a match to light explosives in his shoes on a flight from Paris to Miami, but luckily, he was unsuccessful. He pleaded guilty to eight counts of terrorism, including attempted murder on an aircraft and attempted murder of U.S. nationals overseas. Reid is currently serving a life sentence at the U.S. Penitentiary Administrative Maximum Facility (ADMAX) in Florence, Colorado (Jager, 2018).

Factors Contributing to Radicalization

Although there is limited research on inmate-radicalization patterns, one study examined the characteristics of European jihadists. Results indicated that there was no uniform profile from the sample, but there were patterns. Similar to the statistics we discussed at the beginning of this chapter, all individuals were male and ranged between sixteen through thirty-eight years old (the average age was twenty-five). Most of them were low-level criminals, but 65 percent were involved in violent crimes. Also, 57 percent were incarcerated at least once. Finally, 27 percent of those who spent time in prison radicalized while in prison, and most of them intensified their radicalization after their release from prison (Basra, Neumann, & Bruner, 2016). Given that over one-quarter of these individuals are radicalized in prison, it is clear that prison radicalization is a problem and that more research should be conducted to understand this complex relationship.

Nearly two-thirds of the jihadists in this study had a history of engaging in violent crime. Research suggests that prisoners with a violent disposition may be more prone to radicalization (Borum, 2014). Pro-violent attitudes reinforce the idea that violence is an acceptable way to resolve disputes and come to solutions. Consequently, the concept of violent extremism may be attractive to individuals harboring pro-violent attitudes or having a history of violence. Similarly, inmates who engage in violence toward prison staff and other inmates could also be at increased risk for radicalization (Silke, 2014).

Finally, research suggests that prisoners susceptible to becoming violent extremists typically come from lower-class backgrounds (Silke, 2014). Although most free-world recruits are from the middle or upper class, this is not the case with prisoners. For example, the typical male prisoner is from a lower class and earned less than $20,000 per year before incarceration (Rabuy & Kopf, 2015).

Consequently, inmates have different reasons for converting to Islam, as established in the prior case studies compared to free-world recruits.

Need for Personal Meaning and Identity

Prisoners are denied many of their basic rights while incarcerated, and they cannot control many aspects of their lives that they once could in the free world. They live in small spaces, have no control over whom they share their space with, and have no choice in what they eat, among other privileges that people in the free world take for granted. Adjusting to these new changes can result in a diminished sense of personal value and self-worth (Haney, 2001).

Consequently, many new inmates have the recurring idea that they are looking for something new, and they want to understand their place in the world, which was the case with Mario, Jemahl, and Kevin James. These inmates searched for meaning in their lives, and their identity was driven by finding a sense of purpose and self-worth. Unfortunately, finding personal meaning can be a struggle for many inmates, and some may be attracted to radical beliefs. Thus, the black-and-white nature of extremist ideologies can be attractive for some inmates trying to find meaning in their lives when nothing else seems to make sense for them (Borum, 2014).

Need for Belonging

People in prison are cut off from their family and friends and isolated from the world they once knew. New inmates are afraid and uncertain about the prison experience, and they feel a sense of alienation and isolation. This feeling of isolation causes them to seek protection from prison gangs or religious organizations. As these inmates look for a community and a sense of belonging, they are more susceptible to recruitment and radicalization into extremist Islamic organizations (Brandon, 2009). Joining an extremist group fills their need for belonging and affiliation, helping alleviate their sense of alienation (Borum, 2014). Also, because inmates feel they have a bleak future, they are more apt to join an extremist group because the group provides them with a script on how to think and behave, minimizing some of the uncertainty related to their future (Silke, 2014).

Perceived Injustices

Extremists recognize that most new converts have little knowledge of Islam, allowing them to teach these converts radical beliefs (Brandon, 2009). Moreover, some inmates feel that the United States has discriminated against them or they have been unjustly incarcerated. Consequently, the feeling of oppression, coupled with limited knowledge of Islam, can lead to greater susceptibility for radicalization (Ballas, 2010). Also, al-Qaeda training manuals identify American prisoners as candidates for conversion because they may harbor hostility toward their government. Specifically, African-American offenders may support terrorist goals as payback for their injustices (real and perceived) by the government and the criminal justice system (Hamm, 2007).

Once people think they have been the victim of an injustice, they believe someone is at fault. As soon as they can assign blame for their injustice, they choose a target. The target can be a particular individual or society as a whole (Borum, 2014). Inmates who believe they have been victims of injustice may be more susceptible to radicalization and see their target as the government.

Summary of Causes of Radicalization

Based on the cases above and the existing research, we can determine some patterns among inmates susceptible to radicalization. These characteristics include:

- Being a male in his twenties
- Coming from an impoverished background
- Having a criminal history:
  - Often a history of violence
  - Prior gang involvement
  - Previous incarcerations
  - Violence toward staff or other inmates
- Turning to religion to find meaning in their lives or fill a need for belonging and protection
- Feeling like of victim of a governmental injustice
- Having a father who converted to Islam in prison.

As previous research has mentioned (Basra, Neumann, & Bruner, 2016; Borum, 2014), while it is possible to find common threads among radicalized inmates, it is hard to determine a concrete profile. Such difficulty occurs because most of the characteristics listed above apply to most inmates in American prisons. However, more research is needed to pinpoint common threads among radicalized inmates to prevent future terrorist plots. With more than 70,000 people ready to radicalize in the West (Long, 2015), we will likely see more people convicted of terrorism-related offenses in the coming years. And these individuals will be looking to recruit new inmates to help promote their extremist agendas.

Prison Chaplains and Imams

Correctional facilities are required to ensure that offenders have religious services and appropriate religious reading materials (Sturgeon, 2010). According to the American Correctional Association (ACA), prisons should have at least one chaplain qualified in clinical pastoral education and be endorsed by the appropriate religious certifying body. This chaplain is responsible for coordinating all religious programming within the institution (ACA, 2020).

Unfortunately, there is a shortage of qualified religious providers serving U.S. prisons, so prisons often use individuals with minimal religious training, volunteers from the community, or inmates with limited training in Islam. All of these options create the possibility of individuals spreading extremist views to the inmates. One study found that only one-third of wardens in state prisons nationwide had an adequate number of paid Muslim service providers. Moreover, approximately 65 percent of the wardens in this study believed that volunteer service providers did not have sufficient training. Nearly 70 percent felt that these volunteers posed a threat to their facilities' security. Additionally, approximately 45 percent feared that these volunteers could influence inmates' radicalization (Merola & Vovak, 2012).

Furthermore, this shortage of qualified providers is especially problematic in crowded maximum-security prisons, posing a greater risk for radicalization. According to the ACA, there should be at least one full-time chaplain for facilities with 500 or more inmates (ACA, 2020). However, budget cuts have decreased the number of chaplains in many state prison systems, and many facilities lack the proper number of religious providers. For example, there is only one chaplain for every 2,000 inmates in high-security facilities in California (Hamm, 2007). This deficiency has created opportunities for Islamic prisoners to operate independently, increasing the likelihood of radicalization and recruitment.

An adequate number of qualified chaplains are needed to minimize radicalization, especially in crowded, maximum-security prisons. When this is not feasible due to budgetary constraints, administrators must oversee an extensive screening of religious volunteers and other providers to prevent extremist imams from entering correctional facilities (Atherton & Jurisic, 2015; Neumann, 2010). Additionally, a correctional staff member must be in attendance during all religious services, and if the service is in a foreign language, a translator must be present (Sturgeon, 2010).

Furthermore, as we have advanced throughout this work, prison administrators must continue to stress the need for more chaplains—especially in crowded, maximum-security prisons. The shortage of qualified religious providers serving U.S. prisons presents opportunities for people lacking the proper religious training to enter correctional facilities. One study found that only one-third of state prisons had an adequate number of paid Muslim service providers (Merola & Vovak, 2012). Without the proper number of qualified service providers, prisons invite radicalization into their institutions.

Religious Conversion

Most prisoners in the United States who undergo the radicalization process have little religious or ideological affiliation before their incarceration (Silke, 2014). However, once they are incarcerated, they need to find ways to deal with the prison experience. Many turn to religion to help increase self-discipline and to have more positive interactions with staff and other inmates (Hamm, 2009).

While research on religious conversion in prison is limited, one study examined the motivations for conversions to non-Judean-Christian faith organizations (for example, Islam, Buddhism, Hinduism, and so forth) to determine which motivations were most commonly cited by prisoners and chaplains. This study found that prisoner conversions were primarily motivated by spiritual searching. Prisoners seek meaning in their lives, and religion offers them a way to adjust to prison life by providing them with methods to cope with their surroundings. Additionally, conversion can have a humanizing effect on prison culture and offer prisoners a path to rehabilitation (Hamm, 2007).

Most inmates convert for authentic reasons that involve personal change and reflect upon and acknowledge their criminal pasts. Subsequently, conversion does not typically lead to radicalization. However, for some inmates, conversion can be a step in the radicalization process and may result in terrorist plots and violent attacks (Hamm, 2007, 2009). The following sections discuss what is known about the recruitment process and how that process can turn into radicalization.

CONCLUSIONS

The concern is not about converting to Islam in prison but rather about extremists who use Islam to spread their extremism and justify violent acts (Silke, 2014). A word of caution to correctional personnel at every level: a person's religious preference is guaranteed under the U.S. Constitution. Correctional personnel should seek advice from their legal department before limiting or interfering with any religious activities.

12

Radicalization Recruitment in Facilities

> ISIS terrorists fleeing to their home countries WANT to be sent to prison so they can convert them into 'jihadi universities,' report warns. (Davies, 2017)

Researchers found that the recruitment of inmates is part of the initial phase of the extremist-terrorist inmates' radicalization process. For example, Richard Reid, the shoe bomber, was converted while serving time in a United Kingdom correctional facility (Bucktin, 2015).

This chapter examines from a practitioner's perspective the recruiting process, potential recruits, and extremist-terrorist inmates and recruiters for other extremist organizations. Additionally, we discuss the adjustments to operations, intelligence-gathering practices, security procedures, and the staff training required to manage extremist-terrorist inmates, other extremist inmates, and extremist individuals.

THE RECRUITING PROCESS

Recruiting inmates to join various sub-organizations is not new to correctional personnel. However, what is new is recruiting inmates to be radicalized and perhaps transformed into potential extremist terrorists. The Centre for the Prevention of Radicalization Leading to Violence (2017) defines radicalization as "a process whereby people adopt extremist belief systems—including the willingness to use, encourage, or

DOI: 10.4324/9781003285946-12

facilitate violence—with the aim of promoting an ideology, political project or cause as a means of social transformation."

Initially, the major concentration of this book was on Islamic extremist-terrorist inmates, but the authors also address the growth of White supremacists and other extremist organizations. These organizations hold extreme views and show a willingness to commit violent acts both inside and outside correctional facilities for their causes. While they are criminals and commit crimes, they do not do it in the name of their political, social, and religious causes.

Another difference between criminals and radicalized criminals is that Islamic extremist terrorists and other religious extremist organizations commit their crimes in the name of their God. White supremacists commit their crimes based on their belief that White people should have power over other races. "A White supremacist is someone who believes that one group of people, usually white people, should be more powerful and have more influence than another group" (Anti-Defamation League, n.d.). In some cases, White supremacists use a distorted version of Christianity to promote their philosophy.

Recruiting criminal inmates to join any extremist group is a major concern for correctional administrators, managers, first-line supervisors, and line officers. As the quote at the opening of this chapter states, "ISIS terrorists fleeing to their home countries WANT to be sent to prison so they can convert them into jihadi universities" (Davies, 2017). The recruiting of extremist terrorists from the criminal-inmate population is occurring in correctional facilities worldwide. Prisons are prime locations for identifying, recruiting, converting, and indoctrinating recruits.

Extremist recruiting is one of the priorities that correctional personnel should be trained to identify, report to proper authorities, and employ methods and techniques to interrupt or discontinue the recruiting process. The recruiters from various prison sub-organizations, including extremist-terrorist inmate recruiters, look at inmates' vulnerability, activities, compatibility, value to the group, and propensity for religious conversion when ferreting out potential recruits.

Vulnerability is much more prevalent in a correctional setting, especially for inmates experiencing a penitentiary environment for the first time. This vulnerability is especially prevalent for the first several days and weeks. Many first-time inmates are filled with shock, disbelief, apprehension, and fear. New inmates, extremist-terrorist and non-extremist-terrorist alike, typically arrive in prison insecure, uncertain, and afraid. As a method of approaching the newly arrived inmates, recruiters from some organizations use intimidation, the promise of protection, belonging, kindness, and other means. "In the United Kingdom, some imprisoned Islamists have adopted a proactive strategy to capitalize on this uncertainty by offering goods, friendship, and spiritual support to new arrivals in prison" (Brandon, 2009).

After conversing with a great many inmates, Sturgeon's experience is that many inmates genuinely believed that they would never be "locked up" in anything but a county jail. Inmates have shared that doing time in the county jail was a "piece of cake," but doing time in the "joint" was an entirely different situation. It was a terrifying experience, especially for the first time.

Inmate recruiters look to identify issues of compatibility, showing how the recruit will fit into the group. What are the similarities between the group and the individual/s being recruited?

Some examples of similarities include:

- Similar ethnic background
- Similar religion
- Similar poor socioeconomic backgrounds
- Prior exposure to the criminal justice system
- Difficulties in school
- National origin
- Common language/s
- Similar feelings of disenfranchisement and past abuses by the system
- Same neighborhood
- Family member/s who already belong to the group
- Friends or acquaintances who already belong to the group
- Same schools
- Same/similar crimes
- Same sports team/s

The greater the number of similarities potential recruits have, the more the recruiter/s will exploit them in initial conversations, eventually becoming a brother or sister. The inmate recruiter will promote the advantages and benefits of becoming a brother or sister in the group.

After approaching a potential recruit, the recruiter/s and the group's leaders will conduct a quasi-investigation into the potential recruit's background. While each group wants new members, they also want the "right" members. They want members to follow instructions, complete assignments, be completely loyal to the group, and be true believers in their ideology. They also want members who will eventually become recruiters themselves and who, upon release, will continue to support the group's ideology and activities.

Sometimes people who lack prison-operations experience find it difficult to understand how inmates could find out about other inmates. Correctional facilities are closed environments where information is an extremely valuable commodity. Hence, the various organizations work at placing their inmates through various means, in positions and situations where they can access information helpful to their group. Often, group members will attempt to manipulate the system to be assigned to inmate jobs to be exposed to information. "A report prepared by the Counter-Terrorism Department revealed that terrorists imprisoned at the Central Jail in Karachi had access to the prison's record room and sensitive documents" (CTD report highlights "alarming" security at Karachi Central Jail, 2017).

Staff have shared information with inmates with whom they have built relationships, which is another way inmates can find information about other inmates, information regarding security procedures, individual staff members, and other potentially useful inside knowledge. First-line supervisors need to ensure that staff members maintain a professional relationship with all inmates, especially extremist-terrorist inmates. As the old saying goes, "knowledge is power!"

Inmates belonging to White supremacy organizations have been known to recruit White correctional officers to their belief systems. They do this to compromise the officers, gain knowledge of the facility's workings, obtain better inmate jobs, and learn about staff and inmates.

Before approaching a recruit, the group members will observe their actions, associations, and prison-life adjustment. When observing the potential recruit, the recruiter will be looking for what activities the potential recruit is interested in. The recruiter is looking for ways to approach potential recruits through their actions. For example, if the recruit likes to remain in his cell and appears to be a loner, this could indicate fear. Fear is one of the most common methods of recruiting new members. For an inmate who remains in his cell and is observed reading by the recruiter, the recruiter could solicit information from the inmate librarian and determine what books the potential recruit has checked out. Sturgeon experienced similar scenarios, such as this. For example, an inmate librarian shared information about what an inmate was reading with other inmates within the penitentiary, and the inmates used this information for exploitation.

While extremist-terrorist organizations recruit from the criminal-inmate population, they are very selective about who they recruit. This intense scrutiny during the recruiting process makes it extremely difficult for law enforcement personnel or intelligence agents to infiltrate these extremist-terrorist organizations. Brothers who have joined extremist-terrorist organizations in prison remain scrutinized for several months until they prove their loyalty and commitment.

The process of radicalization of inmate-terrorists requires that criminal-inmate recruits adhere to practicing an extreme variation of the Islamic religion. Though similar to what occurs in other extremist religious organizations, Sturgeon's experience with White supremacists, eco-terrorists, narco-terrorists, and others has shown him what members of these organizations do not embrace, and that is the thought of dying for their causes. They have some profoundly serious and extremist political, racial, and ethnic beliefs. White supremacists adhere to some fringe Christian beliefs to justify their actions. They will, however, commit terroristic and criminal acts against their perceived enemies. Many right-wing religious-extremist organizations believe in their own distorted political and religious views to justify their felonious acts.

Extremist recruiters evaluate whether the potential recruit will enhance the group's activities and, specifically, in what ways. The authors' research into these extremist-terrorist organizations shows that they are structured, cerebral, religious, and political, at least hierarchical. Additionally, like other prison sub-organizations, they can manipulate some of their slower or more violent members to be their intimidators—in other words, their muscles.

The extremist-terrorist recruiters will carefully assess the potential recruit's associations to determine if the potential recruit is associating with infidels, prison gang members, certain ethnic organizations, or gays or lesbians. They will also observe how the potential recruit interacts with staff, including security personnel, programming personnel, medical personnel, and chaplains.

The extremist recruiters will share information with their leaders and assess whether they can separate their current associates' potential recruits. If so, what will it take to separate the potential recruit, and whether it is worth their effort?

The extremist-terrorist organizations, unlike other organizations in prisons, don't recruit just to increase their numbers. Rather, they recruit, intending to radicalize the individuals to blindly follow "their" form of Islam and follow orders while incarcerated and after being released.

In some cases, the potential recruit may have special skills, talents, or characteristics. Recruits with charisma are highly desired. Extremist-terrorist organizations within a prison setting can be more cognitive and manipulative than other sub-organizations. Extremist-terrorist inmates and other extremist inmates have become adept at using religion and religious practices to manipulate prison protocols. In his book *The Fertile Soil of Jihad*, Patrick Dunleavy details how imam chaplains and extremist-terrorist inmates and other extremist inmates collaborated to make phone calls. "When investigators reviewed the phone records from those chaplains, however, they found some oddities about the calls to relatives and associates of suspected terrorists" (Dunleavy, 2011).

Therefore, extremist-terrorist inmates and other extremist inmates are always looking for ways to make their group better, stronger, and more influential within the facility, so that their group can recruit more members, have more influence, and thereby demonstrate power (that they may or may not have) with which to intimidate the other inmates.

al-Qaeda Training Manual Exert

Extremist-terrorist inmates will manipulate the correctional system to advance their activities (see some examples later). An al-Qaeda training manual captured during a raid in Manchester, England, clearly illustrates that extremist-terrorist organizations, specifically al-Qaeda, have been prepared and trained on how to act while incarcerated, being transported, and in courtrooms. How prepared correctional agencies are to manage these extremist-terrorist inmates and other extremist inmates remains a question.

UK/BM-176 TO UK/BM-180 TRANSLATION
Lesson Eighteen
PRISONS AND DETENTION CENTERS

* *IF AN INDICTMENT IS ISSUED AND THE TRIAL BEGINS, THE BROTHER HAS TO PAY ATTENTION TO THE FOLLOWING:*

This document demonstrates that some extremist-terrorist inmates/detainees have been instructed on how to conduct themselves while incarcerated. Reviewing the rest of the confiscated document in Appendix 1 will help identify what new policies and procedures you will need to create and what existing policies and procedures you will need to update or adapt.

*1. *At the beginning of the trial, once more, the brothers must insist on proving that torture was inflicted on them by State Security [investigators] before the judge.*

Correctional officials should take pictures of all incoming extremist terrorists, especially noting injuries, scars, bruises, tattoos, or other body anomalies. Always maintain the dignity of the extremist-terrorist inmate. The rationale for taking pictures of this sort is to show the extremist terrorists' physical condition upon arrival at the facility. These pictures can be used to dispute any allegations of torture an inmate makes to a judge.

Audio and video record all interviews with extremist-terrorist inmates and other extremist inmates to create a record so that they cannot make unsubstantiated claims.

*2. *Complain [to the court] of mistreatment while in prison.*

See above.

*3. *Make arrangements for the brother's defense with the attorney, whether he was retained by the brother's family or court-appointed.*

This entry indicates that the extremist-terrorist inmates and other extremist inmates are aware of the American judicial system and the availability of court-appointed attorneys.

*4. *The brother has to do his best to know the names of the state security officers who participated in his torture and mention their names to the judge. [These names may be obtained from brothers who had to deal with those officers in previous cases.]*

Correctional officials working with their legal department should develop policies and procedures to protect the names and addresses of corrections personnel, directly contacting extremist-terrorist inmates for the personnel and their families' safety. For example, while working at a certain agency, employees practiced using the address of the facility as their official address while testifying in legal proceedings.

*5. *Some brothers may tell and may be lured by the state security investigators to testify against the brothers [i.e., affirmation witness], either by not keeping them together, in the same prison during the trials, or by letting them talk to the media. In this case, they have to be* *treated gently, and should be offered good advice, good treatment, and pray that God may guide them.*

Most correctional agencies have policies and procedures dictating what actions to take should one inmate agree to testify against another. These policies and procedures should be carefully reviewed and updated for extremist-terrorist inmates and other extremist inmates who wish to leave the extremist ideology. Use every precaution to ensure the inmate's safety and security. Additionally, an external agency should work to protect the inmate's family.

*6. *During the trial, the court has to be notified of any mistreatment of the brothers inside the prison.*

Correctional personnel should document every incident, conversation, and event that occurs with extremist-terrorist inmates. If possible, video and audio record any confrontational interactions with extremist-terrorist inmates.

*7. *It is possible to resort to a hunger strike, but that is a tactic that can either succeed or fail.*

Again, most correctional agencies have standard policies and procedures for managing hunger strikes and other criminal correctional emergencies. We recommend that the policies and procedures be reviewed, updated if necessary, and included in the basic and annual training curricula. Provide detailed documentation from the beginning until the end of the incident. If possible, video and audiotape the incident.

*8. *Take advantage of visits to communicate with brothers outside prison and exchange information that may be helpful to them in their work outside prison [according to what occurred during the investigations]. The importance of mastering the art of hiding messages is self-evident here.*

This paragraph is important because it gives insight into how the extremist-terrorist inmates and other extremist inmates pass intelligence between visitors. The visitors keep the extremist-terrorist inmates and other extremist inmates up-to-date on what the group is doing outside. In turn, the extremist-terrorist inmates and other extremist organizations share information about the inner workings of the particular correctional facility they are in. Additionally, and importantly, the extremist terrorists are reporting to their visitors the specific investigative techniques used by the prison's investigators, "… according to what occurred during the investigation." They are passing valuable intelligence to their brothers to train others on what to expect if incarcerated.

* *When the brothers are transported from and to the prison [on their way to the court], they should shout Islamic slogans out loud from inside the prison cars to impress upon the people and their family the need to support Islam.*

Another justification for having courtrooms within a correctional facility is to conduct certain legal procedures that can be achieved via video conferencing. Employing teleconference technology will reduce the danger of transporting extremist-terrorist inmates and other extremist inmates to and from the court for minor judicial matters, thereby reducing escape attempts and offering them an opportunity for publicity. It will also end/reduce the availability of using transport trips to rally support. "Two sheriff's deputies in Kansas were shot while transporting inmates from the jail to court hearing on Friday died of their injuries, Kansas City Kansas Police Department report" (Caron, 2018).

* *Inside the prison, the brother should not accept any work that may belittle or demean him or his brothers, such as the cleaning of the prison bathrooms or hallways.*

As part of the extremist-terrorist inmate's orientation to the facility, work assignments should be thoroughly explained. The explanation should include how inmate jobs are assigned. Refusal to report for a job assignment or not perform a job satisfactorily will result in disciplinary action.

* *The brothers should create an Islamic program for themselves inside the prison and recreational and educational ones, etc.*

Correctional agencies should have detailed policies and procedures to explain how inmates can initiate programs within the facility. These policies should be varied and detailed in what is permitted and applicable to all religions. The agency's legal department should approve this policy before implementation.

* *The brother in prison should be a role model in selflessness. Brothers should also pay attention to each other's needs and should help each other and unite vis-a-vis the prison officers.*

Correctional personnel should pay close attention to ensure that extremist terrorists do not intimidate or extort criminal or other extremist-terrorist inmates.

* *The brothers must take advantage of their presence in prison or obeying and worshiping [God] and memorizing the Qur'an, etc. This is in addition to all guidelines and procedures that were contained in the lesson on interrogation and investigation. Lastly, each of us has to understand that we don't achieve victory against our enemies through these actions and security procedures. Rather, victory is achieved by obeying Almighty and Glorious God and because of their many sins. Every brother has to be careful so as not to commit sins and every one of us has to do his best in obeying Almighty God, Who said in his Holy Book: "We will, without doubt, help Our messengers and those who believe (both) in this world's lie and the one Day when the Witnesses will stand forth." May God guide us.*

In many cases, extremist-terrorist inmates and other extremist inmates do not believe that law enforcement, courts, or correctional personnel have any authority over them. They look at correctional personnel as non-believers because they do not adhere to their ideology. Correctional personnel become the enemy. This section highlights extremist-terrorist inmates' belief that they are warriors in a religious war against non-believers. Correctional agencies should incorporate this extremist-terrorist ideology in their training so that officers can be aware of the view that this inmate population holds of them.

The staff should be cautioned that recruiters often perpetuate many variants of Islam. They may be far afield from the *Koran*—another reason for limiting religious materials to those vetted by accredited members of the faith.

* *To this pure Muslim youth, the believer, the mujahidin (fighter) for God's sake. I present this modest effort as a contribution from me to pave the way that will lead to Almighty God and to establish a caliphate along the lines of the prophet.*

"... the believer, the mujahidin (fighter) for God's sake," explains how deeply this extremist-inmate population believes.

* *The prophet, peace be upon him, said according to what was related by Imam Ahmed: "Let the prophecy that God wants to be in you, yet God may remove it if He so wills, and then there will be a Caliphate according to the prophet's path [instruction], if God so wills it. He will also remove that [the Caliphate] if He so wills, and you will have a disobedient king if God so wills it. Once again, if God so wills, He will remove him [the disobedient king], and you will have an oppressive*

lung. [finally], if God so wills, He will remove him [the oppressive king], and you will have a Caliphate according to the prophet's path [instruction]. He then became silent."

Again, the above paragraph outlines the extremist-terrorist inmates' beliefs that they are working toward establishing their caliphate (a caliphate is an Islamic state under the leadership of an Islamic steward with the title of "caliph").

* *THE IMPORTANCE Of TEAMWORK:*

1. *Teamwork is the only translation of God's command, as well as that of the prophet, to unite and not to disunite. Almighty God says, "And hold fast, all together, by the Rope which Allah (stretches out for or you) and be not divided among yourselves." In "Sahih Muslim," it was reported by Abu Horairah, may Allah look kindly upon him, that the prophet, may Allah's peace and greetings be upon him, said: "Allah approves three [things] for you and disapproves three [things]: He approves that you worship him, that you do not disbelieve in Him, and that you hold fast, all together, by the Rope which Allah, and be not divided among yourselves. He disapproves of three: gossip, asking too much [for help], and squandering money."*
2. *Abandoning "teamwork" or individual and haphazard work means disobeying the orders of God and the prophet and falling victim to disunity.*
3. *Teamwork is conducive to cooperation in righteousness and piety.*

As described in these paragraphs, correctional team members reviewing, writing, or adapting agency policies and procedures for this inmate population should understand the importance of teamwork, brotherhood, and loyalty to all those who follow this extremist ideology.

*4. *Upholding religion, which God has ordered us by His saying, "Uphold religion" will necessarily require an all-out confrontation against all our enemies, who want to recreate darkness. In addition, it is imperative to stand against darkness in all arenas: the media, education, [religious] guidance, and counseling, as well as others. This will make it necessary for us to move on numerous fields so as to enable the Islamic movement to confront ignorance and achieve victory against it in the battle to uphold religion. All these vital goals cannot be adequately achieved without organized teamwork. Therefore, teamwork becomes a necessity, in accordance with the fundamental rule, "Duty*

> *cannot be accomplished without it, and it is a requirement." This way, teamwork is achieved through mustering and organizing the ranks, while putting the Amir (the Prince) before them, and the right man in the right place, making plans or action, organizing work, and obtaining acts of power* (al-Qaeda Manual, n.d.).

The above paragraph clearly states the policy that many extremist-terrorist inmates and other extremist organizations hold. They believe that upholding their religion will necessarily require an all-out confrontation against their enemies (including the prison or other facility) who want to recreate darkness. Besides the extremist beliefs, they claim it is vital to stand against darkness (any areas that conflict with their notions of the Muslim caliphate) in all areas: the media, education, religious guidance and counseling, and others.

These excerpts illustrate the depth of the extremist-terrorist inmates' belief system and how they view correctional staff and other inmates.

These two paragraphs shed light on some reasons why deradicalization programs have struggled to be successful. The extremist-terrorist inmates and other extremist inmates have been trained to reject efforts to deradicalize them. The extremist-terrorist inmates and other extremist inmates constantly reinforce the concepts of "brotherhood, ideology, and movement." Everything they do is for their God.

"Lesson 18" helps to show how extremist-terrorist inmates and other extremists inmates differ from criminal inmates. The extremist terrorists become indoctrinated into believing that everything that they do, they do for their God. As long as they act in God's name and for their ideology, their movement is blessed.

TARGET RECRUITS

Various accounts are available regarding how inmates are identified as possible recruits and how recruiters in correctional facilities approach these potential recruits. Correctional staff should be cautioned not to assume that these prison recruiters would only look to recruit those inmates who appear to be disadvantaged or vulnerable.

As mentioned, anecdotal evidence suggests what characteristics are desirable for selecting potential recruits, but there are many other reasons to recruit. These prison recruiters recruit specific inmates to assist them with their initiatives, both within the correctional facilities and upon release. Since the fall of the Caliphate, the needs of ISIS and other organizations are constantly changing and expanding, and they continually adapt their recruiting efforts to address their needs.

Gang Recruitment Versus Terrorist Group Recruitment. A difference exists between being recruited for a gang rather than for an extremist-terrorist group. Gang members conduct prison-gang recruiting. They accomplish their goal by either the soft approach (become one of us) or by intimidation (threats of physical violence, including severe beatings). In some cases, the inmates recruited into a prison gang are so badly beaten up that they had to be placed in the facility's infirmary. In other cases, recruits must assault or kill someone as part of an initiation into the prison gang.

However, extremist-terrorist group members follow a more religious/conversion model than the violence model used by some gangs when they recruit. Extremist-terrorist recruiters use a conversion approach that encourages recruits to join with them and become a "brother" (Hamm, 2007).

The conversion approach used by recruiters to entice criminal inmates into being radicalized as potential extremists more often than not stresses that the recruits will be joining a "religious brotherhood," and by joining this "religious brotherhood," they will enjoy many benefits. Among the benefits are protection from other inmate organizations and inclusion in a "religious brotherhood." They also may offer special privileges that are not afforded to other inmates because of their religious affiliation, including special "religious" meals, special religious services, and other things. They offer the opportunity to learn new things about their interpretation of religion and being forgiven and embraced by God. They also offer protection—being feared by other inmates and the opportunity to be successful at something.

Some of the recruitment is based on similarities (compatibility).

Because the recruits are not joining a gang but a "religious brotherhood," recruiters want them to believe that they will learn many new things and have very faithful and loyal friends.

> According to a secret CIA/FBI profiling communiqué describing the four-step path for becoming involved with Islamic extremism, the first step for any recruit is to search for a new way of life that offers a sense of meaning and belonging … offers him acceptance 'in the name of Allah, the Compassionate and Merciful.' … then completes the next two steps in textbook order:

> conversion to Islam and indoctrination in radical Islamic ideology. (Dunleavy, 2011)

Thus, the recruitment for extremist-terrorist organizations is a well-thought-out process. The extremist-terrorist recruiting process has checks and balances throughout the entire process.

Prison gangs have a history of evolving, adapting, morphing, and splintering into new gangs because of internal disagreements, perceived better social status, or power struggles among the various gangs such as the Mexican Mafia/Nuestra Familia. Prison gangs continue to expand their numbers within correctional facilities. Gangs change because they are becoming more organized through their chain of command, more sophisticated, prison-wise. They try to outwit and confuse the correctional staff to continue recruiting illegal and illicit activities behind bars. These changes work for a while, but the correctional staff eventually discovers the changes.

Extremist organizations, however, appear to be more ambitious. They want to mold their recruits into individuals who can be radicalized, either in prison or the "free world." Extremists use their time in incarceration to recruit others to their cause, refine their operations, indoctrinate, and plan for the future.

Correctional personnel should be aware that extremist-terrorist inmate radical organizations will use violence. And since many of them are former ISIS fighters, they are very adept and accustomed to using violence, have turned to the Internet to communicate with each other, use technological methods and tactics that sanction the use of violence, to include and recruit lone wolf believers to their ideology. Violence can never be ruled out, especially in correctional institutions. Extremist-terrorist inmates, White supremacy organizations, and prison gangs will use violence just like any other group to protect their religious ideology/beliefs, turf, members, or illicit business operations.

One of the great unknowns is what role returning ISIS/foreign fighters will play in recruiting if/when they are incarcerated. Will they be held up as idols, heroes, soldiers, and religious leaders, or will they use a hardline approach to attracting recruits (Darden, 2019)?

Many of the criminal inmates can be idealistic and naïve, and they are looking for role models. These returning ISIS/foreign fighters could become their role models.

A process that extremist recruiters use begins with observation and targeting. During this initial period of incarceration, the recruiters identify potential recruits and approach them. The recruiter is not necessarily the head recruiter. Initially, the recruiter and the potential recruit will be identified and approached by a recruiter and may or may not have something in common (as discussed in this chapter's compatibility section).

Sturgeon saw an example of this method that involved a gang recruiter approaching a recruit because the recruit had his mother's name tattooed on his forearm. The recruiter told the recruit, "That is my mother's name, too," a move that established the initial bond and began the recruiting process. By the way, official records proved that it was not the recruiter's mother's name.

Enough anecdotal evidence suggests that religious or political beliefs carried to their outer fringes breed extremist terrorists regardless of what faith or belief system a person or group follows. There is no justification for the horrific and nonsensical violent acts that some extremist-terrorist organizations engaged in while fighting in foreign countries. Again, the unknown is how these returning ISIS fighters will act upon returning to their homelands, and if they commit crimes and are incarcerated, how will they conform to prison life? Some evidence is in the captured al-Qaeda document in this chapter and Appendix 1.

Some signs that an inmate is being recruited: "Prisoners suddenly start demanding their food to be made only from Halal products, which are consistent with the requirement of Islam" ("Islamist Recruitment in German Prisons," 2017). Security officers may also observe other lifestyle changes that indicate an inmate being radicalized: changes his name to an Islamic name and changes his behavior to be more religious and adhere to the leader's ideology, including strictly adhering to religious customs. The individual becomes subservient to the group's leadership and stops using vulgar and profane language. The male recruit grows a beard (if permitted). Another clue is when the person starts to attend Islamic religious services and studies the *Koran* intently. Of course, another tipoff is when the person starts to associate with known extremist-terrorist inmates and separates from non-extremist inmates, family, and friends.

Recruitment in Prison

So, how does the recruitment process work? As noted earlier, people in prison are cut off from friends and family and often search for new meaning in their lives. New inmates are afraid and uncertain about the prison experience, and they often feel a sense of alienation and isolation. Extremists prey on this alienation; likewise, the isolation causes prisoners to seek protection from prison gangs or religious organizations. New inmates are looking for a community and a sense of belonging. Terrorist-extremist inmates capitalize on this fear and isolation by trying to befriend them or offer spiritual support (Brandon, 2009).

Furthermore, people often leave prison with no financial or social support system. Radical organizations also prey on this vulnerability, and promise prisoners support to ensure their transition back into society. Thus, it effectively targets newly incarcerated people and those about to be released (Silke, 2014).

Extremists recognize that many new converts have little knowledge of Islam, and they can easily teach converts radical beliefs (Brandon, 2009). Some of these young inmates feel that the United States has discriminated against them or been unjustly incarcerated. Consequently, the feeling of oppression unites with limited knowledge of Islam, leading to a vulnerable population ripe for recruitment (Ballas, 2010).

After radical Islamists have established relationships with new converts, other Muslim prisoners begin preaching their extremist ideologies. They hold prayer circles, including teachings from the *Koran* and radical ideas (Brandon, 2009). Extremists offer recruits a chance to fill their sense of life through being a jihadist and legitimize their criminal acts in the name of jihad (Gutierrez, Jordan, & Trujillo, 2008). Recruiters also persuade inmates that jihadism is similar to their previous criminal behavior. They preach that it can offer redemption from crime and provide power, violence, and identity (Basra, Neumann, & Brunner, 2016).

Jordan Horner, a Muslim extremist, incarcerated in the United Kingdom, revealed how easy it is to convert criminal inmates to radical Islam in prison. He mentioned that recruitment occurs right in front of correctional officers, and there is little they can do about it. Although prison authorities frequently moved Horner to different correctional facilities, he said he could recruit inmates into radical Islam at all new locations (Evans, 2014).

Finally, let's return to Kevin James, who we discussed in a prior chapter, to explain how the recruitment process works. James began converting new inmates in the California prison system, preaching that Muslims should target Islam's enemies, including the U.S. government and Israel's supporters. He recruited other inmates by distributing a document entitled the "JIS Protocol," which described his religious beliefs and required JIS members to take an oath of obedience to him (Hamm, 2007).

James spread the protocol throughout the California prison system from the late 1990s to the early 2000s. He used smuggled letters, mail, and phone calls initiated from people in the free world to help spread his words. At this time, prisoner radicalization was not an issue in American prisons, so there was little communication monitoring. However, in 2003, officials discovered his activities, and they transferred approximately twenty-five JIS members to different institutions within the California state prison system. James then recruited Levar Washington in 2004, who began to hatch a plot from the outside after he was released from prison. Once the plot was discovered, an investigation uncovered another ten JIS members within the California state correctional system (Hamm, 2007).

With JIS, the process began when James converted to the Nation of Islam. James then initiated an alternative version of Islam—Jam'iyyat Ul-Islam Is-Saheed (JIS), a form of prison Islam. Like a prison gang, JIS had its hierarchy, code of conduct, and communication system, which provided members with a sense of meaning and identity, making their prison experience more tolerable (Hamm, 2007).

THE RADICALIZATION PROCESS

We used a model to explain the radicalization process and how it moves into violent extremism in prisons. The first phase of the model involves inmates' factors. As noted earlier, the experience of being incarcerated is shocking, and prisoners feel alienated and isolated from society, so many seek protection in prison gangs or religious organizations. Prisoners experiencing negative personal factors, such as a history of violent behavior, antisocial attitudes, or a sense of victimization, or those who want to wipe away their criminal acts, are more likely to be associated with extremism. Thus, they seek out religion for empowerment and a fresh start (Silke, 2014).

The second phase considers situational factors, pushing vulnerable prisoners into the next phase of radicalization, which usually happens when there is an active presence of extremist social networks within the prison that provide protection and social support to inmates. An example is "prison Islam" or "Prislam," in which gangs interpret parts of the *Koran* to justify the use of violence and recruit new inmates. Prislam bears little resemblance to the Islamic faith. Still, it provides prisoners who feel alienated with a sense of protection and belonging and a charismatic leader to guide them (Silke, 2014).

Phase 3 involves self-identification. This group includes individuals seeking religious or ideological guidance who "self-identify" with other extremists promoting messages they can identify. This phase is the stimulus for the rest of the radicalization process, as inmates begin to explore extremist views. Phase 4 is the indoctrination phase, in which the prisoner starts to learn about the extremist beliefs in depth. Phase 5, or militancy, is when the extremist religion or ideology is fully adopted, and the individual begins to participate in extremist activities (Silke, 2014).

Phase 6 involves post-prison-release terrorism. Most people will not execute any extremist ideas once released from prison; however, we have to be aware of those who have become radicalized and continue their recruitment into the community. Similar to gangs, most people who adopt extremist ideologies in prison do so primarily for protection. Consequently, once they are released from prison, they no longer need protection and support. However, some individuals search for ways to get revenge on their perceived enemies after being released from prison. For some of these people, radicalization intensifies after they are released, and they continue to recruit other extremists on the outside (Silke, 2014).

Finally, in phase 7, or post-attack re-incarceration, former prisoners not killed in their terrorist attacks are re-incarcerated. After phase 7, the cycle begins again in prison (Silke, 2014).

Recruitment

Radicalization is typically associated with extreme Islamist organizations responsible for many of the recent terror attacks across the world. The 9/11 attacks killed approximately 3,000 people, and the 2005 London bombings killed more than 50 people and injured nearly 700 others (Bhui, Hicks, Lashley, & Jones, 2012).

America's Muslim prison population is growing, and it includes many women. The data show that the number of Muslims in state prisons is growing, even though the prison population has decreased in many states. Further, this population includes many women, with 8 percent of female prisoners identifying as Muslim in Pennsylvania and 2.5 percent in Texas and Wisconsin (Muslim Advocates, 2019).

Moreover, prisons are breeding grounds for radicalization, as inmates can explore new beliefs and associations while incarcerated. Because they do not have their former social networks and are isolated from society, they are more susceptible to recruitment and radicalization into extremist Islamic organizations (Neumann, 2010). Consequently, prison staff needs to recognize radicalization to curtail inmates from engaging in this type of violence while incarcerated and when released.

Outside Influences

Other inmates rather than outside influences radicalize most inmates, but radicalization can be aided by external factors, including prison imams, outside visitors, and outside materials.

As we previously discussed, many prisons face a shortage of qualified religious providers serving prisons. As a result, prisons often use contracted-service providers with little or no formal religious training (Silke, 2014), volunteers from the community (Hamm, 2007), or prisoners with limited training in Islam. They assert themselves to be leaders (Ballas, 2010). These options create the potential for misrepresenting the Islamic faith and the possibility of individuals spreading extremist views (Merola & Vovak, 2012).

The United Kingdom faces a similar problem finding qualified prison chaplains, and it is becoming harder to monitor extremists. Imams in Britain have distributed extremist pamphlets and other literature in prisons, leaving inmates at risk for radicalization. Moreover, chaplains at several prisons have encouraged inmates to raise money for Islamic charities associated with terrorism (Hughes & Gye, 2016). Azadul Hussain, a prison imam, has spoken at pro-Taliban events. Meanwhile, another prison imam, Sahib Bleher, was the General Secretary of the Islamic Party of Britain, a group holding extremist views. Finally, in Great Britain, an extreme Islamist organization, the Markfield Institute, prepares Muslim chaplains to work in prisons, educational institutions, and hospitals (Westrop, 2014).

Aside from imams, other people visiting prisons can also contribute to the radicalization process. Most prisons try to prevent inmates from associating with visitors promoting extremist messages, but sometimes it is hard to recognize extremists from the outside. In Spain, for example, prison administrators have little control over who visits prisoners of Muslim origin. There is no database indicating if people visiting prisoners convicted of terrorism have visited others convicted of terrorism. There is also little inspection of visitors, allowing for content exchange with radical messages (Gutierrez, Jordan, & Trujillo, 2008).

Furthermore, as we have previously stated, there is also a shortage of qualified religious leaders or experts to review the content of material entering prisons in the United States, much of which is in foreign languages. Also, no standard procedure is available to determine if the material prisoners receive is appropriate (Silke, 2014). Therefore, it is likely that material promoting violence and extremist ideologies is entering prisons. Without individuals knowledgeable in Islam or the Koran, these materials could easily get into the wrong hands.

Conditions of Prisons

As we noted, maximum-security prisons are more suitable for recruitment than lower-security facilities because they house more violent offenders, are more crowded, have greater gang problems, and have greater shortages of prison chaplains. Some experts claim that "these factors constitute a Petri dish in which terrorism may grow and prosper" (Hamm, 2007, p. 110).

Besides, prisons that are crowded and unorderly exhibit a higher potential for radicalization. Stable prisons require adequate staffing and physical space and have insufficient programming. When prisons are crowded, the staff's ability to recognize radicalization is reduced. Muslim prison gangs and other gangs are more apt to form in crowded prisons where staff cannot adequately supervise inmates (Neumann, 2010).

The correctional officer's role in minimizing radicalization is vital, so training for them is so critical. Correctional officers interact with prisoners daily and have the ability to detect trouble. However, most correctional officers do not have the training to recognize and manage the radicalization process. Also, they cannot always understand the languages spoken by inmates, and there are not always translators on site. Moreover, correctional officers are often on rotation, so it is hard for them to familiarize themselves with and supervise the activities of terrorist-extremist inmates (Gutierrez, Jordan, & Trujillo, 2008).

Although terrorist plots rarely occur inside a prison, the problem is that some inmates embrace extremist ideas, which could lead to terrorist attacks upon their release. While only a few people adopt extremist beliefs solely due to their incarceration, incarceration helps to hasten the radicalization process because inmates who are isolated from society are vulnerable to adopting extreme ideologies. Consequently, it is necessary for prison administrators and staff to understand how the radicalization process works in prison (Brandon, 2009) to prevent terrorist attacks once radicalized inmates are released (Merola & Vovak, 2012).

Correctional administrators must accept the premise that extremist-terrorist inmates and other extremist inmates represent a new inmate population that can create new security, operations, management, and training challenges. These challenges will range from those relatively simple to correct (by developing a policy detailing where and what types of jobs extremist terrorists will be assigned to do) to extremely difficult ones that need to be addressed decisively.

> Inside the prison, the brothers should not accept any work that may be demeaning him or his brothers, such as cleaning of bathrooms or hallways. (al-Qaeda Manual, n.d.)

For example, the issue discussed in a prior chapter, should the agency house extremist-terrorist inmates and other extremist inmates separately? Indecisive or "wishy-washy" management will allow extremist-terrorist inmates and other extremist inmates to fill the management void.

TRAINING

Recruiting occurs in the living areas, recreation yards, religious services, infirmaries, outside work details, and dining facilities. Therefore, first-line supervisors and line correctional officers must receive training in identifying: recruiters, leaders, methods and techniques used to recruit, inmates being recruited, and inmates intimidated into joining extremist-terrorist organizations.

A crucial element in reducing extremist-terrorist inmate recruiting is to have well-trained correctional staff, especially first-line supervisors and line staff, who have direct contact with this classification. They can recognize recruiters and recruiting activities and potential recruits and take the proper steps to interrupt the recruiting process by confronting the recruiter and/or removing the potential recruits. The potential recruits should be sent to a deradicalization class and/or speak with the institution's chaplain of their choice.

Agencies should have an established protocol for correctional staff to follow if an extremist-terrorist inmate informs a staff member that he does not want to be radicalized or separate from the organization. There should be a designated housing area, which should be considered protective custody for these inmates until staff can determine if their desires are real.

The staffer who learns about the inmate's decision to leave the extremist-terrorist organization should immediately inform deradicalization personnel. Continuous evaluation of the extremist-terrorist inmate's progress in the deradicalization process is crucial. Only authorized correctional personnel should be permitted to access this unit.

The personal safety of inmates wishing to leave the extremist-terrorist organization or any other group must be paramount! Deradicalization personnel should conduct an intake interview to determine if the inmate is sincere about leaving the extremist-terrorist organization. If the deradicalization personnel believe that the inmate is sincere about leaving, they should develop an individualized program. Individualized programs are necessary because many of the extremist-terrorist inmates and other extremist inmates come from varying backgrounds.

Some questions to consider when interviewing these extremist-terrorist inmates:

- Why do they want to leave the extremist-terrorist organization now? Has something happened? What are the extremist-terrorist inmate's feelings about the ideology/belief system as a whole? What was good about the ideology, and what was difficult about the ideology?
- How long have they been radicalized?
- How does the inmate see his or her future unfolding?
- Has the inmate belonged to other organizations in the past, and why has he/she left that group?

Those considering alternative housing for inmates seeking deradicalization should examine these inmates' criminal history and their past behavior while incarcerated, if available. Line supervisors and line staff can provide valuable information to the deradicalization team.

"Although radicalization research has grown substantially over the years, more research is needed to understand the causes, processes, and mechanisms of radicalization to be able to develop effective preventative measures and countermeasures" (RAN Centre of Excellence, 2016).

We have much to learn about the intricacies of the recruiting processes for extremist-terrorist inmates. What the authors found intriguing were the religious implications associated with recruiting criminal inmates to become extremist terrorists. Recruiting for other gangs or subversive organizations does not involve a religious commitment.

Although terrorist plots rarely occur inside a prison, some inmates embrace extremist ideas, leading to terrorist attacks upon their release. While only a few people adopt extremist beliefs solely due to incarceration, incarceration helps to hasten the radicalization process because inmates are isolated from society and vulnerable to adapting extreme ideologies. Consequently, prison administrators and staff need to understand how the radicalization process works in prison (Brandon, 2009). Such knowledge will help prevent terrorist attacks once radicalized inmates are released (Merola & Vovak, 2012).

CONCLUSIONS

Criminal inmates' radicalization and recruitment will be a constant problem for correctional administrators, managers, first-line supervisors, and line staff. If correctional personnel do not intercede to disrupt or curtail radicalization and recruitment, the extremist-terrorist inmate population will grow. The authors warn that the prison gang problem got out of control because not enough correctional personnel took its growth seriously and moved to interrupt and curtail its growth until it was too late and the prison gangs had gotten a foothold and organized! Correctional administrators and others can get ahead of the problem, devise programs, and train staff to handle these extremist-terrorist inmates.

13

Inmate Vulnerability and Correctional Facility Practices

Common threads exist among correctional agencies worldwide, and extremist-terrorist inmates and other extremist inmates can use these common threads to their advantage while incarcerated. Examples of these common threads are in day-to-day operations, such as how official counts are conducted, when a change of shifts occurs, visiting procedures, and other areas. Correctional personnel must embrace the reality that extremist-terrorist inmates and other extremist inmates represent a new breed of inmate. Chapter 12 (Captured al-Qaeda Training Manual) detailed that many extremist-terrorist inmates and other extremist inmates are well-versed in jail and prison operations and security practices and procedures.

Some extremist-terrorist inmates and other extremist inmates were incarcerated in prisons where they were severely mistreated and possibly tortured, reinforcing their extremism and radical beliefs. Because of their prior abuses, this inmate population initially may be defensive.

Correctional professionals throughout the industrialized world understand how important the living conditions are within some prisons. Prisons with poor living conditions and abuse can contribute to inmates being converted and radicalized while incarcerated. "Former detainees said they were routinely subjected to (invasive) full-nudity body searches

DOI: 10.4324/9781003285946-13

and confined for up to 22 hours a day" (Gerretsen, 2017). Poor living conditions and prison crowding can generate resentment and provide the ground for antisocial narratives to take root.

No matter how heinous their crime/s, the nation's judicial system meted out the extremist-terrorist inmates' punishment. Staff must refrain from inflicting any type of physical harm as additional punishment. Additionally, it is a criminal offense for staff to inflict physical punishment on an inmate in most industrialized countries. The common thread among professional correctional personnel is ensuring the facility's security and safety for the staff and the public. Another common thread is to encourage extremist-terrorist inmates and other extremist inmates to enter deradicalization programs and ensure all inmates' safety, including extremist-terrorist inmates.

In the United States, several different stakeholders oversee prisons and conditions of confinement. Governing bodies and standard-setting agencies ensure that facilities are well maintained and that the inmates receive proper nutrition, healthcare and are not mistreated. State and federal courts impose laws that define how inmates in the United States must be treated and cared for. The "Totality of Conditions of Confinement" was detailed in a Texas case, *Ruiz v Estelle* 1972 (Texas Politics Project, n.d.). The team needs to review the agency's policies and procedures to become familiar with the *Ruiz* case's tenets to consider everyone's civil rights.

If correctional personnel mistreat, abuse, or cause harm in any way to inmates, they can be punished and could end up in prison themselves. If the violation/s rises to the level that the U.S. Department of Justice gets involved, one of the most common statutes used to charge correctional agencies or individual correctional employees is *Code 42. Section 1983:*

> Every person who, under color of any statute, ordinance, regulation, custom, or usage, of any State or Territory or the District of Columbia, subjects, or causes to be subjected, any citizen of the United States or other person within the jurisdiction thereof to the deprivation of any rights, privileges, or immunities secured by the Constitution and laws, shall be liable to the party injured in an action at law, suit in equity, or other proper proceeding for redress, except that in any action brought against a judicial officer for an act or omission taken in such officer's judicial capacity, injunctive relief shall not be granted unless a declaratory

decree was violated or declaratory relief was unavailable. For the purposes of this section, any Act of Congress applicable exclusively to the District of Columbia shall be a statute of the District of Columbia.

Additionally, several nonprofit organizations oversee prison operations, conditions, and inmate care. A few examples are as follows:

- American Correctional Association
- International Correctional Association
- American Jail Association
- Irish Prison Service
- Netherlands–Dutch Custodial Institutions Agency
- South African Department of Correctional Services
- Her Majesty Prison and Probation Service

Many other nations have similar organizations and governmental agencies that oversee their prison systems. Yet even with these safeguards, radicalization occurs in American prisons and prisons all over the world. "One of the things I have learned [is] that one of the places to look for the radicalization of people who become terrorists is the prison" (Greninger, 2017).

By their very nature and the people that every nation incarcerates, prisons foster subcultures, such as extremist terrorists, gangs, and radical groups (Hamm, 2008). Violent behaviors associated with prison gangs, extremism, and radicalism, while not condoned, occur often. These types of antisocial and violent behaviors are fostered in part by:

1. Overcrowded facilities and specific housing classifications
2. Outdated, misused, and nonexistent classification systems are driven more by available bed space than by the accepted classification rubric of the facility/agency. The result is over-classification or under-classification, both of which create operations and security issues.
3. Inmates with mental health issues that go undiagnosed and untreated
4. Inadequate or outdated staff training
5. Inadequate staff supervision

Prisoners' classification and categorization are essential to decide their allocation to a suitable prison or unit within a prison and,

> together with the findings of their risk and needs assessment, provide the basis for the development of individualized sentence plans. These basic rules apply to the management of all prisoners...They are particularly important to the case of violent extremist prisoners, where any shortcomings in their classification, categorization, and allocation can have far-reaching consequences both for the prisoner and the public. (Bryans, 2016)

Personal experience demonstrates that when inmates are assigned to a unit that is more restrictive than needed for their risk level, the inmates, for the most part, will adapt to the conditions of the unit; it is called "survival." In contrast, when inmates are assigned to a less-restrictive unit than they need, a strong possibility exists that the inmates may be recruited into either an extremist-terrorist group or a prison gang. Possibly, the security of the unit may be compromised. For example, if a medium-custody inmate is placed in a high-security housing unit, the inmate will take on a high-security inmate's characteristics. If an inmate is assigned to a unit that does not consider his or her "risk factor" and sends the inmate to a less-restrictive housing unit, that inmate could take over the unit and jeopardize the other inmates.

Before the need arises, each agency should establish an extremist-terrorist inmate monthly review committee. This review committee should be a multidisciplinary group consisting of the deputy warden for security, the security-threat-group manager, first-line supervisor/s from units that are housing extremist-terrorist inmates, the supervisor of the perimeter patrol activities, a vetted imam or other religious personnel, and representatives of inmate work assignments. The committee should review incident reports with special attention to what happened before the incident and what might have caused the incident.

Another goal is to identify all parties (staff, inmates, and others) involved. Did one or more inmates appear to be the leader/s?

Another aspect for consideration: Was the incident pre-planned? If yes, what led to that conclusion? Did staff or other inmates say anything to provoke the incident? If a weapon or weapons were involved, has the origin of the weapon/s been determined?

Was anyone injured? If so, what was the extent of the injuries?

This committee should also review all intelligence reports submitted by correctional staff and forward them to the appropriate internal and external agency personnel. After the monthly meeting, the committee should write a report and submit it to all appropriate departments and the facility administration.

SIGNS OF INMATE UNREST

From these reviews, the team should determine if there are issues within the extremist-terrorist inmates' group/s transpiring, such as any of the following:

- Their questioning of the current leader/s
- Members of the group becoming disheartened with their living arrangements
- Issues about access to religious services and activities
- More confrontations with correctional staff and threats against staff
- More confrontations with other extremist-terrorist inmates and other extremist organizations within the same group/other organizations
- Complaints about food
- Demanding to see a sergeant or above before complying with a correctional officer's instructions. (This is a tactic used by White supremacists on occasion when interacting with correctional officers of color and female correctional officers.)

Staff burnout is another major common thread that occurs with correctional staff assigned to special-inmate-management living units. The burned-out staff member may become a weak link. Therefore, supervisors have to spot such burned-out staff and get them help or medical leave because they could endanger the rest of the staff and inmates.

The facility or agency should establish an extremist-terrorist inmate secure "Intelligence Network" for sharing information within the facility, the agency, and with other parties who have a "need to know."

While we discussed recruiting throughout this book, we again state that correctional agencies and facilities should constantly be vigilant for the recruiters and recruiting activities. European correctional sources report an upswing in recruiting and radicalization activities because of the returning ISIL fighters.

> The problem of radicalization in German prisons is getting more and more serious due to a large number of radicals returning to Germany from Syria, an expert on Islam and Islamism, Sigrid Herrmann-Marschall, said, commenting on a recent German police report on recruitment attempts in the country's prisons. (Islamist recruitment in German Prisons: How to Identify Radicalization, 2017)

The administration and all staff members must be prepared to address any eventuality that may arise within the facility, on the facility's perimeter, or in the facility's visiting areas. Most correctional facilities are well prepared to manage traditional correctional emergencies. With the introduction of extremist-terrorist inmates, the potential exists for situations that do not fall within traditional emergencies. Additionally, few correctional facilities were built considering terrorist attacks using explosives; therefore, they are especially vulnerable to this attack style. Figures 13.1 and 13.2, on pages 143–144, are useful reminders of how to prepare for such an eventuality.

CONCLUSIONS

Correctional agencies, institutions, and staff responsible for incarcerating extremist-terrorist inmates and other extremist inmates will require that correctional administrators and correctional staff at every level and discipline be more vigilant, better informed, better trained, and more proactive. All staff must be better prepared to manage correctional emergencies, day-to-day operations, training and staffing needs—especially under media and political scrutiny. Correctional administrators, managers, and first-line supervisors must be continuously vigilant and able to think outside the box as the terrorist inmates often do not follow the behaviors of other inmates. Complacency is the nemesis of corrections.

BOMB THREAT STAND-OFF CARD

Threat Description	Explosives Capacity	Mandatory Evacuation Distance	Shelter-in-Place Zone	Preferred Evacuation Distance
Pipe Bomb	5 lbs	70 ft	71-1199 ft	+1200 ft
Suicide Bomber	20 lbs	110 ft	111-1699 ft	+1700 ft
Briefcase/Suitcase	50 lbs	150 ft	151-1849 ft	+1850 ft
Car	500 lbs	320 ft	321-1899 ft	+1900 ft
SUV/Van	1,000 lbs	400 ft	401-2399 ft	+2400 ft
Small Delivery Truck	4,000 lbs	640 ft	641-3799 ft	+3800 ft
Container/Water Truck	10,000 lbs	860 ft	861-5099 ft	+5100 ft
Semi-Trailer	60,000 lbs	1570 ft	1571-9299 ft	+9300 ft

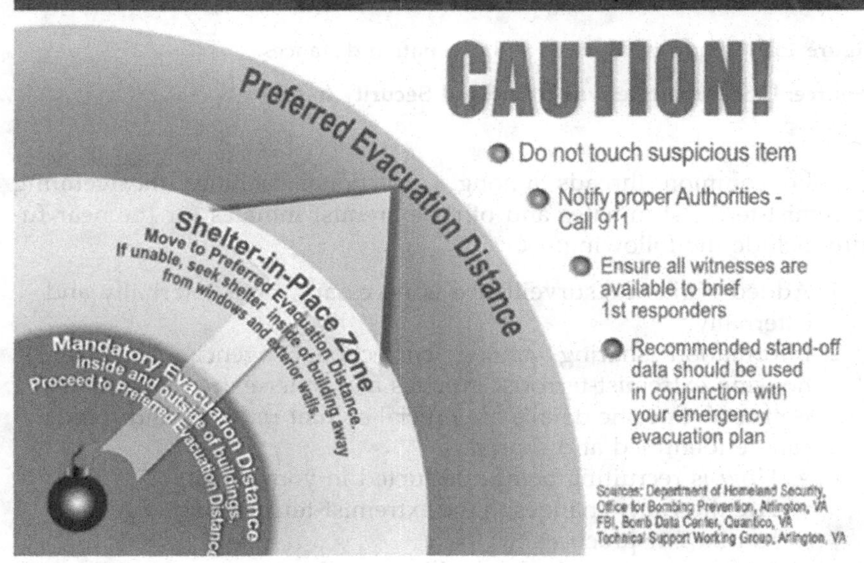

CAUTION!
Do not touch suspicious item
Notify proper Authorities - Call 911
Ensure all witnesses are available to brief 1st responders
Recommended stand-off data should be used in conjunction with your emergency evacuation plan
Preferred Evacuation Distance
Shelter-in-Place Zone
Move to Preferred Evacuation Distance.
If unable, seek shelter inside of building away from windows and exterior walls.
Mandatory Evacuation Distance
inside and outside of buildings.
Proceed to Preferred Evacuation Distance
Sources: Department of Homeland Security, Office for Bombing Prevention, Arlington, VA
FBI, Bomb Data Center, Quantico, VA
Technical Support Working Group, Arlington, VA

Figure 13.1 Bomb Threat Stand-Off Card guidelines.

(Source: U.S. Department of Homeland Security, Office for Bombing Prevention, FBI Bomb Data Center, and Technical Support Work Group, (n.d.))

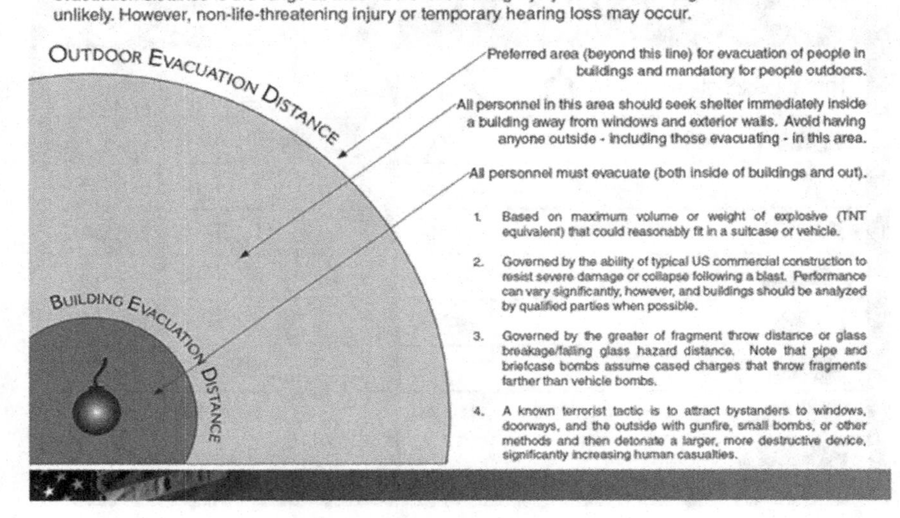

Figure 13.2 Explosive devices and evacuation distances.

(Source: U.S. Department of Homeland Security (n.d.).)

The common threads among correctional facilities incarcerating extremist-terrorist inmates and other extremist inmates for the near future include the following:

1. Added vigilance/surveillance is necessary, both internally and externally.
2. Information sharing among correctional agencies that are housing extremist-terrorist inmates and other extremist inmates is crucial. Specific details are crucial so that patterns and trends can be identified and shared.
   - How is recruiting being conducted in your facility?
   - Are there any changes to the extremist-terrorist inmates' daily routines or practices?
   - Do inmates have body markings, such as tattoos, brandings, scars, and combat injuries?

- Report any/all confrontations with staff or other inmates, especially if it involves one of their brothers or sisters. What caused the confrontation?
- Are there any changes to visiting activities?
- Who is providing funding for their canteen accounts and what types of things are they buying from the canteen?
- Are there any changes in staff attitudes, staff physical wellness, calling in sick, or requesting a transfer?
- Were any staff members compromised and terminated? Before termination, debrief any compromised staff members about the methods used to convert them. This debriefing is crucial so that training programs can be developed to prevent staff from being future recruits.
- Are there any changes in the incoming or outgoing mail activities?
- Are there any changes in visiting and visitors?
- Are there any changes in telephone activities? How do extremist-terrorist inmates and other extremist inmates interact with other inmates?
- What are the personal characteristics of extremist-terrorist inmate leaders and recruiters?

While appearing to be tedious, these examples of questions to ask and follow up on are methods of gaining intelligence that could lead to better policies, procedures, and a more secure and safe facility.

The authors avoid using the term "best practice" to share what is working, why it is working, and, more importantly, what is not working and why. Rather than "best practices," perhaps the goal is to find policies, procedures, and practices that appear to be working well with this population. What may work very well in one correctional setting might not work so well in another. Several reasons for this include cultural differences—and institutional culture, staffing and training, differences in the way inmates adhere to their ideology, and prison living conditions. Other important issues include prior conditions of confinement, including prior abuse while incarcerated. Additional variables include budget issues, gender issues, and political, religious, and racial bias.

Remember, worldwide corrections are always on a continuous learning curve for managing extremist-terrorist inmates and determining how jihadists, White supremacists, and yet-to-be-identified organizations co-exist. That area is still being explored and documented.

14
Future Challenges

Correctional institutions worldwide will, for the foreseeable future, be asked to incarcerate and manage constantly changing and unique extremist organizations of inmates that, for the most part, are ideologically driven. The extremist-terrorist inmates and other extremist organizations currently represent various international, domestic, and yet unknown extremist organizations! Certainly, these organizations span a large spectrum of extremist ideologies, from numerous Jihadi organizations, far-right organizations, White supremacist extremists, far-left groups, and extremist drug cartels. Also represented are a variety of gangs (Belz, 2020).

The Anti-Defamation League (ADL, n.d.) defines White supremacy:

> White supremacy is a term used to characterize various religious beliefs central to which are one or more of the following key tenets: 1) Whites should have dominance over people of other backgrounds, especially where they may coexist; 2) Whites should live by themselves in White-only societies; 3) White people have their own culture that is superior to other cultures; 4) White people are genetically superior to other people. As a full-fledged ideology, White supremacy is far more encompassing than simple racism and bigotry.
>
> Most White supremacists today further believe that the White race is in danger of extinction due to the rising flood of non-Whites who are controlled and manipulated by Jews, and their imminent action is needed to save the White race. (ADL, n.d.)

DOI: 10.4324/9781003285946-14

WHITE SUPREMACISTS/NEO-NAZIS

White supremacists' resurgence in the United States and neo-Nazi and nationalist organizations throughout Europe and Asia put additional strain on law enforcement, and correctional agencies already stretched thin.

Correctional agencies have, for years, dealt with prison gangs and racial and ethnic gangs labeled "Known Enemies/Keep Separate," but the numbers were, in most cases, manageable. The possibility exists that the sheer number of individuals representing numerous "Known Enemies" organizations could create management, operations, and security issues for correctional agencies/facilities, which are not prepared to deal with these diverse extremist organizations.

What can correctional agencies take from this book that could assist them in getting ready for what could be the most challenging times for corrections since the prison riots at Attica, New York State Prison in 1971 (Riot at Attica Prison, 2019), and the New Mexico State Prison in 1980?

Another group of terrorists, the "Jihadi," or jihadist, refers to a person who believes that an Islamic state governing the entire community of Muslims must be created, even violently" (Zalman, 2019).

Because these organizations of extremist terrorists continue to engage in illegal activities, at some point, many of their members will enter the criminal justice system. In the United States, possibly, the extremist-terrorist arrestee/s will be composed of domestic terrorists and subversive groups. The correctional odyssey will start in local jails and then, if found guilty, be sentenced to either federal or state prisons.

Extremist-terrorist ideologies and political and religious views are spreading worldwide and gaining members (Gehrke, 2019). Organizations include al-Qaeda, ISIS, Al-Shabaab, al-Qaida in the Islamic Maghreb (AQIM), Boko Haram, and Ansar Bayt Al-Maqdis (ABM). al-Qaeda has branched out into central Africa, the Arabian Peninsula, and the Philippines to date. ISIS fighters are returning to their home countries.

> Then, the White supremacy ideology is growing rapidly. "White supremacy extremism (WSE) is a transnational challenge—its tentacles reach from Canada to Australia, and the United States to Ukraine—but it has evolved at a different pace in different parts of the world." (Soufan Center, 2019)
>
> While White supremacy organizations are well known to American correctional personnel, White supremacists for many years represented a relatively small but dangerous number of inmates.

> In my experience, their numbers and ideologies have fluctuated over the years. Now, however, White supremacist organizations are growing in number and are carrying out violent attacks, both in and out of the correctional environment. (Wilson, 2020)
>
> "Leaders of the Aryan Brotherhood prison gang were charged Thursday with directing killings and drug smuggling from within California's most secure prisons, U.S. prosecutors said. The charges detailed five slayings and accused an attorney of helping smuggle drugs and cell phones to a white supremacist gang. Sixteen Aryan Brotherhood members and associates are accused of running a criminal enterprise using contraband cell phones, encrypted chats, text messages, multimedia messages, and emails." (Thompson, 2019)
>
> "Violent right-wing extremists maintain international links, for example, through participation in concerts and rallies marking historical events in a variety of E.U. member states. Right-wing extremist ideology is not uniform and is fed from different sub currents, united in their rejection of diversity and minority rights. One element of violent right-wing ideology is the belief in the superiority of the white race, which will have to fight a race war. Right-wing extremists deem this confrontation unavoidable to stop the alleged conspiracy by the system to replace the white population through migration." (Bielby, 2020)
>
> "Over 1,000 hate groups are now active in the United States," and "most hate organizations in the United States, including the Ku Klux Klan neo-Confederates and white nationalists, espouse some form of White supremacist ideology," according to the Southern Poverty Law Center, a civil rights group. (Stack, 2019)

Regardless of where the terrorists are incarcerated, correctional agencies, from county jails to state or federal prisons, must be prepared to manage White supremacists and other inmates and keep them and the correctional staff safe. One method of maintaining security is to separate the various extremist organizations from each other.

Additionally, correctional agencies must take proactive steps to protect criminal inmates from being recruited, intimidated, exploited, or physically harmed by extremist-terrorist inmates. Danish prisons' inmates are overwhelmingly Islamic, and non-Muslim inmates are abused and forced to participate in Islamic prayer. Muslim inmates take control of what other inmates can eat. Brutal assaults on ethnic Danes are also common, according to Bo Yde Sørensen, a Prison Federation leader (Danish Inmates Abused and Forced to Participate in Islamic Prayers, 2020).

Denmark is not alone in growing inmate violence. Attacks against correctional personnel and inmates are escalating in several countries. According to Penal Reform International (n.d.), the root cause of this violence is overcrowding.

> Prison overcrowding is one of the key contributing factors to poor prison conditions around the world. It is also arguably the biggest single problem facing prison systems, and its consequences can at worst be life-threatening at best prevent prisons from fulfilling their proper function. Data suggests that the number of prisoners exceeds official prison capacity in at least 115 countries. Overcrowding is a consequence of criminal justice policy not of rising crime rates, and undermines the ability of prison systems to meet basic human needs, such as healthcare, food, and accommodation. It also compromises the provision and effectiveness of rehabilitation programs, educational and vocational training, and recreational activities. (Penal Reform International, n.d.)

The disrespect and direct assaults on law enforcement personnel in the free world have spilled into correctional systems. When this attitude is coupled with issues of terrorism, the situation in corrections becomes stark. Still, this book's objective is to demonstrate how to handle the terrorist inmates so that the staff remains safe and the facility remains secure!

The authors believe that correctional agencies should take this opportunity to begin updating, creating, or adapting new policies and procedures and specifically examine their security operations, intelligence-gathering techniques and methods, and training curriculum to meet the new challenges facing twenty-first-century corrections. The old phrase, "We've always done it that way," could have disastrous consequences in today's world.

WHAT-IF SCENARIOS

A productive method for assessing policies, procedures, operations, security ops, and training is to conduct "What-If" scenario drills. Take some of these "What-If" scenarios from news videos of street disturbances/riots. For example, terrorists use lasers to blind officers, balloon bombs, Molotov cocktails, and firework bombs to injure police officers.

Here are a few other examples of non-criminal correctional What-Ifs:

1. A vehicle loaded with explosives drives into the sally port of the facility and detonates. Simultaneously, there is a major disturbance in the yard. What is your plan?
2. A woman enters the visitors' reception area of the facility wearing a vest bomb and detonates it, killing or injuring all the other visitors and staff. What is your plan?
3. Extremist-terrorist inmates, who have killed in the past, take correctional officers hostage and threaten to kill them if their demands are not met. What is your plan?
4. There is an all-out assault of the perimeter of the facility by a well-armed and well-trained team. The outside patrol officer has been dispatched, and the attackers have penetrated the perimeter with a vehicle bomb. What is your plan?
5. Violent incidents occur in various areas around the facility as the perimeter is attacked. What is your plan?
6. A drone is adapted to drop an explosive within a facility's interior while a vehicle simultaneously crashes through the sally port. Drones are being adapted to do many things, some of which are illegal and may affect correctional facilities' security. "Drone drops drugs into Ohio prison yard, spurring inmate fight" (CBS News, 2015).
7. Perimeter patrol officer/s or tower officers are blinded by laser beams, thereby leaving the perimeter vulnerable. What is your plan?

When developing "What-If" scenarios, keep in mind that extremist organizations often conduct simultaneous incidents so that something could be occurring on the facility's perimeter, and a major disturbance/hostage situation occurs within the facility. We know from experience that extremist terrorists use explosives, automatic weapons and conduct well-planned operations. Conducting an attack on a correctional facility will certainly draw media attention (Scott, 2010).

Another concern for correctional facilities is extremist terrorists' ability to adapt their methods to compromise security operations changes.

> Every time security is changed to adapt to a new threat; the terrorist planner must come up with a new attack plan (often involving a new type of improvised explosive device to defeat the enhanced security measures). For example, terrorist planners, such as Imad Mughniyeh's team in Lebanon, adjusted to increased perimeter security at embassies and government buildings by developing very large vehicle-borne improvised explosive devices. Jihadist planners have responded to changes in the airline security measures by adopting baby doll bombs, shoe bombs, liquid bombs, and underwear bombs. (Stewart, 2013)

Thus, correctional personnel must constantly update their security operations, policies/procedures, and training initiatives.

Correctional facilities incarcerate individuals representing various extremist-terrorist organizations with conflicting social, religious, and political ideologies, which could mean warring factions. However, both profess belief in the same ideology/religion, yet have a profound hatred for each other. Correctional personnel must be aware of these warring organizations so that housing arrangements do not jeopardize the inmates' and staff's safety and the integrity of the facility's security.

Correctional agencies, globally, are experiencing an upsurge in the extremist-terrorist inmate populations. These include returning foreign fighters from the Middle East, Africa, and other volatile locations. "A study by the Soufan Center and the Global Strategy Network has tracked 5,600 fighters who have returned to their home countries" (Meko, 2018).

Another group increasingly incarcerated include lone wolves who have become converts, either through the Internet or local affiliations such as religious sources, family members, and friends.

WOMEN

According to Audrey Alexander of the George Washington University Program on Extremism, women play a more active role in the various jihadist organizations. "The self-proclaimed Islamic State and other actors have identified several unique roles for Western women in their radicalization and recruitment efforts" (2016). Alexander's report finds that a few women conduct violent plots, many disseminate propaganda, donate resources, or travel abroad to offer their support. The rate of American female involvement in jihadist movements is on the rise.

In Alexander's (2016) study, the profile of the American female jihadist revealed vast differences among its members. Individuals hailed from fourteen different states and ranged from fifteen to forty-four years old, with an average age of twenty-seven. Women aligned themselves with a range of organizations, including, but not limited to, the Islamic State, al Shabaab, the Taliban, and al-Qaeda.

Commonalities among the twenty-five cases inform a framework that sorts women's contributions into three overlapping categories: Plotters, Supporters, and Travelers. Plotters design, attempt, or carry out domestic attacks. Supporters garner material support within U.S. borders by disseminating propaganda or concealing information about impending threats to advance jihadist organizations' agendas. Travelers migrate to participate in the movement directly.

While a few women appear to act alone, many conduct activities in pairs, trios, or clusters alongside friends, siblings, or romantic partners. Online and offline dynamics complement one another and remain influential among jihadi women in America. Social media platforms are an especially common medium through which women are active, highlighting a vital opportunity for online detection and disruption.

Alexander's findings contribute to the necessity for policy development to respond to the threat, which must be met with various responses. Moreover, the diverse background of these cases renders monolithic approaches ineffective.

Though "legal redress is the primary means to mitigate the threat, complementary strategies offer alternatives to arrest, explore deradicalization, and emphasize prevention are necessary steps to counter violent extremism by women," Alexander (2016) contends.

Propaganda to women terrorists is carried in some of the more popular magazines for women along with tips on house and beauty (New Jersey Office of Homeland Security and Preparedness, 2018).

Children also are being groomed to play a more active role in the various jihadist organizations.

Recently,

> a video surfaced on the internet that depicted a ten-year-old Kazakh boy using a gun to execute two Russian members of the Islamic State of Iraq and al-Sham (ISIS) who had been accused of being spies ... Only a few days earlier, twin suicide bombings rocked northern Nigeria, involving three girls, who appeared to have been only ten years old, all wearing explosives that may

> have been remotely detonated by members of Boko Haram. A year before, a nine-year-old girl named Spozhmai, who is the sibling of an Afghan Taliban commander, was detained at a border checkpoint in Kandahar. Rather than go through with her mission, she confessed to the authorities that she had been forced to wear a suicide belt. (Bloom & Horgan, 2015)

Prisons across the world are releasing extremist-terrorist inmates. Nations worldwide are re-examining their housing and sentencing structures for convicted extremist terrorists.

However, if the past is prologue, most of those will not be high-profile inmates serving life sentences for plotting or carrying out attacks such as Zacarias Moussaoui (direct links to 9/11) or Dzhokhar Tsarnaev (one of the Boston Marathon bombers).

We look at the implications of the majority of released convicted terrorists in Chapter 15.

CHECKLIST OF ACTIONS

Throughout this work, the authors stressed:

The need for updating or creating policies and procedures that address issues specific to extremist-terrorist inmates. Extremist-terrorist inmates and other extremist organizations include new organizations with varying ideologies while professing beliefs in the same deity. They often have diametrically opposing ideologies steeped in schisms, which have transpired hundreds perhaps thousands of years ago. As for the far White organizations, they too have split and morphed over the years.

Hardening of the physical facility, both exterior and interior, is a vital step. Some of the hardenings can be accomplished using technology to augment a well-trained staff.

The best people to recruit for the hardening of the facility are line staff from every department. The correctional personnel from every department know the facility's weak points. Remember to use the "Matrix" (Paper–People–Places–Equipment, Technology, Materials).

Giving special attention to the exterior-security perimeter could be something new to American and other industrial nations' correctional systems. In today's world, there is the possibility of an armed assault on a correctional facility. These extremist organizations have the ability, technology, and funds to use their followers or hire individuals to attack a correctional facility. Security of a correctional facility means paying attention to a 360-degree circumference, including air space above and adjacent to the facility and sub-ground. The agency/facility's information technology personnel must constantly be on guard for internal and external hackers. Many of today's correctional operating security systems are automated, wireless, and web-based and are susceptible to hackers.

Sutter (2011) explains, "Hackers aim at prison locks and other real-world targets." In recent months, America has seen police stations (precincts) attacked, and evacuated; federal buildings including a Federal Courthouse were attacked.

Special attention to contraband control is important in all correctional facilities but is especially crucial when incarcerating extremist-terrorist inmates.

In Israel, the inspections were conducted simultaneously, of dozens of cells of security prisoners suspected of harboring contraband, to prevent attempts by the prisoners to hide the items. Among the items confiscated were cell phones, SIM cards, knives and even explosives. Prisoners who were found with contraband were punished with some put in isolation. Most of the prisoners with contraband were terrorists belonging to Fatah, Hamas, and Islamic Jihad. (Benovodia, 2019)

Among the extremist-terrorist inmate population are some sophisticated, well-educated, and well-trained inmates. These inmates will be able to find the weak points associated with every operational procedure and staff members. They will use these weak links to their advantage.

These organizations also present the ability to create non-criminal correctional situations and emergencies. While criminal inmates are streetwise, cunning, deceitful, and devious, they concern themselves, for the most part, with playing prison games. They rarely have a higher purpose other than to serve themselves. These various extremist-terrorist organizations have competing ideologies, goals, and objectives, but they do have some things in common.

Terrorists and other extremist organizations want to be considered a "presence/force" within the facility. For these organizations, being a "presence/force" can have multiple meanings, including the following: intimidating, getting respect, controlling turf, displaying open hostility toward staff, prison gangs, other extremist organizations, and other inmates, which also includes constantly challenging officers and other staff's authority, intentionally breaking the facility's rules and regulations to see how far they can push. Such behavior may also include demanding special privileges because of their religious beliefs and affiliations.

The violent inmate extremist terrorists also recruit new members/ brothers as followers using whatever means they deem appropriate. Regardless of what group it is, recruiting is the priority. Recruiting becomes especially important when "their" group is in the minority.

They strategically position themselves to get inmate jobs that can lead to intelligence, food, special privileges, and the ability to intimidate other inmates' organizations and staff by giving the facility's appearance of power.

All these organized organizations have some form of a hierarchy that gives the orders. The natural flow is from top to bottom. Anything other than top to bottom is frowned upon and dealt with immediately.

ROLE OF STAFF

Before developing or adapting policies and procedures, selecting new technology, or adapting training curricula and staffing patterns, select a team to spearhead the changes. Team members should come from a cross-section of the agency facility, including from the following disciplines: the administration, security staff–administration, first-line supervisors, and line staff. First-line supervisors and line staff must be an integral part of this process because they must implement it.

The advice of legal staff is needed for the hiring of imams and setting standards on religious materials, diets, dress, and so forth. Be sure to pass changed regulations, policies, and procedures through the legal staff.

Programs staff, administration, program supervisors, and deradicalization program staff will determine what programs will be delivered to the extremist-inmate populations and where they will be delivered. Because the extremist-terrorist inmate population will be made up of different and diverse organizations, the will have to be different deradicalization programming for each group; for example, deradicalizing members of ISIS and a White supremacist will require different programs.

The security-threat-group intelligence section needs to be aware of and contribute to intelligence gathering, analysis, and dissemination of intelligence concerning these organizations. Intelligence that directly affects what is happening in the living unit and the entire facility should be decimated to those who "Need to Know" as quickly as possible. In the past, the Intelligence division kept some information from staff for "security" reasons:

1. Staff would leak it to the inmates.
2. Staff would share information with other staff who did not need to know.
3. Staff, by their actions, would alert the inmates, etc.

The canteen staff should track the purchases of extremist terrorists and other extremists. The business office should work to determine who is contributing to the extremist-terrorist inmates' canteen fund. A long-established criminal justice practice of "Follow the Money" also applies when following who is contributing money to this population's canteen fund. Any information gained from this activity should be shared with the Joint Terrorism Task Force.

Individuals who are responsible for inmate job assignments should ensure that the system does not get manipulated. The authors recommend that a committee establishes a committee to review all inmate work assignments if the facility does not have such a committee. A committee of this type ensures oversight of inmate job assignments.

The head steward will submit special diets to the appropriate correctional personnel and diets for special religious observances:

a. Religious diets to the appropriate prison chaplain for approval
b. Medical diets to the prison's medical or nutritionist for approval

Throughout the process, the team should meet with the director of the agency or the warden at the facility to keep them appraised of the process and what needs must be fulfilled. The team should then tour the entire facility to identify vulnerabilities and assess what corrective actions need to be taken.

While these precautions are geared to agencies and facilities that are already housing or who are preparing to house extremist-terrorist inmates, they could, or perhaps, should be used by other correctional facilities to analyze and evaluate operations.

CONCLUSIONS

The world has become an extremely complex place full of competing ideologies about how things should be according to various belief systems. Correctional facilities are not exempt from the mass diversity, anger, and hatred present in the free world. The difference is that in a correctional facility, the staff is responsible for keeping all the staff, inmates/prisoners, and volunteers safe and secure, regardless of their beliefs.

The authors believe that now is the time to move corrections into the twenty-first century to face the new challenges. We still have time to get ready for these important challenges. A significant part of this twenty-first-century preparation will be the enhanced use of technology to monitor staff and inmates' safety and security. Technology will play an enhanced role in correctional facilities' operations, and security because it is becoming difficult to recruit and maintain correctional staff.

Just like everything else that happens in the free world, the COVID-19 virus has breached the perimeter of correctional facilities and infected and killed both staff and inmates. As the novel coronavirus ravages prisons worldwide, more than 5,000 state and federal correctional officers tested positive for the virus (Barr, 2020). At least 8,471 cases were reported among prison staff; 5,079 staff have recovered, while at least 34 deaths from coronavirus were reported among prison staff as of June 4, 2020 (Marshall Project, July 2020).

Epidemics and pandemics will be with humankind for the foreseeable future. The management of extremist-terrorist inmates and other extremist organizations during medical emergencies is another area that will take intense planning and staff training to maintain safety and security while delivering in-depth medical care and trying to prevent other inmates from contracting the disease. The old saying "We've always done it that way!" time has passed!

The authors remind correctional personnel: "Change is the only constant in life," according to the Greek philosopher Heraclitus (ca. 500 BC).

15

Inmate Release and Probation and Parole

PREPARATION FOR RELEASE

Probation and parole departments are another part of the criminal justice community that must begin developing policies, procedures, and training initiatives for dealing with these terrorist inmates when released from correctional agencies. The critical role of the probation and parole departments has yet to be recognized.

> The overwhelming majority of the more than 450 convicted terrorists currently in jail in the United States, most will be charged with lesser, non-violent offenses and serve sentences of 13 years on average. Given that the average age of those charged with ISIS-related crimes is only 27, this means that they will be released in the United States with decades of life to live. This raises a critical and but little examined question regarding U.S. counterterrorism strategy: what is being done in U.S. prisons to prepare this growing and unique segment of the prison population for re-entry into society? (Rosand, 2017)

With the early release of John Walker Lindh, aka "The American Taliban", from prison after serving seventeen years of a twenty-year sentence, and the press coverage surrounding his early release, the reality of extremist-terrorist inmates being released from prisons back into society hit home.

DOI: 10.4324/9781003285946-15

"According to data compiled by the Program on Extremism at George Washington University, over 80 individuals convicted of jihadist-related activity alone will be released from federal custody within the next five years" (Clifford, 2018).

In the United Kingdom, after the London Bridge attack, the monitoring and reporting requirements for probationers were tightened. Janice Grierson (2020) notes:

> The number of counter-terrorism specialist probation officers will double and they will work to a set of updated national standards for managing terrorists on licence, with closer monitoring and reporting requirements including polygraph tests, the Home Office and Ministry of Justice said in a joint announcement.
>
> Polygraphs, commonly known as lie-detector tests, remain inadmissible in UK courts but their use within the probation service for monitoring offenders is increasing. Sex offenders and domestic abuse perpetrators are already subject to the technology, and failures to pass a test can lead to further investigation or supervision.

PROBATION AND PAROLE

First and foremost, prisons must share information with probation departments and parole boards. As more terrorists are released from prison, probation and parole officers must become familiar with supervising former extremist-terrorist inmates within the community. Not only will this require additional efforts regarding the sharing of information, but it will also require additional staff training. Like line staff in correctional institutions, probation and parole officers must know about terrorism and counterterrorism efforts, the inmates' religious and cultural backgrounds, and circumstances leading to violent extremism (Williams, 2016).

Until now, there has been a minimal focus on the aftercare of terrorists in the United States. However, probation departments and parole boards must be provided with adequate resources to effectively deal with these populations to prevent acts of terrorism in the community (Basra, Neumann, & Brunner, 2016). These former inmates will need intensive supervision, and staff needs the tools to meet this challenge.

POST-RELEASE

Finally, there must also be a comprehensive database that tracks terrorists after they are released from prison (Basra, Neumann, & Brunner, 2016; Riechmann, 2017; Silke, 2014). Thus far, it has been hard to track these individuals because of a lack of proper data (Jones & Morales, 2012). If they are monitored in the community upon release, the probation department or parole board supervising them could maintain a database, including information on recidivism. This information should then be shared with relevant agencies and actors, including law enforcement, prisons, counterterrorism units, and researchers. This information is necessary to determine which programs and policies in prison help prevent recidivism among this special population.

Once again, Sturgeon cautions, "We don't know what we don't know!" For probation and parole departments, supervising extremist terrorists and members of other extremist organizations is a relatively new endeavor. Like correctional agencies, probation and parole departments will have to review their existing policies and procedures thoroughly. Additionally, probation and parole departments will have to assess their current training programs to ensure that their training programs address extremist terrorists and other extremist individuals' supervision.

The safety and security of probation and parole personnel should be prioritized in the review and planning initiatives! Safety should be divided into the following subdivisions:

1. Personal Safety
    - Be vigilant when in the public.
    - Be conscious of your situational awareness at all times.
    - Always secure your vehicle.
2. Office Safety
    - Prescreening clients before entering the office area.
    - Develop a list of Dos and Don'ts for the client. For example, do not bring a backpack, do not bring friends/s to your office visits, and other rules.
3. Home Visit Safety
    - Become familiar with the neighborhood.
    - Inform your supervisor when the officer/s are entering the domicile. Inform your supervisor when the officer/s are back in the vehicle.

- If possible, have more than one officer go on home visits.
- Be attentive to cultural and gender issues.
- Be concerned with situational awareness issues.
- If things go south, know an escape route.
- Follow all department policies and procedures.

4. Violation/Apprehension Safety Plan
    - Develop a plan to do the following:
        - Determine the best possible location to effect the arrest.
        - Ensure that there are sufficient officers present to effect the arrest employing the minimal amount of force.
        - Be prepared for any eventuality.
        - Exit the area as quickly as possible.
        - Coordinate with local law enforcement.

CONCLUSIONS

These extremist terrorists and other extremists commit criminal offenses, for which they were incarcerated as part of their ideology/religious beliefs. Their ideology and belief system alone separates them from criminal probationers and parolees. It would be a serious error on the management of probation or parole departments to consider these individuals the same as other clients.

As the authors have continuously mentioned throughout this book, extremist terrorists are a unique population that will present new challenges to probation and parole departments across the nation and the world, just as they have to law enforcement and corrections.

Much research and experiential learning need to be done before the criminal justice community has an in-depth understanding of how to best interact with extremist terrorists and other extremist individuals. The issues associated with extremist terrorists and other extremist organizations cannot be resolved overnight or in one book! These issues will take years, perhaps generations, to understand and to resolve.

In the interim, the criminal justice community must continue to improve its methods, techniques, and training.

1. Law enforcement, parole, probation personnel will protect the general public and arrest those who use terroristic violence to kill or injure innocent civilians.

2. Judges will conduct fair and impartial trials.
3. Correctional staff will operate safe, secure, and humane correctional facilities.
4. Upon release under parole guidelines, parole personnel will carry out their duties in a professional manner.

As the Chinese saying goes, "May you live in interesting times!"

16

The Next Steps

Prisoner radicalization in Western correctional facilities is a serious issue that is not going away anytime soon and is increasing and diversifying. Local, state, and federal criminal justice and government agencies must continue working together to share intelligence, engage in information sharing and best practices, to prevent the spread of violent extremism throughout correctional facilities.

Most importantly, although prisons are known as breeding grounds for all types of antisocial recruiting, they are also known as environments that promote positive change and transformation (Hill, 2016). Incapacitation alone will not solve violent extremism. Therefore, prisons must look for ways to play a positive role in minimizing the spread of violent extremism, radicalization, and extremism.

Society must find the means to rehabilitate terrorists, provided they maintain their facilities' security and operations and the public's safety. As responsible correctional leaders and staff, they need to ensure that they are doing everything possible to prepare for the release of these individuals and their monitoring in the community.

Researchers must continue studying the relationship between religious conversion and radicalization. Researchers must also explore the connection between adequate programming and education and derailing radicalism.

When the authors submitted this book to their editor, they concluded:

> We are having very real concerns about what the future challenges in the field of corrections will be. The current street demonstrations/riots, attacks on police precinct stations, police officers, citizens,

DOI: 10.4324/9781003285946-16

correctional personnel, both inside and outside of correctional facilities, could be a harbinger of what is to come for correctional facilities. What is happening in the civilian world today will be played out in correctional facilities in the future!

Correctional administrators, security, operations, and training personnel must note what transpires on America's streets and other countries worldwide. As the saying goes, "Coming to a place near you" could be a true statement when it comes to extremist-terrorist behavior/activities.

Much attention and planning need to occur in jails, police lockups, and detention facilities. These facilities will be the first to incarcerate extremist terrorists and other extremists. Perhaps many of these arrestees will be people who have committed arson, physical assaults, destruction of property, looting, and intimidation of others.

How can county jail and detention facilities prepare for these arrestees? Correctional administrators can develop and use the following preemptive measures.

1. Train staff in the following areas:
   - De-escalation techniques.
   - Self-restraint.
   - Extremist-terrorist harassment techniques.
   - Practice in the application and removal of restraints (mechanical and soft) on non-cooperative persons.
   - Reinforce and practice use-of-force policies, procedures, and techniques.
   - Install and ensure the working of additional video and audio recording equipment in vulnerable areas, along with proper signage, with the warnings that there are always audio and video-recording devices in use.
   - Review the intake process, policies, and procedures.
   - Review the (detainee) property-inventory process and policies.
   - Review bail policies and procedures.
2. To ensure staff and detainee safety, increase staffing in specific areas, such as booking and holding areas.
   - Ensure that there is an adequate number of supervisors/managers assigned during peak booking and bail events.
   - Ensure sufficient medical personnel are on duty during peak booking events.

3. Before a mass arrest event, the management of all the agencies involved should meet and develop a plan of action. This plan should have a variety of contingencies, such as what to do if:
   - Extremist terrorists armed with Molotov cocktails, industrial-grade fireworks, and other weapons attack the perimeter of their facility.
   - A large group storms the perimeter to free colleagues.
   - The detainees take correctional staff hostage(s).
   - The detainees cause a major disturbance in the booking (intake) area, causing damage to the facility.
   - Detainees turn on each other and begin fighting.
   - Detainees start fires in the booking (intake) area and holding cells where they are held.
   - Something should happen to a detainee held in a cell with other detainees. You need an established policy and procedure for what the officers should do. Remember, this situation could trap the officers into unlocking the door and taking the officers hostage. One of the details in this policy and procedure should ensure that sufficient staff are present before unlocking the cell door.
   - Teams of lawyers arrive and demand to see their clients.
4. Who should be on duty if a mass arrest takes place:
   - The sheriff, chief, or designee.
   - The head of security.
   - The agency's attorney.
   - The medical director.
   - The food service manager.
   - The chaplains.
   - The representatives of the local fire service, emergency medical services (EMS), and local enforcement.
5. Post-incident documentation needed:
   - Video and still photography of damage to the facility.
   - Video and still photography of any injuries to staff and detainee(s).
   - Managers/supervisors to ensure that officers and others submit written reports before leaving the facilities.
   - Managers/supervisors to review and approve all written reports before releasing officers from duty.

6. Regroup as soon as possible and be prepared for additional incidents affecting the facility, law enforcement, correctional personnel, and all other first responders.
7. Conduct an "After Action" within a reasonable timeframe to determine staff performance following an exercise, training session, or major event. The "After Action" exercise should include discussions and evaluations of the agency (or multiple agencies). The following components should be examined:
   - How the staff performed throughout the incident.
   - Whether any breach occurred in the security of the facility.
   - Whether any additional policies and procedures are needed.
     - If so, what are they? Identify what new policies and procedures are needed.
     - Identify what current policies and procedures need to be updated.
     - Identify what policies and procedures are outdated and need to be replaced.
   - Identify areas where additional training is required.

Meet with local community leaders from the political, religious, racial, public safety organizations and the media. As part of an agency's preparation process, it would be advisable to meet with local community leaders from the political, religious, racial, public safety organizations and the media to develop its effort. Doing so will allow the process to be transparent. All correctional agencies and courts must begin to prepare now! Those who doubt that there is a need to prepare watch what is happening on several American cities' streets. Staff should review videotapes of street disturbances, riots, attacks on police, attacks on buildings, and see how rioters negate barriers such as fences.

Those agencies unprepared for future eventualities will experience the possibility of injured staff, detainees, inmates, and excessive damage to the facility. And, of course, there will be those looking to blame someone or some organization. Media scrutiny of everything that was done, or wasn't done, will be grounds for negative news stories and costly lawsuits.

CONCLUSIONS

Correctional agencies still have time to get ahead of what could be the most rebellious and challenging inmate populations ever to be incarcerated in correctional facilities. These new and challenging populations span the extremist spectrum, from extremist terrorists (domestic and foreign) to the extreme right- and left-wing organizations that believe in various ideologies. Many extremist organizations have demonstrated on the streets of American cities, showing their disrespect for law and order, their willingness to commit arson, assault law enforcement officers and others, and make and use improvised explosives and weapons.

For now and for the immediate future, the action words for correctional personnel are flexibility, adaptability, spontaneity, and react! "We don't know what we don't know."

Appendix I: The Captured al-Qaeda Training Manual*

The attached manual was located by the Manchester (England) Metropolitan Police during a search of an al-Qaeda member's home. The manual was found in a computer file described as "the military series" related to the "Declaration of Jihad." The manual was translated into English and was introduced earlier this year at the New York embassy bombing trial. UK/BM-2TRANSLATION Declaration Of Jihad [holy War] Against The Country's Tyrants Military Series [Emblem]: A drawing of the globe emphasizing the Middle East and Africa with a sword through the globe [On the emblem] Military Studies in the Jihad [Holy War] Against the Tyrants.

UK/BM-3 TRANSLATION [E] 19/220 In the name of Allah, the merciful and compassionate PRESENTATION to those champions who avowed the truth day and night…And wrote with their blood and sufferings these phrases … -*- The confrontation that we are calling for with the apostate regimes does not know Socratic debates…, Platonic ideals…, nor Aristotelian diplomacy. But it knows the dialogue of bullets, the ideals of assassination, bombing, and destruction, and the diplomacy of the cannon and machine-gun. ***… Islamic governments have never and will never be established through peaceful solutions and cooperative councils. They are established as they [always] have been by pen and gun by word and bullet by tongue and teeth.

In the name of Allah, the merciful and compassionate belongs to the guest house. Please do not remove it from the house except with permission. [Emblem and signature, illegible]

UK/BM-5 TRANSLATION Pledge, OSister To the sister believer whose clothes the criminals have stripped off. To the sister believer whose hair the oppressors have shaved. To the sister believer whose body has been abused by the human dogs. To the sister believer whose…Pledge, OSister Covenant, OSister…to make their women widows and their

* It is filled with errors and is included here without corrections.

children orphans. Covenant, OSister...to make them desire death and hate appointments and prestige. Covenant, OSister...to slaughter them like lambs and let the Nile, al-Asi, and Euphrates rivers flow with their blood. Covenant, OSister...to be a pick of destruction for every godless and apostate regime. Covenant, OSister...to retaliate for you against every dog who touch you even with a bad word.

In the name of Allah, the merciful and compassionate thanks be to Allah. We thank him, turn to him, ask his forgiveness, and seek refuge in him from our wicked souls and bad deeds. Whomever Allah enlightens will not be misguided, and the deceiver will never be guided. I declare that there is no god but Allah alone; he has no partners. I also declare that Mohammed is his servant and prophet. [Koranic verses]: ye who believe! Fear Allah as he should be feared, and die not except in a state of Islam" "O mankind! Fear your guardian lord who created you from a single person. Created, out of it, his mate, and from them twain scattered [like seeds] countless men and women; fear Allah, through whom ye demand your mutual [rights], and be heedful of the wombs [that bore you]: for Allah ever watches over you." "0ye who believe! Fear Allah, and make your utterance straight forward: That he may make your conduct whole and sound and forgive you your sins. He that obeys Allah and his messenger, has already attained the great victory." Afterward, the most truthful saying is the book of Allah and the best guidance is that of Mohammed, God bless and keep him. [Therefore,]the worst thing is to introduce something new, for every novelty is an act of heresy and each heresy is a deception.

Introduction Martyrs were killed, women were widowed, children were orphaned, men were handcuffed, chaste women's heads were shaved, harlots' heads were crowned, atrocities were inflicted on the innocent, gifts were given to the wicked, virgins were raped on the prostitution alter... After the fall of our orthodox caliphates on March 3, 1924 and after expelling the colonialists, our Islamic nation was afflicted with apostate rulers who took over in the Moslem nation. These rulers turned out to be more infidel and criminal than the colonialists themselves. Moslems have endured all kinds of harm, oppression, and torture at their hands. Those apostate rulers threw thousands of the Haraka Al-Islamyia (Islamic Movement) youth in gloomy jails and detention centers that were equipped with the most modern torture devices and [manned with] experts in oppression and torture. Those youth had refused to move in the rulers' orbit, obscure matters to the youth, and oppose the idea of rebelling against the rulers. But they [the rulers] did not stop there; they started to fragment the essence of the Islamic nation by trying to eradicate its Moslem identity. Thus, they started spreading godless and atheistic views among the youth. We found some that claimed that socialism was from Islam, democracy was the [religious] council, and the prophet-God bless and keep him-propagandized communism. Colonialism and its followers, the apostate rulers, then started to openly erect crusader centers, societies, and organizations like Masonic Lodges, Lions and Rotary clubs, and foreign schools. They aimed at producing a wasted generation that pursued everything that is western and produced rulers, ministers, leaders, physicians, engineers, businessmen, politicians, journalists, and information specialists. [Koranic verse:] "And Allah's enemies plotted and planned, and Allah too planned, and the best of planners is Allah."

They [the rulers] tried, using every means and [kind of] seduction, to produce a generation of young men that did not know [anything] except what they [the rulers] want, did not say except what they [the rulers] think about, did not live except according to their [the rulers') way, and did not dress except in their [the rulers'] clothes. However, majestic Allah turned their deception back on them, as a large group of those young men who were raised by them [the rulers] woke up from their sleep and returned to Allah, regretting and repenting. The young men returning to Allah realized that Islam is not just performing rituals but a complete system: Religion and government, worship and Jihad [holy war], ethics and dealing with people, and the *Koran* and sword. The bitter situation that the nation has reached is a result of its divergence from Allah's course and his righteous law for all places and times. That [bitter situation] came about as a result of its children's love for the world, their loathing of death, and their abandonment of Jihad [holy war]. Unbelief is still the same. It pushed Abou Jahl—may Allah curse him—and Kureish's valiant infidels to battle the prophet—God bless and keep him—and to torture his companions—may Allah's grace be on them. It is the same unbelief that drove Sadat, Hosni Mubarak, Gadhafi, Hafez Assad, Saleh, Fahed—Allah's curse be upon the non-believing leaders—and all the apostate Arab rulers to torture, kill, imprison, and torment Moslems. These young men realized that an Islamic government would never be established except by the bomb and rifle. Islam does not coincide or make a truce with unbelief, but rather confronts it. The confrontation that Islam calls for with these godless and apostate regimes, does not know Socratic debates, Platonic ideals nor Aristotelian diplomacy. But it knows the dialogue of bullets, the ideals of assassination, bombing, and destruction, and the diplomacy of the cannon and machine-guns. The young came to prepare themselves for Jihad [holy war], commanded by the majestic Allah's order in the holy *Koran*. [Koranic verse:] "Against them make ready your strength to the utmost of your power, including steeds of war, to strike terror into (the hearts of) the enemies of Allah and your enemies, and others besides whom ye may not know, but whom Allah doth know."

I present this humble effort to these young Moslem men who are pure, believing, and fighting for the cause of Allah. It is my contribution toward paving the road that leads to majestic Allah and establishes a caliphate according to the prophecy. According to Imam Ahmad's account, the prophet—God bless and keep him—said, ... [A few lines of Hadith verses, not translated]

FIRST LESSON: GENERAL INTRODUCTION

5. We cannot resist this state of ignorance unless we unite our ranks, and adhere to our religion. Without that, the establishment of religion would be a dream or illusion that is impossible to achieve or even imagine its achievement. Sheik Ibn Taimia—may Allah have mercy on him—said,

> The interests of all Adam's children would not be realized in the present life, nor in the next, except through assembly, cooperation, and mutual assistance. Cooperation is for achieving their interests and mutual assistance is for overcoming their adversities. That is why it has been said, 'man is civilized by nature.' Therefore, if they unite there will be favorable matters that they do, and corrupting matters to avoid. They will be obedient to the commandment of those goals and avoidant of those immoralities. It is necessary that all Adam's children obey.

He [Sheik Ibn Taimia] then says,

> It should be understood that governing the people's affairs is one of the greatest religious obligations. In fact, without it, religion and world [affairs] could not be established. The interests of Adam's children would not be achieved except in assembly, because of their mutual need. When they assemble, it is necessary to [have] a leader. Allah's prophet—God bless and keep

> him—even said, 'If three [people] come together let them pick a leader.' He then necessitated the rule by one of a small, non-essential travel assembly in order to draw attention to the remaining types of assembly. Since Allah has obligated us to do good and avoid the unlawful, that would not be done except through force and lording. Likewise, the rest of what he [God] obligated [us with] would not be accomplished except by force and lordship, be it Jihad [holy war], justice, pilgrimage, assembly, holidays, support of the oppressed, or the establishment of boundaries. That is why it has been said, 'the sultan is Allah's shadow on earth.'

The book *Tharwat Al-Sinam Fe Al-Ta'at wa Al-Nizam*, by Ibrahim Al-Masri, copying from Al-Fannawi Ibn Taimi's collection, 28–380. UK/BM-12 TRANSLATION

Principles of Military Organization: Military Organization has three main principles without which it cannot be established. 1. Military Organization commander and advisory council. 2. The soldiers (individual members). 3. A clearly defined strategy Military Organization Requirements: The Military Organization dictates a number of requirements to assist it in confrontation and endurance. These are: 1. Forged documents and counterfeit currency. 2. Apartments and hiding places. 3. Communication means. 4. Transportation means. 5. Information. 6. Arms and ammunition. 7. Transport Missions Required of the Military Organization: The main mission for which the Military Organization is responsible is: The overthrow of the godless regimes and their replacement with an Islamic regime. Other missions consist of the following: 1. Gathering information about the enemy, the land, the installations, and the neighbors. 2. Kidnapping enemy personnel, documents, secrets, and arms. 3. Assassinating enemy personnel as well as foreign tourists. 4. Freeing the brothers who are captured by the enemy. 5. Spreading rumors and writing statements that instigate people against the enemy. 6. Blasting and destroying the places of amusement, immorality, and sin; not a vital target. 7. Blasting and destroying the embassies and attacking vital economic centers. 8. Blasting and destroying bridges leading into and out of the cities.

Importance of the Military Organization: 1. Removal of those personalities that block the call's path. [A different handwriting:] All types of military and civilian intellectuals and thinkers for the state. 2. Proper utilization of the individuals' unused capabilities. 3. Precision in performing tasks, and using collective views on completing a job from all aspects, not just one. 4. Controlling the work and not fragmenting it or deviating from it. 5. Achieving long-term goals such as the establishment of an Islamic state and short-term goals such as operations against enemy individuals and sectors. 6. Establishing the conditions for possible confrontation with the regressive regimes and their persistence. 7. Achieving discipline in secrecy and through tasks.

SECOND LESSON: NECESSARY QUALIFICATIONS

Necessary Qualifications for the Organization's members: 1. Islam: The member of the Organization must be Moslem. How can an unbeliever, someone from a revealed religion [Christian, Jew], a secular person, a communist, etc. protect Islam and Moslems and defend their goals and secrets when he does not believe in that religion [Islam]? The Israeli Army requires that a fighter be of the Jewish religion. Likewise, the command leadership in the Afghan and Russian armies requires any one with an officer's position to be a member of the communist party. 2. Commitment to the Organization's Ideology: This commitment frees the Organization's members from conceptional problems. 3. Maturity: The requirements of military work are numerous, and a minor cannot perform them. The nature of hard and continuous work in dangerous conditions requires a great deal of psychological, mental, and intellectual fitness, which are not usually found in a minor. It is reported that Ibn Omar—may Allah be pleased with him—said, "During Ahad [battle] when I was fourteen years of age, I was submitted [as a volunteer] to the prophet—God bless and keep him. He refused me and did not throw me in the battle. During Khandak [trench] Day [battle] when I was fifteen years of age, I was also submitted to him, and he permitted me [to fight]. 4. Sacrifice: He [the member] has to be willing to do the work and undergo martyrdom for the purpose of achieving the goal and establishing the religion of majestic Allah on earth. 5. Listening and Obedience: In the military, this is known today as discipline. It is expressed by how the member obeys the orders given to him. That is what our religion urges. The Glorious says, "O, ye who believe! Obey Allah and obey the messenger and those charged with authority among you." In the story of Hazifa Ben Al-Yaman—may Allah have mercy on him—who was exemplary in his obedience to Allah's messenger—Allah bless and keep him. When he [Mohammed]—Allah bless and keep him—sent him to spy on the Kureish and their allies during their siege of Madina, Hazifa said,

"As he [Mohammed] called me by name to stand, he said, 'Go get me information about those people and do not alarm them about me.

As I departed, I saw Abou Soufian and I placed an arrow in the bow. I [then] remembered the words of the messenger—Allah bless and keep him—'do not alarm them about me.' If I had shot I would have hit him." 6. Keeping Secrets and Concealing Information [This secrecy should be used] even with the closest people, for deceiving the enemies is not easy. Allah says, "Even though their plots were such that as to shake the hills! [Koranic verse]." Allah's messenger—God bless and keep him—says, "Seek Allah's help in doing your affairs in secrecy." It was said in the proverbs, "The hearts of freemen are the tombs of secrets" and "Moslems' secrecy is faithfulness, and talking about it is faithlessness." [Mohammed]—God bless and keep him—used to keep work secrets from the closest people, even from his wife A'isha—may Allah's grace be on her. 7. Free of Illness The Military Organization's member must fulfill this important requirement. Allah says, "There is no blame for those who are infirm, or ill, or who have no resources to spend." 8. Patience [The member] should have plenty of patience for [enduring] afflictions if he is overcome by the enemies. He should not abandon this great path and sell himself and his religion to the enemies for his freedom. He should be patient in performing the work, even if it lasts a long time. 9. Tranquility and "Unflappability" [The member] should have a calm personality that allows him to endure psychological traumas such as those involving bloodshed, murder, arrest, imprisonment, and reverse psychological traumas such as killing one or all of his Organization's comrades. [He should be able] to carry out the work. 10. Intelligence and Insight When the prophet—Allah bless and keep him—sent Hazifa Ben Al-Yaman to spy on the polytheist and [Hafiza] sat among them, Abou Soufian said, "Let each one of you look at his companion." Hazifa said to his companion, "Who are you?" The companion replied, "So-and-so son of so-and-so."

In World War I, the German spy, Julius Seelber [PH]managed to enter Britain and work as a mail examiner due to the many languages he had mastered. From the letters, he succeeded in obtaining important information and sent it to the Germans. One of the letters that he checked was from a lady who had written to her brother's friend in the fleet. She mentioned that her brother used to live with her until he was transferred to a secret project that involved commercial ships. When Seelber read that letter, he went to meet that young woman and blamed her for her loose tongue in talking about military secrets. He, skillfully, managed to draw out of her that her brother worked in a secret project for arming old commercial ships. These ships were to be used as decoys in the submarine war in such a way that they could come close to the submarines, as they appeared innocent. Suddenly, cannonballs would be fired from the ships' hidden cannons on top of the ships, which would destroy the submarines. 48 hours later that secret was handed to the Germans. 11. Caution and Prudence In his battle against the king of Tomedia [PHI, the Roman general Speer [PH]sent an emissary to discuss with that king the matter of truce between the two armies. In reality, he had sent him to learn about the Tomedians' ability to fight. The general picked, Lilius [PH], one of his top commanders, for that task and sent with him some of his officers, disguised as slaves. During that mission, one of the king's officers, Sifax [PH]pointed to one of the [disguised] slaves and yelled, "That slave is a Roman officer I had met in a neighboring city. He was wearing a Roman uniform." At that point, Lilius used a clever trick and managed to divert the attention of the Tomedians from that by turning to the disguised officer and quickly slapping him on the face a number of times. He reprimanded him for wearing a Roman officer's uniform when he was a slave and for claiming a status that he did not deserve.

The officer accepted the slaps quietly. He bowed his head in humility and shame, as slaves do. Thus, Sifax men thought that officer was really a slave because they could not imagine that a Roman officer would accept these hits without defending himself. King Sifax prepared a big feast for Lilius and his entourage and placed them in a house far away from his camp so they could not learn about his fortifications. They [the Romans] made another clever trick on top of the first one. They freed one of their horses and started chasing him in and around the camp. After they learned about the extent of the fortifications they caught the horse and, as planned, managed to abort their mission about the truce agreement. Shortly after their return, the Roman general attacked King Sifax' camp and burned the fortifications. Sifax was forced to seek reconciliation. B. There was a secret agent who disguised himself as an American fur merchant. As the agent was playing cards aboard a boat with some passengers, one of the players asked him about his profession. He replied that he was a "fur merchant." The women showed interest [in him] and began asking the agent—the disguised fur merchant—many questions about the types and prices of fur. He mentioned fur price figures that amazed the women. They started avoiding and regarding him with suspicion, as though he were a thief, or crazy. 12. Truthfulness and Counsel The Commander of the faithful, Omar Ibn Al-Khattab—may

Allah be pleased with him—asserted that this characteristic was vital in those who gather information and work as spies against the Moslems' enemies. He [Omar] sent a letter to Saad Ibn Abou Wakkas—may Allah be pleased with him—saying, "If you step foot on your enemies' land, get spies on them. Choose those whom you count on for their truthfulness and advice, whether Arabs or inhabitants of that land. Liars' accounts would not benefit you, even if some of them were true; the deceiver is a spy against you and not for you.

Ability to Observe and Analyze: The Israeli Mossad received news that some Palestinians were going to attack an Israeli El Al airplane. That plane was going to Rome with Golda Meir—Allah's curse upon her—the Prime Minister at the time, on board. The Palestinians had managed to use a clever trick that allowed them to wait for the arrival of the plane without being questioned by anyone. They had beaten a man who sold potatoes, kidnaped him, and hidden him. They made two holes in the top of that peddler's cart and placed two tubes next to the chimney through which two Russian-made "Strella" [PH]missiles could be launched. The Mossad officers traveled the airport back and forth looking for that lead them to the Palestinians. One officer passed the potato cart twice without noticing anything. On his third time, he noticed three chimneys, but only one of them was working with spoke coming out of it. He quickly steered toward the cart and hit it hard. The cart overturned, and the Palestinians were captured.

14. Ability to Act, Change Positions and Conceal Oneself a. [An example] is what Noaim Ibn Masoud had done in his mission to cause agitation among the tribes of Koraish, those of Ghatfan, and the Jews of Koreitha. He would control his reactions and managed to skillfully play his role. Without showing signs of inconsistency, he would show his interest and zeal towards the Jews one time and show his concern about the Koraish at another. b. In 1960, a car driven by an American colonel collided with a truck. The colonel lost consciousness, and while unconscious at the hospital, he started speaking Russian 1. This story is found in the book A'n Tarik Al-Khida' *By Way of Deception Methods*, by Victor Ostrovsky [PH]. The author claims that Mossad wants to kill him for writing that book. However, I believe that the book was authorized by the Israeli Mossad. UK/BM-20 TRANSLATION fluently. It was later discovered that the colonel was a Soviet spy who was planted in the United States. He had fought in Korea in order to conceal his true identity and to gather information and critical secrets. If not for the collision, no one would have suspected or confronted him.

THIRD LESSON: COUNTERFEIT CURRENCY AND FORGED DOCUMENTS

Financial Security Precautions: 1. Dividing operational funds into two parts: One part is to be invested in projects that offer financial return, and the other is to be saved and not spent except during operations. 2. Not placing operational funds [all] in one place. 3. Not telling the Organization members about the location of the funds. 4. Having proper protection while carrying large amounts of money. 5. Leaving the money with non-members and spending it as needed. Forged Documents (Identity Cards, Records Books, Passports): The following security precautions should be taken: 1. Keeping the passport in a safe place so it would not be ceized by the security apparatus, and the brother it belongs to would have to negotiate its return (I'll give you your passport if you give me information). 2. All documents of the undercover brother, such as identity cards and passport, should be falsified. 3. When the undercover brother is traveling with a certain identity card or passport, he should know all pertinent [information] such as the name, profession, and place of residence. 4. The brother who has special work status (commander, communication link, ...) should have more than one identity card and passport. He should learn the contents of each, the nature of the [indicated] profession, and the dialect of the residence area listed in the document. 5. The photograph of the brother in these documents should be without a beard. It is preferable that the brother's public photograph [on these documents] be also without a beard. If he already has one [document] showing a photograph with a beard, he should replace it. 6. When using an identity document in different names, no more than one such document should be carried at one time.

7. The validity of the falsified travel documents should always be confirmed. 8. All falsification matters should be carried out through the command and not haphazardly (procedure control) 9. Married brothers should not add their wives to their passports. 10. When a brother is carrying the forged passport of a certain country, he should not travel to that country. It is easy to detect forgery at the airport, and the dialect of the brother is different from that of the people from that country. Security Precautions Related to the Organizations' Given Names: 1. The name given by the Organization [to the brother] should not be odd in comparison with other names used around him. 2. A brother should not have more than one name in the area where he lives {the undercover work place).

FOURTH LESSON: ORGANIZATION MILITARY BASES "APARTMENTS-HIDING PLACES"

Definition of Bases: * These are apartments, hiding places, command centers, etc. in which secret operations are executed against the enemy. These bases may be in cities, and are [then] called homes or apartments. They may be in mountainous, harsh terrain far from the enemy, and are [then] called hiding places or bases. During the initial stages, the Military Organization usually uses apartments in cities as places for launching assigned missions, such as collecting information, observing members of the ruling regime, etc. Hiding places and bases in mountains and harsh terrain are used at later stages, from which Jihad [holy war] organizations are dispatched to execute assassination operations of enemy individuals, bomb their centers, and capture their weapons. In some Arab countries such as Egypt, where there are no mountains or harsh terrain, all stages of Jihad work would take place in cities. The opposite was true in Afghanistan, where initially Jihad work was in the cities, then the warriors shifted to mountains and harsh terrain. There, they started battling the Communists.

Security Precautions Related to Apartments: 1. Choosing the apartment carefully as far as the location, the size for the work necessary (meetings, storage, arms, fugitives, work preparation). 2. It is preferable to rent apartments on the ground floor to facilitate escape and digging of trenches. 3. Preparing secret locations in the apartment for securing documents, records, arms, and other important items. 4. Preparing ways of vacating the apartment in case of a surprise attack (stands, wooden ladders).

5. [sic] Under no circumstances should anyone know about the apartment except those who use it. 6. Providing the necessary cover for the people who frequent the apartment (students, workers, employees, etc.) 7. Avoiding seclusion and isolation from the population and refraining from going to the apartment at suspicious times. 8. It is preferable to rent these apartments using false names, appropriate cover, and non-Moslem appearance. 9. A single brother should not rent more than one apartment in the same area, from the same agent, or using the same rental office. 10. Care should be exercised not to rent apartments that are known to the security apparatus [such as] those used for immoral or prior Jihad activities. 11. Avoiding police stations and government buildings. Apartments should not be rented near those places. 12. When renting these apartments, one should avoid isolated or deserted locations so the

enemy would not be able to catch those living there easily. 13. It is preferable to rent apartments in newly developed areas where people do not know one another. Usually, in older quarters people know one another and strangers are easily identified, especially since these quarters have many informers. 14. Ensuring that there is has been no surveillance prior to the members entering the apartment. 15. Agreement among those living in the apartment on special ways of knocking on the door and special signs prior to entry into the building's main gate to indicate to those who wish to enter that the place is safe and not being monitored. Such signs include hanging out a towel, opening a curtain, placing a cushion in a special way, etc.

16. If there is a telephone in the apartment, calls should be answered in an agreed-upon manner among those who use the apartment. That would prevent mistakes that would, otherwise, lead to revealing the names and nature of the occupants. 17. For apartments, replacing the locks and keys with new ones. As for the other entities (camps, shops, mosques), appropriate security precautions should be taken depending on the entity's importance and role in the work. 18. Apartments used for undercover work should not be visible from higher apartments in order not to expose the nature of the work. 19. In a newer apartment, avoid talking loud because prefabricated ceilings and walls [used in the apartments] do not have the same thickness as those in old ones. 20. It is necessary to have at hand documents supporting the undercover [member]. In the case of a physician, there should be an actual medical diploma, membership in the [medical] union, the government permit, and the rest of the routine procedures known in that country. 21. The cover should blend well [with the environment]. For example, selecting a doctor's clinic in an area where there are clinics, or in a location suitable for it. 22. The cover of those who frequent the location should match the cover of that location. For example, a common laborer should not enter a fancy hotel because that would be suspicious and draw attention.

See the section of the manual in Chapter 12 dealing with Prisons and Detention Centers.

Appendix 2: Radicalization and Intelligence Gathering in Correctional Institutions

PART I: AWARENESS OF INMATES

Inmates who are doing the radicalization of other inmates are not doing it in a vacuum. They are continuously updated and are very familiar and aware of what is happening in the free world. They must interact with their terrorist organizations:

1. To conduct background checks on new recruits.
2. To get current information, they can use it to recruit new members.
3. To get information to their organizations about when the new recruits will be released.
4. To receive information from the free world telling the recruits were to report upon release.

Correctional personnel can be valuable in gathering intelligence and sharing that intelligence with other criminal justice and intelligence agencies by:

1. Discovering recruiting techniques
2. Sharing the identities of (suspected and confirmed) recruits
3. Sharing the identities of those inmates who were approached but didn't buy into the radicalization so that they can be questioned on what methods and techniques were used to recruit them
4. Identifying characteristics that the terrorist recruiters were looking for before approaching a person to be a new recruit

5. Informing criminal justice and intelligence agencies of release dates of those inmates doing the recruiting and those recruited
6. Sharing the names (and other information contained in the inmates' official visitors lists) of those inmates doing the recruiting and confirmed and suspected recruits.
7. Sharing a video of visitors who visit recruiters and recruits
8. Sharing audio recordings from visits and telephone conversations.

To be successful against these terrorist organizations, agencies must learn to work more closely together than ever before. These terrorist organizations are waging war with no guidelines or boundaries; therefore, we must use all the assets we have at our disposal.

PART II: COMMON THEMES

I started researching the materials about incarcerated terrorists and their impact on correctional facilities' operations shortly after 9/11. I conducted my first workshop about Terrorists and Corrections at an American Correctional Conference in California (August 2002). Several years later, prisons worldwide are now incarcerating more terrorists. We also now know that some of these incarcerated terrorists are recruiters for their various causes. They work to radicalize other inmates, most of whom are disenfranchised and who, in previous times, would have been recruited to join a gang.

A few common themes have manifested themselves over the years. Some of these themes dovetail with what much experienced correctional staff will recognize as gang-recruiting activities. The difference between radicalizing inmates for religious purposes and gang membership is that each has a different outcome.

Correctional line staff receiving specialized training in "intelligence gathering" can readily observe many of these common themes.

January 2015, killings of the French staff employees of *Charlie Hebdo Magazine* (Vinogard et al., 2015) and the murder of innocent people in a French Kosher market (Sieczkowski, 2017) by individuals purportedly radicalized while in jail ("How to Prevent Radicalization in Prisons," 2019) has caused governments and the criminal justice communities to closely look at what role(s) correctional facilities are playing in the furthering of radical Islam. For example, this information about French prisons and a California State Prison further reinforces the belief that terrorists use prisons and jails to recruit and radicalize new followers.

The vital questions are how prevalent and successful such radicalization is and will radicalized offenders continue to follow their free-world leaders, and to what extent? Are our correctional facilities becoming the "recruiting stations" for radicalized lone wolves?

By being more attentive to what is going on throughout their correctional facilities, correctional personnel, especially line staff, can help identify those doing the radicalizing and those undergoing radicalization.

Seasoned correctional personnel can develop a sixth sense of the feel of certain correctional environments. They know when something is not right or normal. Gathering intelligence is just refining those learned traits and reporting and documenting observations, conversations, associations, changes in offenders' actions and behaviors, and similar actions.

Most correctional facilities have well-established "strategic threat organizations/gang units," which should be the collection point for all intelligence regarding inmates' radicalization. My rationale for recommending these units is because they are already experienced in gathering, assessing, and disseminating information to internal and external departments.

As I mentioned earlier, there are many similarities in the early stages of joining a gang and being radicalized. Some examples of the similarities between gang recruitment and radicalization are as follows:

- The recruits begin to hang around with the group that they are aligning with at that time.
- The recruits either grow their hair/beard or cut their hair and have their beards, again depending on the group they align with at that time.
- They distance themselves from the correctional staff unless instructed to become more familiar with "certain" staff personnel. These are usually staff which the group believes can assist them in getting jobs, better living conditions, favors, and so forth.
- The recruits for gangs may start to use the vernacular, get tattoos, and wear certain clothing in certain ways of the group they align themselves with at that time.

SIMILARITY OF GANG RECRUITMENT AND RADICALIZATION

When an offender begins to associate with those offenders who have been identified as already radicalized and gang members, correctional personnel making this observation should leave reports stating:

1. The name(s) of the offender(s) observed and of the radicalized offenders
2. The time(s) that someone saw them together and when these offenders started meeting/hanging around together, or when correctional staff first observed their association
3. Identification of every location where they were seen together, such as eating together, walking together in the yard, changing seats in school areas to sit closer to each other.

Research demonstrates that offender-recruiters who radicalize other offenders use a series of methods and techniques. The recruiters look for vulnerable, "disenfranchised" offenders. Sturgeon believes that the recruiters seek those who are afraid, looking for protection, looking to belong to something, and vulnerable to kindness.

The steps or phases include the following:

1. Approach target person in an open setting (yard, dayroom, gym, school).
2. Engage in light conversation.
3. Discuss the benefits of the group/gang (protection, belonging to something bigger than self, believing in a higher spiritual being, becoming someone, to mention a few benefits. Of course, these examples will manifest themselves differently, depending on whether the recruits are joining a gang, a subversive group, or if they are undergoing radicalization as part of joining a terrorist group.
4. One of the recruits demonstrates an interest as the recruiter becomes increasingly more engaging. The conversation will focus more on religion and the recruit's relationship with God, the cause, the religion, and so forth. Note: many of the recruiters are "NOT" trained in the study of Islam, and in many cases, what they are preaching/teaching is their interpretation of the *Quran*.
5. In the case of the recruit undergoing radicalization, the recruiter will start to share literature with the recruit; again, the literature may not be based on official teachings contained in the *Quran*.
6. Once the recruiter believes that he/she has the recruit's confidence and trust, he/she will make a move to involve the recruit fully in the movement.
7. From the time that the recruit is fully engaged, the recruiter will continue to recruit further and further into the fold.

For the most part, alert line staff could see this recruiting process occurring. Line staff should be leaving reports detailing everything that they witness. Sturgeon's experience shows that it is easier to stop people's radicalization than de-radicalize them.

CONCLUSIONS

Sturgeon states that in his fifty years in the criminal justice community, he has seen several new challenges come into the field. Initially, some of these challenges caused the field to make some adjustments, some minor and some major. Terrorism is here with all of its manifestations: lone wolves, returning fighters from the Middle East, White supremacists, and other far right and left splinter organizations. Radicalization is occurring both inside prisons and on the streets of America and the world. Correctional personnel can play a major role in the process of limiting the reach of radicalism.

Law enforcement will have to adopt military-style tactics. Correctional facilities will have to adjust their intelligence-gathering techniques and their offender-management strategies for dealing with terrorists and those identified as recruiters.

Appendix 3: Religious Issues

1. The selection of agency chaplains and other community religious leaders representing all the religions of the inmates' population is extremely important because they set the religious standard for the inmates' religions. These chaplains and religious leaders will compose the *Committee for Religious Involvement.*
2. A committee of religious leaders, correctional management, security, legal personnel, and civilian religious leaders should research, review, and approve all entries for inclusion into *The Manual for Approved Religious Materials*. This manual should contain at least the following: approved religious articles, other approved reading, audio materials, symbols, and other items for every religion. Correctional personnel should receive training in the contents of this manual.
3. The *Manual for Approved Religious Materials* shall be reviewed and updated, if needed, at least every six months or as needed.
4. The facility should outline what security measures will be taken during any holiday prior to any observance of religious holidays. (Past incidents should be reviewed on a worldwide basis.)
5. Any religious articles, other reading, audio, symbols, and so forth found in any inmates' possession but not included in *The Manual for Approved Religious Materials* shall be considered contraband and seized with the possibility of disciplinary actions.
6. All correctional staff shall receive training in religious beliefs, customs, and practices pertinent to the facility's inmates.
7. Any changes in religious policies and procedures shall be approved by the agency's legal department.
8. At no time should correctional personnel make any disparaging remarks about any inmates' religious beliefs. There should be policies and procedures addressing staff making disparaging remarks accompanied by what types of disciplinary action can be taken against the staff member who violated his policy.

9. Outline what security measures the staff will use before any observance of religious holidays.
10. Officers who are assigned to religious service will leave a report that should contain:
    - The number of inmates at the service.
    - Any situations that occurred during the service. This should contain a narrative exactly describing what happened.
    - The person conducting the service and the names of any religious volunteers attending the service.
    - Attest that the officer(s) conduct a thorough search of the area, before and after, where the religious service took place. As information or reports are accumulated, officers assigned to religious services should review past reports.

Appendix 4: "Posse Comitatus"

APPENDIX 4

"Posse Comitatus" is a Latin term meaning "Power of the County". A county chapter of the posse is usually chartered with the county clerk.

Named in this charter are seven charter members. These members must be Christian, U. S. citizens, and Anglo-Saxon. They also must be male. This posse must follow the constitution of the posse. Some later formed chapters probably will not follow the guidelines of the "Posse" constitution. After filing the charter with the county clerk, they then notify the county sheriff. They advise the sheriff of their availability to him for service. The Posse feels that they should notify the Sheriff of any unlawful act. After notification of the Sheriff, they are free to take care of the situation in any manner they see fit. The posse feels that the Sheriff is the only true Jaw enforcement. This is because the office of Sheriff is an elected position. Also, the power of the posse can override the authority of the Sheriff.

The first known group of the posse comitatus was formed in Portland, Oregon in 1972. The group was known as the "Portland Identity Group." Since 1972, Posse and various "splinter" groups have been formed across the country. In the earlier Posse organizations, many of the members were well–meaning people. After discovering that the Posse advocated violence, killing and destruction of property, the well–meaning people left the Posse. Most members of the Posse now are just using the cover of the posse to raise hell, or are very militant in their feelings.

Members of the posse now are extreme believers in para-military training, survivalist methods, and the Constitution of the United States. The Posse Comitatus members totally distort the meaning of the U. S. Constitution. The posse also does not believe in the Federal Reserve System. They still base their monetary value on the Gold and Silver standard. They believe that the Federal Reserve notes are valueless.

In some areas, the posse members have attempted to use "Public Office money Certificates." These certificates are totally worthless. They use these to buy tags and pay taxes. Some members do not buy tags, they use "Kansas Constitution gs". These tags are white over blue in color (Figure 1). It is advisable to confiscate the tags if one is located.

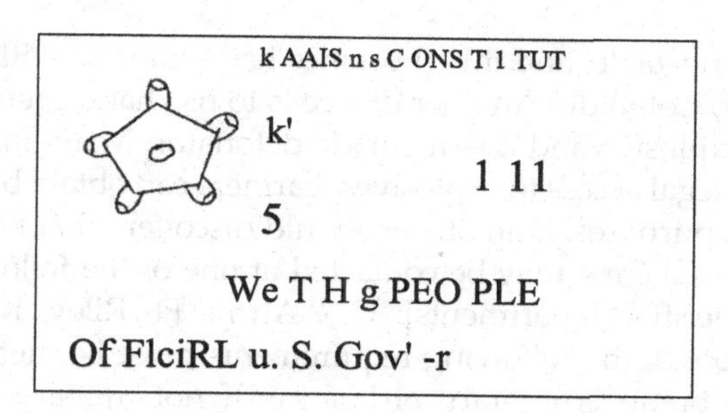

Figure A4.1 White lettering, blue background.

Posse members also use "CONSTITUTIONAL DRIVERS LICENSES." These are printed cards that have no identification value. The cards state on them that the possessor can drive under his rights of the constitution. Possession of these drivers' licenses is also illegal.

Posse Comitatus is considered to be an extreme right wing militant organization. They advocate the killing of Jews, Negroes, IRS agents, and other state and federal officials. Many posse members stockpile guns and ammunition, explosives (both homemade and factory made), food, and military equipment (helmets, clothing, belts, etc., and reloading equipment).

The Posse Comitatus has been associated with many other militant organizations. Some of these are the American Nazi Party, the United Klansmen (branch of the KKK), the Christian Defense League, Farmers Liberation Army, the American Agriculture Movement and many others.

The Posse Comitatus was very active within the State of Kansas at this time. There is much activity occurring in the northeast part of the state; however, many incidents have occurred statewide. In the northwest part of the state, near Colby, many members have been receiving papa—military training. Only a few of the extremely militant members are reported to own fully automatic weapons. As outlined in the posse constitution, they prefer to have legally owned and legally obtained weapons. Also their constitution even specifies what type of weapons to have. They specify that each member should possess a .45 auto sidearm, and a rifle of some type in 30.06 cal. The top of the list for the rifle is the Ml—I Garand. In areas of Colorado, many homemade bombs have been recovered. These bombs are made of PVC plastic pipe. PVC pipe ends have explosive contents. Some homemade explosives are in plastic form. The contents of the plastic explosives are black powder, petroleum jelly and wax. These ingredients are mixed together. This combination is unstable, and this substance has exploded with detonation at a lab in Denver, Colorado. Another device is to use hand grenade hulls with a homemade explosive and a homemade detonator. Many farmers who are members have legal access to explosives. Farmers can obtain blasting permits for agricultural purposes. If an officer should discover what he believes to be a bomb, a disposal crew may be contacted at one of the following agencies: [list of local sheriff's departments]. U.S. Army, Ft. Riley, Kansas. For the military to respond, the following requirements must be met: Ft. Riley Will respond if the bomb is military ordinance. If not military ordinance, the bomb MUST represent an eminent danger to human life, and you must have exhausted all other means of obtaining a bomb squad. Other means of handling this bomb will be normal procedure. If you discover a bomb, also notify the Alcohol, Tobacco and Firearms (ATF) agent in your area. The ATF agent can help you identify the type of explosives and blasting equipment used. The posse will not hesitate to resort to violence. Members feel that they are in the right. One advantage to keeping on top of the situation is to develop an informant who is a member of the posse. Most posse groups are very loosely organized. It is reported to be very easy to develop an informant. Most posse members will talk freely about their group's activities. This is due to the fact that they like to brag and promote the posse. Posse groups have a very effective "counter-intelligence." They are very devoted to their cause. They may go to extreme measures to gain information. They push very hard for police officers to join their group. They try to use these officers to gain information about the activities of the police department or other agency.

The KB I and other agencies advise to listen for rumors about upcoming sales and auctions in the area. A recent incident of violence in Springfield, Colorado is a good example of this. Sheriff Goff had prior information about a demonstration occurring in the area of a sale. This gave him time to prepare for the posse. It may also be advisable to keep a file on known members and suspected members.

It is reportedly very easy to infiltrate the ranks of the posse. Many agencies are using an undercover officer within the posse. To get into the posse, some agencies say, all you have to do is ask.

The Kansas Highway Patrol has made themselves available to assist in any needed situation where manpower is needed. If assistance is needed, either contact a Trooper or the Captain of the Division. A trooper can advise you of the proper steps to take. If the assistance of the National Guard is needed, a request in writing must be made by the Chief to the Governor of the state.

Bibliography

"Six Palestinian prisoners escape Israeli jail through tunnel." *BBC News*. September 6, 2021. https://www.bbc.com/news/world-middle-east-58460702

"13 dangerous prison gangs correctional officers should know about." Corrections1, May 12, 2015. https://www.correctionsone.com/corrections/articles/13-dangerous-prison-gangs-correctional-officers-should-know-about-RdHAOeXAsCLY4RLl/

"2015 Paris terror attacks fast facts." *CNN.com Editorial Research*, November 13, 2019. https://www.cnn.com/2015/12/08/europe/2015-paris-terror-attacks-fast-facts/index.html

Abrams, Joseph. "Homegrown terror suspects turned toward radicalism in US prisons." *Fox News*. May 22, 2009. http://www.truthandgrace.com/muslimloveforcriminals.htm

al-Qaeda Manual, Part 21. United States Border Patrol. (n.d.). http://www.usborderpatrol.com/Border_Patrol1803_21.htm

"al-Qa'ida supporters target women with female-focused propaganda." Intelligence Note, New Jersey Office of Homeland Security and Preparedness, September 4, 2018. https://static1.squarespace.com/static/54d79f88e4b0db3478a04405/t/5b8ea9f90e2e721ef38a24af/1536076282888/Al-Qa%E2%80%99ida+Supporters+Target+Women+With+Female-Focused+Propaganda.pdf

Alexander, Audrey. "Cruel intentions, female Jihadists in America." Program on Extremism, George Washington University, November 2016. https://extremism.gwu.edu/sites/g/files/zaxdzs2191/f/downloads/Female%20Jihadists%20in%20America.pdf.

American Correctional Association. *Performance-Based Standards for Adult Correctional Institutions*, 5th ed. Alexandria, VA: American Correctional Association, 2020.

American Correctional Association. Standards for Adult Correctional Institutions. (n.d.). http://www.correctionalchaplains.org/aca_prison_standards.pdf.

Andrews, Donald A., James Bonta, & J. Stephen Wormith. "The recent past and near future of risk and/or need assessment." *Crime & Delinquency* 52 (2006): 7–27. doi:10.1177/0011128705281756

Anti-Defamation League, "White supremacy" (n.d.). https://www.adl.org/resources/glossary-terms/white-supremacy

Atherton, Eugene, & Andjela Jurisic. "5 principles of managing terrorists in prison." *Corrections1*, August 7, 2015. Retrieved July 29, 2017. https://www.correctionsone.com/column/articles/8694916-5-principles-of-managing-terrorists-in-prison/

Atherton, Eugene, & Richard L. Phillips. *Guidelines for the Development of a Security Program*, 3rd ed. Alexandria, Virginia: American Correctional Association, 2007.
"Audit of the Federal Bureau of Prisons' monitoring of inmate communications to prevent radicalization." U.S. Department of Justice, Office of the Inspector General, March 25, 2020. https://www.oversight.gov/report/doj/audit-federal-bureau-prisons%E2%80%99-monitoring-inmate-communications-prevent-radicalization
Baggio, Stephanie, Nicolas Peigné, Patrick Heller, Laurent Gétaz, Michael Liebrenz, & Hans Wolff. "Do overcrowding and turnover cause violence in prison." *Frontiers of Psychiatry*, January 24, 2020. doi:10.3389/fpsyt.2019.01015
Ballas, Dennis A. "Prisoner radicalization." *Law Enforcement Bulletin*, October 1, 2010. Retrieved June 9, 2017. https://leb.fbi.gov/2010/october/prisoner-radicalization.
Barr, Luke. "Over 5,000 corrections officers have contracted COVID-19." *ABC News* Online, May 5, 2020. https://abcnews.go.com/US/5000-corrections-officers-contracted-covid-19/story?id=70520117
Basra, Rajan, Peter R. Neumann, & Claudia Brunner. "Criminal pasts, terrorist futures: European jihadists and the new crime-terror nexus." *International Centre for the Study of Radicalisation and Political Violence*, 2016. https://icsr.info/wp-content/uploads/2016/10/ICSR-Report-Criminal-Pasts-Terrorist-Futures-European-Jihadists-and-the-New-Crime-Terror-Nexus.pdf
Beardsley, Eleanor. "Inside French prisons, a struggle to combat radicalization." *National Public Radio*, June 25, 2017. https://www.npr.org/sections/parallels/2017/06/25/534122917/inside-french-prisons-a-struggle-to-combat-radicalization
Beckford, Martin. "Revealed: First UK jail where half the inmates are Muslim, and others are pressured to convert to Islamic 'protection racket.'" *Daily Mail*, October 18, 2015. https://www.dailymail.co.uk/news/article-3277502/First-UK-jail-half-inmates-Muslim--convert-Islamic-protection-racket.html
Belz, Bradford. "Disrupt and destroy MS-13: DOJ announces first-ever terrorism charges in nationwide gang crackdown." *Fox News* Online, July 15, 2020. https://www.foxnews.com/us/ms13-doj-first-terrorism-charges-gang-crackdown
Bennett, Clifford. "Radicalization in custody: Towards a data-driven terrorism prevention in the United States Federal Correctional System." Program on Extremism Policy Paper, George Washington University, November 2018. https://extremism.gwu.edu/sites/g/files/zaxdzs2191/f/Prisons%20Policy%20Paper.pdf?mod=article_inline
Benovadia, Don. "Phones, weapons found in surprise inspection of terrorists' cells." *Hamodia*, January 21, 2019. https://hamodia.com/2019/01/21/phones-weapons-found-surprise-inspection-terrorists-cells/
Bhui, Kamaldeep S., Madelyn H. Hicks, Myrna Lashley, & Edgar Jones. "A public health approach to understanding and preventing violent radicalization." *BMC Medicine* 10 (2012): 1–8. https://pubmed.ncbi.nlm.nih.gov/22332998/
Bielby, Kylie. "Europol's annual terrorism trends report reveals growing interest in explosives and firearms." *Homeland Security Today*, June 27, 2020.

https://www.hstoday.us/subject-matter-areas/border-security/europols-annual-terrorism-trends-report-reveals-growing-interest-in-explosives-and-firearms/

Binelli, Mark. "Inside America's toughest federal prison." *New York Times*, March 26, 2015. Retrieved August 8, 2017. https://www.nytimes.com/2015/03/29/magazine/inside-americas-toughest-federal-prison.html

Birnbaum, Michael. "French prisons, long hotbeds of radical Islam, get new scrutiny after Paris attacks." *Washington Post*, January 28, 2015. https://www.washingtonpost.com/world/europe/paris-killers-radicalized-in-prison-now-leaders-want-to-fix-that-problem/2015/01/28/52271e28-a307-11e4-91fc-7dff95a14458_story.html

Bjelopera, Jerome. "Committee on Homeland Security Subcommittee on Counterterrorism and Intelligence U.S. House of Representative," *Terror Inmates: Countering Violent Extremism in Prison and Beyond*, October 28, 2015. https://docs.house.gov/meetings/HM/HM05/20151028/104102/HHRG-114-HM05-Wstate-BjeloperaJ-20151028.pdf

Bloom, Mia, & John Horgan. "The rise of the child terrorist: The young faces at the frontlines." *Foreign Affairs*, February 9, 2015. https://www.foreignaffairs.com/articles/middle-east/2015-02-09/rise-child-terrorist

Borum, Randy. "Psychological vulnerabilities and propensities for involvement in violent extremism." *Behavioral Sciences and the Law* 32 (2014): 286–305. doi:10.1002/bsl.2110

Brandon, James. "The danger of prison radicalization in the West." *Combating Terrorism Center*, Vol. 2 (12), December 2009. https://ctc.usma.edu/the-danger-of-prison-radicalization-in-the-west/

Bronson, Jennifer, & Marcus Berzofsky. "Indicators of mental health problems reported by prisoners and jail inmates, 2011-12." Bureau of Justice Statistics (NCJ 250612), 2017a. https://www.bjs.gov/content/pub/pdf/imhprpji1112.pdf

Bronson, Jennifer, Jessica Stroop, Stephanie Zimmer, & Marcus Berzofsky. "Drug Use, Dependence, and Abuse Among State Prisoners and Jail Inmates, 2007-2009."(NCJ 250546). Bureau of Justice Statistics, 2017b. https://www.bjs.gov/content/pub/pdf/dudaspji0709.pdf

Bryans, Shane. *Handbook on the Management of Violent Extremist Prisoners and the Prevention of Radicalization to Violence in Prisons*. United Nations Office on Drugs and Crime, 2016. https://www.unodc.org/pdf/criminal_justice/Handbook_on_VEPs.pdf

Bryans, Shane, & Tomris Atabay. *Handbook on the Management of High-Risk Prisoners*. Vienna: United Nations Office on Drugs and Crime, 2016. https://www.unodc.org/documents/justice-and-prison-reform/HB_on_High_Risk_Prisoners_Ebook_appr.pdf?source=post_page

Bryant, Lisa. "France looks at its prisons as ground zero in terror battle." *VOA News* Online, September 13, 2016. https://www.voanews.com/a/france-prisons-deradicalization-terrorism/3505805.html

Bucci, Steven, James Carafano, & Jessica Zuckerman. "60 terrorist plots since 9/11: Continued lessons in domestic counterterrorism." *The Heritage*

Foundation, July 22, 2013. https://www.heritage.org/terrorism/report/60-terrorist-plots-911-continued-lessons-domestic-counterterrorism

Bucktin, Christopher. "Shoe-bomber Richard Reid: 'My plot to attack plane failed because God decided it wasn't my time to die.'" *Daily Mirror* Online, February 3, 2015. https://www.mirror.co.uk/news/world-news/shoe-bomber-richard-reid-my-plot-5098027

Bukay, David. "Defensive or offensive jihad: History exegesis vs. contemporary propagation. Part I—The religious aspect." *Jerusalem Post*, February 13, 2004. https://www.jpost.com/Opinion/Op-Ed-Contributors/Defensive-or-Offensive-Jihad-History-Exegesis-vs-Contemporary-Propagation-341308

Bukay, David. "The religious foundations of suicide bombings: Islamic terrorism and Islamist ideology." *The Progressive Conservative USA*, Vol viii, 172, September 6, 2006a. https://www.proconservative.net/PCVol8Is172BukaySuicideBombings.shtml

Bukay, David. "The religious foundation of suicide bombings." *Middle East Quarterly* 13, 4 (2006b): 27–36. https://www.meforum.org/1003/the-religious-foundations-of-suicide-bombings.

Bukay, David. "Essay: It is written." Australian/Israel Jewish Affairs Council. *Australia/Israel Review*. October 2, 2006c. https://aijac.org.au/australia-israel-review/essay-it-is-written/

Burrows-Taylor, Evie. "Why the upcoming release of 40 racialized inmates presents 'a major risk' to France." *The Local fr*, May 29, 2018. https://www.thelocal.fr/20180529/french-prisons-release-of-radicalised-inmates-is-major-risk-paris-prosecutor-warns

Byman, Daniel L., & Jeremy Shapiro, "Homeward bound: Don't hype the threat of returning jihadists." *Brookings*. September 30, 2014. https://www.brookings.edu/articles/homeward-bounddont-hype-the-threat-of-returning-jihadists/

Caron, Christina. "2 deputies in Kansas are fatally shot while transporting inmates." *New York Times*, June 16, 2018. https://www.nytimes.com/2018/06/16/us/sheriff-deputies-kansas-shooting.html

Carson, E. A. "Prisoners in 2015." Bureau of Justice Statistics (NCJ 250229), 2016. https://www.bjs.gov/content/pub/pdf/p15.pdf

Central Intelligence Agency. "Terrorist organizations—Home based." *The World Factbook*, September 22, 2020. https://www.cia.gov/library/publications/the-world-factbook/fields/397.html

Centre for the Prevention of Radicalism Leading to Violence. "Radicalization" (n.d.). https://info-radical.org/en/definition-2/

"Chérif Kouachi." Counter Extremism Project (n.d.). https://www.counterextremism.com/extremists/ch%C3%A9rif-kouachi

Chitty, Alex. "Al Qaeda prison breaks could lead to a new wave of terror attacks." *Vice*, August 6, 2013. https://www.vice.com/en_us/article/yv5ayj/will-al-qaeda-prison-breaks-lead-to-a-new-wave-of-terror-attacks

Clifford, Bennett. "Radicalization in custody: Towards data driven terrorism prevention in the United States Federal Correctional System." Program on Extremism,

George Washington University, November 2018. https://extremism.gwu.edu/sites/g/files/zaxdzs2191/f/Prisons%20Policy%20Paper.pdf

Clutterback, Linda. "Deradicalization programs and counterterrorism: A perspective on the challenges and benefits." *Middle East Institute*, June 10, 2015. https://www.mei.edu/publications/deradicalization-programs-and-counterterrorism-perspective-challenges-and-benefits

Coronavirus Staff. "A state-by-state look at Coronavirus in prisons." The Marshall Project, July 16, 2020. https://www.themarshallproject.org/2020/05/01/a-state-by-state-look-at-coronavirus-in-prisons#staff-cases

Corrections1 Staff. "13 dangerous prison gangs correctional officers should know about." *Corrections1.com*, May 12, 2015. https://www.corrections1.com/corrections/articles/13-dangerous-prison-gangs-correctional-officers-should-know-about-RdHAOeXAsCLY4RLI/

Cosker, Glynn. "New 'terror threat snapshot' reports terror events increased in 2015." September 14, 2015. https://inhomelandsecurity.com/new-terror-threat-snapshot-reports-terror-events-increased-in-2015/

"Countering violent extremism in prisons." The Commonwealth (n.d.). http://thecommonwealth.org/sites/default/files/inline/ComSec%20CVE%20in%20Prisons%20Presentation.pdf

Cronin, Cat. "The necessity of prison programs to deradicalize terrorists." *American Security Project*, May 30, 2019. https://www.americansecurityproject.org/the-necessity-of-prison-programs-to-deradicalize-terrorists/

"Cruel and unusual punishment: Ruiz." The Texas Politics Project (n.d.). https://texaspolitics.utexas.edu/archive/html/just/features/0505_01/ruiz.html

"CTD report highlights 'alarming' security at Karachi Central Jail." *Geo News*, September 26, 2017. https://www.geo.tv/latest/159970-ctd-report-spotlights-alarming-security-at-karachi-central-jail

Cybersecurity and Infrastructure Security Agency. *Security of Soft Targets and Crowded Places Resource Guide*. Department of Homeland Security, 2019. https://www.cisa.gov/publication/securing-soft-targets-and-crowded-places-resources

"Danish inmates abused and forced to participate in Islamic prayers." *European Union Times*, May 7, 2020. https://www.eutimes.net/2020/03/danish-inmates-abused-and-forced-to-participate-in-islamic-prayers/

Darden, Jessica Trisko. *Tackling Terrorists' Exploitation of Youth*. American Enterprise Institute, May 2019. https://www.un.org/sexualviolenceinconflict/wp-content/uploads/2019/05/report/tackling-terrorists-exploitation-of-youth/Tackling-Terrorists-Exploitation-of-Youth.pdf

Darden, Michael. *Isis Returnees: Can Ex-Fighters Be Rehabilitated?*, U.S. Institute of Peace. February 25, 2019. https://www.usip.org/publications/2019/02/isis-returnees-can-ex-fighters-be-rehabilitated

Davies, Caroline. "UK Judge orders right wing extremist to read classic literature or face prison." *The Guardian*. September 1, 2021. https://www.theguardian.com/politics/2021/sep/01/judge-orders-rightwing-extremist-to-read-classic-literature-or-face-prison

Davies, Gareth. "ISIS terrorists fleeing to their home countries WANT to be sent to prison so they can convert them into 'jihadi universities,' report warns." *Daily Mail* Online, July 19, 2017. https://www.dailymail.co.uk/news/article-4711114/Fleeing-ISIS-terrorists-WANT-sent-prison.html

Davis, Lois M., Robert Bozick, Jennifer L. Steele, Jessica Saunders, & Jeremy N. V. Miles. *Evaluating the Effectiveness of Correctional Education: A Meta-Analysis of Programs That Provide Education to Incarcerated Adults.* 2016. https://www.bja.gov/publications/rand_correctional-education-meta-analysis.pdf

Dean, Christopher, Merel Molenkamp, & Elaine Pressman. *Council of Europe Handbook for Prison and Probation Services Regarding Radicalisation and Violent Extremism*, 2016. https://www.researchgate.net/publication/322100931_Council_of_Europe_Handbook_for_Prison_and_Probation_Services_Regarding_Radicalisation_and_Violent_Extremism

Dearden, Lizzie. "Terrorists to take lie detector tests as part of major overhaul after London Bridge Attack." *Independent*, January 21, 2020. https://www.independent.co.uk/news/uk/crime/terrorists-lie-detector-tests-attacks-london-bridge-probation-prisons-sentences-law-a9293481.html.

De Armond, Paul. "Right-wing terrorism and weapons of mass destruction, motives, strategies, and movements." Office of Justice Programs, U.S. Department of Justice (NCJRS 194399), 1999. https://www.ojp.gov/ncjrs/virtual-library/abstracts/right-wing-terrorism-and-weapons-mass-destruction-motives

Detro, Chris. "Finton pleads guilty to Federal Courthouse bomb plot." *Press Mentor*, May 9, 2011. https://www.pressmentor.com/article/20110509/NEWS/305099833

"Drone drops drugs in Ohio prison yard, sparking inmate fight." *CBS News* Online, August 4, 2015. https://www.cbsnews.com/news/drone-drops-drugs-in-ohio-prison-yard-sparking-inmate-fight/

Dugas, M., & A. W. Kruglanski. "The quest for significance model of radicalization: Implications for the management of terrorist detainees." *Behavioral Sciences and the Law* 32 (2014): 423–439. doi:10.1002/bsl.2122

Dunleavy, Patrick T. *The Fertile Soil of Jihad: Terrorism's Prison Connection.* Washington, D.C.: Potomac Books, 2011.

Durkin, Erin. "New stats show surge in violence at Rikers Island." *Politico New York*, September 17, 2019. https://www.politico.com/states/new-york/albany/story/2019/09/17/new-stats-show-surge-in-violence-at-rikers-island-1193798

Elliott, Michael. "The shoe bomber's world." 2002. Retrieved July 28, 2017. http://content.time.com/time/world/article/0,8599,203478,00.html

Evans, Martin. "It's easy to recruit extremists in prison, notorious convert claims." *The Telegraph*, May 12, 2014. http://www.telegraph.co.uk/news/uknews/terrorism-in-the-uk/10823517/Its-easy-to-recruit-extremists-in-prison-notorious-convert-claims.html

Extremist Files. Southern Poverty Law Center. https://www.splcenter.org/fighting-hate/extremist-files

Fadel, Leila. "Muslims over-represented in state prisons, report finds." *NPR* Online, July 25, 2019. https://www.npr.org/2019/07/25/745226402/muslims-over-represented-in-state-prisons-report-finds

Fagenson, Zachary. "U.S. judge re-sentences Jose Padilla to 21 years on terrorism charges." July 28, 2017. http://www.reuters.com/article/us-usa-florida-padilla-idUSKBN0H41TW20140909

Faiola, Anthony, Naveena Kottoor, & Stefano Pitrelli. "Suspect in Berlin market attack was radicalized in an Italian jail." *Washington Post*, December 22, 2016. https://www.washingtonpost.com/world/europe-searches-for-suspect-berlin-christmas-market-attack/2016/12/22/78502d7e-c7e0-11e6-acda-59924caa2450_story.html

Fairfield, Hannah, & Tim Wallace. "The terrorists in U.S. prisons." *New York Times*, April 7, 2016. https://www.nytimes.com/interactive/2016/04/07/us/terrorists-in-us-prisons.html

Farley, Robert. "The facts on White nationalism." *FactCheck.org*, March 20, 2019. https://www.factcheck.org/2019/03/the-facts-on-white-nationalism/

Farrell, Helen M. "Terrorism and mental health." *Psychology Today*, May 3, 2013. https://www.psychologytoday.com/us/blog/frontpage-forensics/201305/terrorism-and-mental-health

Fausset, Richard, Alan Blinder, & Michael S. Schmidt. "Gunman kills 4 marines at military site in Chattanooga." *New York Times*, July 16, 2015. https://www.nytimes.com/2015/07/17/us/chattanooga-tennessee-shooting.html

"Fears of extremists being recruited into German jails." *Deutsche Welle*, February 3, 2015. https://www.dw.com/en/fears-of-extremists-being-recruited-in-german-jails/a-18289581

Federal Bureau of Investigation. "What are known extremist organizations." (n.d.). https://www.fbi.gov/cve508/teen-website/what-are-known-violent-extremist-organizations#:~:text=%20International%20Violent%20Extremist%20Organizations%20%201%20Al,God%2C%E2%80%9D%20is%20an%20extremist%20group%20based...%20More%20

Federal Bureau of Prisons. *Communications Management Units*, 2015. Retrieved August 9, 2017. https://www.bop.gov/policy/progstat/5214_002.pdf

Federal Bureau of Prisons. *Custody and Care Designations*. (n.d.). Retrieved August 8, 2017. https://www.bop.gov/inmates/custody_and_care/designations.jsp.

Federal Bureau of Prisons. *Inmate Security and Classification Manual*.

Federal Bureau of Prisons. *Visiting Procedures*, 2014. https://www.bop.gov/locations/institutions/flm/FLM_visit_hours.pdf

Fielitz, Mark. "A new wave of right-wing terrorism." *Insights*. June 30, 2020. Centre for Analysis of the Radical Right. A New Wave of Right-Wing Terrorism – Centre for Analysis of the Radical Right (radicalrightanalysis.com).

Foges, Clare. "Prisons must not tiptoe around extremism." *The Times*, January 13, 2020. https://www.thetimes.co.uk/article/prisons-must-not-tiptoe-around-extremism-f6lrs2vml

"France Isla protest after jail prison attack." *BBC News* Online, March 6, 2019. https://www.bbc.com/news/world-europe-47467821

Fuchs, Michael H. "The American right wing is enabling a dual crises: Gun violence and white supremacy. *The Guardian*, August 7, 2019. https://www.theguardian.com/commentisfree/2019/aug/07/gun-violence-white-supremacy-right-wing

Gaubatz, Dave. "The strategy and objectives of Al-Qaeda." *American Thinker*, February 9, 2007. https://www.americanthinker.com/articles/2007/02/the_strategy_and_objectives_of.html

Gehrke, Joel. "Al Qaeda 'as strong as it has ever been' and ISIS spreading, top US counterterrorism official warns." *Washington Examiner*, August 1, 2019. https://www.washingtonexaminer.com/policy/defense-national-security/al-qaeda-as-strong-as-it-has-ever-been-and-isis-spreading-top-us-counterterrorism-official-warns

George, Susannah, Aziz Tassal, & Sharif Hassan. Coronavirus sweeps through Afghanistan's security forces. June 25, 2020. Washington Post. https://www.washingtonpost.com › world › 2020/06/24

George, Susannah, Aziz Tassal, & Sharif Hassan. "Islamic state attack on Afghan prison ends on second day with at least 29 dead." *Washington Post*, August 3, 2020. https://www.washingtonpost.com/world/islamic-state-attack-on-an-afghan-prison-stretches-into-its-second-day-with-21-dead/2020/08/03/69e7146e-d556-11ea-a788-2ce86ce81129_story.html

Gerretsen, Isabelle. "Terrorists searched naked and kept in cells 22 hours a day in 'inhuman' Dutch prisons, amnesty warns." *International Business Times*, October 31, 2017. http://www.ibtimes.co.uk/amnesty-slams-inhuman-conditions-dutch-terrorist-prisons-1645291

Gettys, Travis. "Leaked police documents show violent plots continued following January 6 insurrection." *Salon*, May 24, 2021.

Gonderme, Yorum, Sonraki Kayt, Anya Safya, Onecki Kayet, & Kayt Yorunia. "Hero or terrorist; ethno-nationalist terrorism." *MegaLinks in Criminal Justice*, September 13, 2008. http://www.apsu.edu/oconnort/rest

Grassley, Sen. Charles. Federal prisons enlisted terrorist-linked group to review and endorse Islamic chaplains, 2016. https://www.grassley.senate.gov/news/news-releases/federal-prisons-enlisted-terrorist-linked-group-review-and-endorse-islamic

Gregory, Andy, & Borzou Daragahi. "Syria: Already 800 Isis-affiliated women and children escape from camp." *Independent*, October 13, 2009. https://www.independent.co.uk/news/world/middle-east/isis-syria-kurds-turkey-escape-camp-sd-ain-issa-a9153816.html

Greninger, Howard. "Professor: American prisons creating terrorists." *Tribune-Star*, September 6, 2017. https://www.tribstar.com/news/local_news/professor-american-prisons-creating-terrorists/article_94884174-4c9b-59d1-829e-07de176c377f.html

Grierson, Janice. "Lie-detector tests planned for convicted terrorists freed on license." *The Guardian*, January 20, 2020. https://www.theguardian.com/politics/2020/jan/21/lie-detector-tests-planned-for-convicted-terrorists-freed-on-licence

"Guantanamo bay naval station fast facts." Retrieved July 29, 2017. http://www.cnn.com/2013/09/09/world/guantanamo-bay-naval-station-fast-facts/index.html

"Guantanamo by the numbers." https://www.humanrightsfirst.org/sites/default/files/gtmo-by-the-numbers.pdf

Gunaratna, Rohan. "Terrorist rehabilitation: An introduction to concepts and practices." *Pakistan Journal of Criminology* 3 (2012): 143–157.

Gutierrez, Jose A., Javier Jordan, & Humberto Trujillo. "Prevention of jihadist radicalization in Spanish prisons. Current situation, challenges and dysfunctions of the penitentiary system." *Athena Intelligence Journal* 3, 1–9 (2008). https://www.researchgate.net/publication/268183992_Prevention_of_Jihadist_Radicalization_in_Spanish_Prisons_Current_Situation_Challenges_and_Dysfunctions_of_the_Penitentiary_System

Hamm, Mark S. "Terrorist recruitment in American correctional institutions: An exploratory study of non-criminal faith organizations final report." Washington, D.C.: U.S. Government Printing Office, Document No. 220957, December 2007. https://www.ojp.gov/pdffiles1/nij/grants/220957.pdf

Hamm, Mark S. "Prisoner radicalization: Assessing the threat in U.S. correctional institutions." *NIJ Journal*, 261 (2008). https://nij.ojp.gov/topics/articles/prisoner-radicalization-assessing-threat-us-correctional-institutions

Hamm, Mark S. "Prison Islam in the age of sacred terror." *The British Journal of Criminology* 49, 5 (2009): 667–685. https://academic.oup.com/bjc/article-abstract/49/5/667/499567?redirectedFrom=fulltext.ncjrs.gov/pdffiles1/nij/grants/220957.pdf

Haney, Craig. "The psychological impact of incarceration: Implications for post-prison adjustment." December 1, 2001. U.S. Department of Health and Human Services https://aspe.hhs.gov/basic-report/psychological-impact-incarceration-implications-post-prison-a

Haverluck, Michael F. "UK record 400-terror arrest in 17 up 54%." *NE News Now*, December 8, 2017. https://onenewsnow.com/national-security/2017/12/08/uk-record-400-terror-arrests-in-17-up-54

Hill, Gary. "Rehabilitating terrorists." *Journal of Eastern-European Criminal Law* 1 (2016): 154–158.

Hogan, Bernadette. "Assaults on NYC correction officers surges over past year." *New York Post*, September 17, 2020. https://nypost-com.cdn.ampproject.org/c/s/nypost.com/2020/09/17/assaults-on-nyc-correction-officers-surges-over-

Hoke, Scott, & Randy Demory. "Inmate behavior management: Guide to meeting basic needs." *U.S. Department of Justice, National Institute of Corrections*, 2014. https://info.nicic.gov/nicrp/system/files/027704.pdf

"How two prisoners escaped from a maximum-security prison." *New York Times*. June 8, 2015. https://www.nytimes.com/interactive/2015/06/08/nyregion/prison-escape.html

Hsieh, Steven. "Colorado's Federal Supermax Prison is force-feeding inmates on hunger strike." *The Nation*, February 27, 2014. https://www.thenation.com/article/colorados-federal-supermax-prison-force-feeding-inmates-hunger-strike/

Huda. "Halal and haram: The Islamic dietary laws." *Learn Religions*, February 11, 2020. https://learnreligions.com/islamic-dietary-law-2004234

Hughes, Tammy, & Hugo Gye. "UK prison imams are free to spread hatred: Preachers found to be distributing extremist literature including homophobic and misogynistic leaflets." *The Daily Mail*, April 18, 2016. http://www.dailymail.co.uk/news/article-3546919/Prison-imams-free-spread-hatred-jails-Preachers-distributing-extremist-literature-including-homophobic-misogynistic-leaflets.html

ICF Consulting, 2019. "How to prevent radicalization in prisons." *ICF Consulting*, March 4, 2019. https://www.icf.com/insights/public-policy/preventing-radicalization-in-prisons

Information Institute. "42 U.S. code section 1983, civil action for deprivation of rights." Legal Information Institute, Cornell Law School (n.d.). https://www.law.cornell.edu/uscode/text/42/1983

International Institute for Justice and Rule of the Law. "Prison Management Recommendation to Counter and address Prison Radicalization." (n.d.). https://theiij.org/wp-content/uploads/Prison-Recommendations-FINAL-1.pdf

"Involvement of minors in terrorist attacks likely to endure." National Counterterrorism Center, November 2018. https://www.dni.gov/files/NCTC/documents/jcat/firstresponderstoolbox/62us—Involvement-of-Minors-in-Terrorist-Plots-and-Attacks-Likely-To-Endure-survey.pdf

"Islamist recruitment in German prisons: How to identify radicalization." *Sputnik News*, December 9, 2017. https://sputniknews.com/europe/201709121057314437-islamist-recruitment-german-prisons/

Ives, Mike, & Isabella Kwai. "1,300 prisoners escape from Congo jail after an attack caused by ISIS." *New York Times*, October 20, 2020. https://www.nytimes.com/2020/10/20/world/africa/congo-jail-attack-prisoners-freed.html

Jager, Avraham. "The 'shoe bomber' Richard Reid - His radicalization explained." *International Institute for Counter Terrorism*, February 2018. https://www.ict.org.il/images/Richard%20Reid%20-20His%20Radicalization%20Explained.pdf

Johnson, Daryl. "Holy hate: The far rights' radicalization of religion." Southern Poverty Law Center, February 10, 2018. https://www.splcenter.org/fighting-hate/intelligence-report/2018/holy-hate-far-right's-radicalization-religion

Johnson, Dirk. "Suspect in Illinois bomb plot 'didn't like America very much.'" *New York Times*, September 27, 2009. http://www.nytimes.com/2009/09/28/us/28springfield.html

Johnson, Kevin. "FBI director says Islamic state influence growing in U.S." *USA Today*, May 7, 2015. https://www.usatoday.com/story/news/nation/2015/05/07/isis-attacks-us/70945534/

Jones, Clarke R., & Resurrecion R. Morales. "Integration versus segregation: A preliminary examination of Philippine correctional facilities for de-radicalization." *Studies in Conflict & Terrorism* 35 (2012): 211–228. doi:10.1080/1057610X.2012.648157. https://www.researchgate.net/publication/233456923_Integration_versus_Segregation_A_Preliminary_Examination_of_Philippine_Correctional_Facilities_for_De-radicalization/citation/download

Jones, Seth G., Catrina Doxsee, & Nicholas Harrington. "The escalating terrorism problem in the United States." Center for Strategic and International Studies, June 2020. https://csis-website-prod.s3.amazonaws.com/s3fs-public/publication/200612_Jones_DomesticTerrorism_v6.pdf

Jordan, Freddie. "ISIS reborn: Terror group forming new caliphate extending to India—Shock report." *Express*, June 11, 2019. https://www.express.co.uk/news/world/1139028/isis-latest-afghanistan-kashmir-afghanistan-update-rt-video

Joscelyn, Thomas. "Islamic state claims prison raid in Eastern Afghanistan." *FDD's Long War Journal*, August 3, 2020. https://www.longwarjournal.org/archives/2020/08/islamic-state-claims-prison-raid-in-eastern-afghanistan.php?utm_source=feedburner&utm_medium=email&utm_campaign=Feed%3A+LongWarJournalSiteWide+%28FDD%27s+Long+War+Journal+Update%29

Kaeble, Danielle, & Lauren Glaze. "Correctional populations in the United States, 2015." Bureau of Justice Statistics (NCJ 250374), December 2016. https://bjs.ojp.gov/library/publications/correctional-populations-united-states-2015

Kaplan, Ivy. "An inside look at the first US domestic deradicalization program." *Defense Post*, February 12, 2019. https://www.thedefensepost.com/2019/02/12/us-minnesota-deradicalization-program-inside-look/

Kern, Soeren. "Britain: Muslim prison population up 200%." *Gatestone Institute International Policy Council*, August 2, 2013. https://www.gatestoneinstitute.org/3913/uk-muslim-prison-population

Kheel, Rebecca. "Intel report: 121 former Gitmo detainees returned to terrorism." *The Hill*, March 7, 2017. https://thehill.com/policy/defense/322768-intel-report-121-former-gitmo-detainees-returned-to-terrorism

Kirby, Jen. "The strangest details from that report on the Dannemora Prison escape." *New York Intelligencer*. June 8, 2016. https://nymag.com/intelligencer/2016/06/how-two-inmates-escaped-from-dannemora-prison.html

Knox, Patricia, & Nika Shakhnazarova. "El Trapo—Inside El Chapol's Hellhole Prison dubbed the 'Alcatraz of the Rockies' where he'll be shut off from all contact with the outside world for the rest of his life." *The Sun*, July 17, 2019. https://www.thesun.co.uk/news/8417329/el-chapo-prison-alcatraz-rockies-jailed-life/

LaFree, Gary. "A comparative study of violent extremism and gangs." Final Report to the National Institute of Justice, 2019. National Institute of Justice, 2020.

Lefebvre, Stephane. "Perspectives on ethno-nationalist/separatist terrorism." Conflict Studies Research Center, 2003. https://www.files.ethz.ch/isn/39989/06_Aug.pdf

Legal Information Institute. "22 U.S. Code Section 1656f, Annual Country Reports" (n.d.). https://www.law.cornell.edu/uscode/text/22/2656f

Levin, Sam. "US Capitol riot police have a long history of aiding neo-Nazis and extremists." *Guardian*. January 16, 2021.

Lincoln, Abraham. Annual message to Congress, 1862. http://www.abrahamlincolnonline.org/lincoln/speeches/congress.htm

Liu, J. "Religion in prisons–A 50-state survey of prison chaplains." 2012. http://www.pewforum.org/2012/03/22/prison-chaplains-exec/

Lonas, Lexi. "Nearly a dozen correction officers injured in inmate attack at Rikers." *The Hill*, March 27, 2021. https://thehill.com/homenews/state-watch/545217-nearly-a-dozen-correction-officers-injured-in-inmate-attack-at-rikers

Long, Heather. "Who's joining ISIS? It might surprise you." *CNN*, December 15, 2015. http://money.cnn.com/2015/12/15/news/economy/isis-recruit-characteristics/index.html

Luymes, Glenda. "Violence in prisons will rise with the end of solitary confinement, warns guards' union." *Vancouver Sun*, October 21, 2018. https://vancouversun.com/news/local-news/violence-in-prisons-will-rise-with-the-end-of-solitary-confinement-warns-guards-union/

Mahoney, Charles W. "Splinters and schisms: Rebel Group fragmentation and the durability of insurgencies." pp. 345–364, November 2, 2017. doi:10.1080/09546553.2017.1374254

"Man who formed terrorist group that plotted attacks on military and jewish facilities sentenced to 16 years in Federal prison." Federal Bureau of Investigation, Los Angeles Division, March 6, 2009. https://archives.fbi.gov/archives/losangeles/press-releases/2009/la030609ausa.htm

Mann, Brian. "1 year after New York prison break, what went wrong at Dannemora?" *National Public Radio*, June 5, 2016. https://www.npr.org/2016/06/05/480820198/1-year-after-new-york-prison-break-what-went-wrong-at-dannemora

Marchese, Joseph J. "Managing gangs in a correctional facility: What wardens and superintendents need to know." *Corrections Today* 71, 1 (2009): 44–47.

McKinley, Jesse. "The prison escape that riveted the nation." *New York Times*, 2015. https://www.bing.com/search?q=McKinley%2C+The+Prison+Escape+that+Riveted+the+Nation.%E2%80%9D+New+York+Times.+2015.&form=WNSGPH&qs=SW&cvid=0c9b3129f58542999693698308f2246e&pq=McKinley%2C+The+Prison+Escape+that+Riveted+the+Nation.%E2%80%9D+New+York+Times.+2015.&cc=US&setlang=en-US&nclid=2DEBBD4602D759F6DB18632792ED4158&ts=1603452116723&wsso=Moderate

McSmith, Andy. "Jailed Islamist terrorists to be isolated in UK prisons despite risk of comparisons with Guantanamo Bay." *Independent*, August 21, 2016. http://www.independent.co.uk/news/uk/crime/isis-islamist-terrorists-isolated-in-uk-prisons-a7201101.html

Meko, Tim. "Now that Islamic state has fallen in Iraq and Syria, where are all the fighters going?" *Washington Post*, February 22, 2018. https://www.washingtonpost.com/graphics/2018/world/isis-returning-fighters/

Meredith, Charlotte. "Muslim inmates who 'beat up on prison guard demand release of radicalised women." *Express*, May 20, 2019. https://www.express.co.uk/news/uk/403320/Muslim-inmates-who-beat-up-prison-guard-demanded-release-of-radicalised-women

Merola, Linda M., & Heather Vovak. "The challenges of terrorist and extremist prisoners: A survey of U.S. prisons." *Criminal Justice Policy Review* 24 (2012): 735–758.

Miller-Idriss, Cynthia. "The global rise of right-wing extremism. Ask the expert: Professor Cynthia Miller-Idriss weighs." American University, Washington, D.C., April 3, 2019.

Morales, Mark. "Boston Marathon bomber appeals death sentence, alleging juror bias." *CNN*, December 12, 2019. https://www.cnn.com/2019/12/12/us/boston-marathon-bomber-appeal/index.html

Moser, Andrea. *Handbook on Classification of Prisoners*. United Nations Office on Drugs and Crime, 2020. https://www.unodc.org/documents/dohadeclaration/Prisons/HandBookPrisonerClassification/20-01921_Classification_of_Prisoners_Ebook.pdf

Mouras, Tamara. "Lone wolves: Are they really alone in the radicalization process?" *InHomelandSecurity.com*, February 4, 2015. https://inhomelandsecurity.com/lone-wolf-alone-in-the-radicalization-process/

Mullin, Gemma. "Muslim extremists turn prison block into 'no-go zone' as inmates fear being forced to convert." *Mirror*, April 4, 2016. https://www.mirror.co.uk/news/uk-news/muslim-extremists-turn-prison-block-7690460.

Muslim Advocates. "New report offers comprehensive view of America's Muslim prison population." July 25, 2019. https://muslimadvocates.org/2019/07/new-report-offers-comprehensive-view-of-americas-muslim-prison-population/

Myers, Lisa. "Jihad letters from prison went far, wide." *NBC News* Online, March 9, 2005. http://www.nbcnews.com/id/7140883/ns/nbc_nightly_news_with_brian_williams-nbc_news_investigates/t/jihad-letters-prison-went-far-wide/#.X2u4Jz-SlPY.

Myre, Greg. "Americans in ISIS: Some 300 tried to join; 12 have returned to U.S." *NPR*, February 5, 2018.

National Institute of Justice. "Gangs vs. extremists: Solutions for gangs may not work against extremists." NIJ.OJP.gov, October 26, 2020. https://nij.ojp.gov/topics/articles/gangs-vs-extremists-solutions-gangs-may-not-work-against-extremism

National Public Radio Staff. *Taliban Help Nearly 500 Escape from Afghan Prison*, April 25, 2011. https://www.npr.org/2011/04/25/135693601/nearly-500-inmates-escape-from-afghan-prison

Neumann, Peter R. "Prisons and terrorism: Radicalisation and de-radicalisation in 15 countries." *International Centre for the Study of Radicalisation and Political Violence*, July 2010. https://www.clingendael.org/sites/default/files/pdfs/Prisons-and-terrorism-15-countries.pdf

NIDA. "Principles." National Institute on Drug Abuse, June 16, 2020. Retrieved October 21, 2020. https://www.drugabuse.gov/publications/principles-drug-abuse-treatment-criminal-justice-populations-research-based-guide/principles.

Nomani, Asra Q. "This is Danny Pearl's final story." *Washingtonian*. (n.d.). https://www.washingtonian.com/projects/KSM/

Office of Inspector General. "Audit of the Federal Bureau of Prisons' monitoring of inmate communications to prevent radicalization." March 2020.

O'Hanlon, Michael. "The limitations of imagination." *Prepared Testimony before the House Select Committee on Intelligence,* August 4, 2004. https://www.globalsecurity.org/intell/library/congress/2004_hr/040804-ohanlon.pdf

O'Harrow, Robert Jr., Andrew Ba Tran, & Derek Hawkins. "The rise of domestic extremism in America." *Washington Post,* April 12, 2021. https://www.washingtonpost.com/investigations/interactive/2021/domestic-terrorism-data/

Paiwels, Annelies. "Rising right-wing violence and its impact on the fight against terrorism." *Vision of Humanity,* Institute for Strategic Dialogue, August 12, 2021. https://www.isdglobal.org/digital_dispatches/rising-right-wing-violence-and-its-impact-on-the-fight-against-terrorism/

Pavlo, Walter. "Will cell phones be the downfall of prisons?" *Forbes.* August 19, 2020. https://www.forbes.com/sites/walterpavlo/2020/04/19/will-cell-phones-be-the-downfall-of-prisons/?sh=bfc6d611be46

Penal Reform International, "Overcrowding." (n.d.). https://www.penalreform.org/issues/prison-conditions/key-facts/overcrowding/

Picinu, Andra. "The disadvantages of being a correctional officer." *Houston Chronicle,* March 24, 2019. https://work.chron.com/disadvantages-being-correctional-officer-10287.html

Pilkington, Ed, & Dan Roberts. "FBI and Obama confirm Omar Mateen was radicalized on the Internet." *Guardian,* June 2016. https://www.theguardian.com/us-news/2016/jun/13/pulse-nightclub-attack-shooter-radicalized-internet-orlando

Potter, Will. "Communications Management Units: The secret prisons you've never heard of, TED Talk." (n.d.). http://willpotter.com/CMU/

Qureshi, Aisha Javed. "Understanding Domestic Radicalism and Terrorism." *National Institute of Justice Journal,* August 14, 2020. https://nij.ojp.gov/topics/articles/understanding-domestic-radicalization-and-terrorism

Rabuy, Bernadette, & Daniel Kopf. "Prisons of poverty: Uncovering the pre-incarceration incomes of the imprisoned." *Prison Policy Initiative,* July 9, 2015. https://www.prisonpolicy.org/reports/income.html

"Radical inmates moved as first separation centre opens." Ministry of Justice, July 6, 2017. https://www.gov.uk/government/news/radical-extremists-moved-as-first-separation-centre-opens

"Radicalised prisoner held after French prison attack." *France* 24, May 3, 2019. https://www.france24.com/en/20190305-radicalised-prisoner-guards-french-jail-attack-jihad.

RAN Centre of Excellence, 2016. "RAN Centre of Excellence, Radicalization Research Gap Analysis" Radicalisation Awareness Network, Ran Centre of Excellence, December 2016. https://ec.europa.eu/home-affairs/sites/homeaffairs/files/docs/pages/201612_radicalisation_research_gap_analysis_en.pdf#:~:text=RAN%20RESEARCH%20PAPER%20December%202016%20Radicalisation%20Research%20%E2%80%93,European%20Union%20that%20explore%20online%20aspects%20of%20radicalisation%2C#:~:text=RAN%20RESEARCH

%20PAPER%20December%202016%20Radicalisation%20Research%20%E2%80%93,European%20Union%20that%20explore%20online%2.

Radicalisation Awareness Network. "RAN collection of approaches and practices preventing radicalisation to terrorism and violent extremism: Prison and probation interventions." 2019. https://ec.europa.eu/home-affairs/sites/homeaffairs/files/what-we-do/networks/radicalisation_awareness_network/ran-best-practices/docs/prison-and-probation-interventions_en.pdf#:~:text=However%2C%20since%202012%2C%20the%20context%20of%20terrorism%20has,EU%20over%20the%20past%20three%20years%20%281%29%20is

Rapoport, David C. "Before the bombs, there were the Mobs: American experiences with terror." *Terrorism & Political Violence* 20, 2 (2008): 167–194. doi:10.1080/09546550701856045

Real ID. Homeland Security. https://www.dhs.gov/real-id

"Release of 40 radicalized prisoners a 'major risk'—French counter-terrorism prosecutor." *RT*, May 29, 2018. https://www.rt.com/news/428162-france-radicalized-inmates-released/

"Religion in prisons–A 50-state survey of prison chaplains." Pew Research Center, March 22, 2012. http://www.pewforum.org/2012/03/22/prison-chaplains-exec/

"Research on domestic radicalization and terrorism." National Institute on Justice, January 16, 2020. https://www.nij.gov/topics/crime/terrorism/pages/welcome.aspx

Reid, Richard. (n.d.). https://www.britannica.com/biography/Richard-Reid

Reid, Richard. Fast Facts, 2016. http://www.cnn.com/2013/03/25/us/richard-reid-fast-facts/index.html

Richards, Lauren, Peter Molinaro, John Wyman, & Sarah Craun. "Lone offender: A study of lone offender terrorism in the United States (1972–2015)." U.S. Department of Justice, Federal Bureau of Investigation, Behavioral Threat Assessment Center, November 2019. https://www.fbi.gov/file-repository/lone-offender-terrorism-report-111319.pdf/view

Riechmann, Deb. "International, domestic terrorism convicts set to be released in U.S." *Los Angeles Daily News*, 2017. http://www.dailynews.com/general-news/20170805/international-domestic-terrorism-convicts-set-to-be-released-in-us

"Riot at Attica Prison, September 9, 1971." A&E Television Network, July 27, 2019. https://www.history.com/this-day-in-history/riot-at-attica-prison

"Rome memorandum on good practices for rehabilitation and reintegration of violent extremist offenders." (n.d.). August 22, 2017, https://www.thegctf.org/Portals/1/Documents/Frameworkpercent20Documents/A/GCTF-Rome- Memorandum-ENG.pdf

Rosand, Eric. "We need to prepare for the inevitable: When terrorists leave prison." *Time*, March 8, 2017. https://time.com/4715307/terrorists-get-out-of-prison/

Rosenblatt, Kalhan, Nancy Ing, & David K. Li. "Deadly shooting near Christmas Market in Strasbourg, France." *NBC News* Online, December 12, 2018.

https://www.nbcnews.com/news/world/1-dead-3-injured-shooting-strasbourg-france-german-border-n946656

Rubin, Alissa J., Adam Nossiter, & Christopher Mele. "Scores die in nice, France as truck plows into Bastille Day crowd." *New York Times*, July 14, 2016. https://www.nytimes.com/2016/07/15/world/europe/nice-france-truck-bastille-day.html

Ruschenkeo, Julia. "Terrorist recruitment and prison radicalization: Assessing the UK experiment in separation centres." *European Journal of Criminology*, February 20, 2019. https://journals.sagepub.com/doi/abs/10.1177/1477370819828946

"Salford prison van escape gang jailed for armed ambush." *BBC News* Online, April 29, 2014. http://www.bbc.com/news/uk-england-manchester-27210081

Saunders, Debra. "Padilla's life and times." *SFGate*, April 27, 2004. Retrieved July 14, 2017, from http://www.sfgate.com/opinion/saunders/article/Padilla-s-life-and-Times-3313935.php.

Schweitzer, Yoram, Aviad Mendelboim, & Yotam Rosner. "Suicide attacks in 2016: The highest number of fatalities." Institute for National Security Studies, INSS Insight No. 887, January 5, 2017. http://www.inss.org.il/publication/suicide-attacks-2016-highest-number-fatalities/

Schweitzer, Yoram, Aviad Mendelboim, & Dana Ayalon. "Suicide bombings worldwide in 2019. Signs of decline following the military defeat of Islamic state." Institute for National Security Studies, INSS Insight No. 1244, January 2, 2020. https://www.inss.org.il/publication/suicide-bombings-worldwide-in-2019-signs-of-decline-following-the-military-defeat-of-the-islamic-state/

Scott, Stewart. *Stratford Global Security & Intelligence Report*. April 8, 2010. www.stratfor.com?fn=9615985979

"Security soft targets and crowded places—Resource guide." Department of Homeland Security, Cybersecurity and Infrastructure Security Agency (CISA), April 2019. https://www.cisa.gov/publication/securing-soft-targets-and-crowded-places-resources

Shane, Leo III. "Signs of White supremacy, extremism up again in poll of active-duty troops." *Yahoo News* Online, February 6, 2020. https://news.yahoo.com/signs-white-supremacy-extremism-again-100042578.html

Shortell, David. "American Taliban released from prison, a key case for questions about radicals re-entering society." *CNN Politics*, September 27, 2019. https://www.cnn.com/2019/05/22/politics/john-walker-lindh-american-taliban/index.html

Sieczkowski, Cavan. "Gunman kills 4 in Kosher Market attack in Paris." *Huffington Post*, December 6, 2017. https://www.huffpost.com/entry/kosher-market-hostages-killed-paris-amedy-coulibaly_n_6444404

Silke, Andrew. *Prisons, Terrorism and Extremism: Critical Issues in Management, Radicalization*. London: Routledge, 2014.

Skarbek, David, & Courtney Michaluk. "To end prison gangs, it's time to break up the largest prisons." *Politico*, May 13, 2015. https://www.politico.com/agenda/story/2015/05/end-prison-gangs-break-largest-prisons-000034

Skillicorn, D., C. Leuprecht, Y. Stys, & R. Gobeil. "Structural differences of violent extremist offenders in correctional settings." *Global Crime* 16, 3 (2015): 238–258.

Smith, Alison. "Risk factors and indicators associated with radicalization to terrorism in the United States: What research sponsored by the National Institute of Justice tells us." *NIJ.ojp.gov*, National Institute of Justice, June 2018. https://www.ojp.gov/pdffiles1/nij/251789.pdf

Smith, Andy. "Jailed Islamist terrorists to be isolated in the UK prisons despite rest of comparisons with Guantanamo Bay." *Independent*. August 21, 2011.

Smith, Marc, Tracy Connor, & Richard Engel. "The ISIS files: What leaked documents reveal about terror recruits." *NBC News* Online, April 18, 2016. http://www.nbcnews.com/storyline/isis-uncovered/isis-files-what-leaked-documents-reveal-about-terror-recruits-n557411?cid=eml_onsite

Sotto, Philippe. "French prison guards protest violent work conditions." *Daily Herald*, January 16, 2018. https://www.dailyherald.com/article/20180116/news/301169877

Speckhard, Anne. "Prison: Militant jihadist recruiting grounds or refuge for rehabilitation?" *Security*, February 2019. https://www.securitysolutionsmedia.com/2019/02/12/jihadist-recruiting-grounds-refuge-rehabilitation/

Speckhard, Anne, & Ardian Shajkovci. "Prison militant jihadist recruiting grounds or refuge rehabilitation." *Homeland Security Today*, December 11, 2018. https://www.hstoday.us/subject-matter-areas/terrorism-study/prison-militant-jihadist-recruiting-grounds-or-refuge-for-rehabilitation/

Spencer, Robert. "Washington state Muslim prisoner screaming 'Allahu Akbar' hits guard on head repeatedly with metal stool." *Jihad Watch*, February 11, 2016. https://www.jihadwatch.org/2016/0213/washington-state-muslim-prisoner-scream

Stack, Liam. "Over 1,000 hate organizations are now active in the United States, Civil Rights Group says." *New York Times*, February 20, 2019. https://www.nytimes.com/2019/02/20/us/hate-organizations-rise.html

State of New Jersey, Office of Homeland Security and Preparedness. "Analysis: Al-Qaida supporters target women with female focused propaganda." September 4, 2018. https://www.njhomelandsecurity.gov/analysis/al-qaida-supporters-target-women-with-female-focused-propaganda

Stempel, Jonathan. "After two escapes, 'El Chapo" may go to supermax prison to avoid a third." *Reuters*. July 17, 2019. https://www.reuters.com/article/us-usa-mexico-el-chapo-supermax/after-two-escapes-el-chapo-may-go-to-supermax-prison-to-avoid-a-third-idUSKCN1UC142day.

Stewart, Scott. "The role of improvised explosive devices in terrorism." *Stratford WorldView*, May 23, 2013. https://worldview.stratfor.com/article/role-improvised-explosive-devices-terrorism

Stojkovic, Stan, ed. *Managing Special Populations in Jails and Prisons*, Vol. II. Kingston, NJ: Civic Research Institute Inc, 2010.

Sturgeon, William "Terrorism and 21st century corrections." *Corrections.com*, September 26, 2005. http://www.corrections.com/articles/5689-terrorism-and-21st-century-corrections

Sturgeon, William. "From Gitmo to a place near YOU!: All that glitters is not gold." *Corrections.com*, August 25, 2009.

Sturgeon, William. "Terrorism and correctional security programs." In *Guidelines for the Development of a Security Program*, by Eugene E. Atherton & Richard L. Phillips. Alexandria, Virginia: American Correctional Association, 2007.

Sturgeon, William. "17 terrorist inmates–The new challenge for correctional administrators." In *Managing Special Populations in Jail and Prisons*, Vol. II, by Stan Stojkovic, ed. Kingston, NJ: Civic Research Institute, 2010.

Sturgeon, William. "Checking for tunnels." *Corrections.com*, March 2012. http://www.corrections.com/ezine/show?id=384

Sturgeon, William. "Security new year's resolutions for 2015." *Corrections.com*, December 30, 2014. http://www.corrections.com/bill_sturgeon/?s=Operational+Functional+

Sullivan, Mike. "Terror cells: Leicestershire jail is 'no-go zone' due to Muslim extremists." *The Sun*, April 4, 2016. https://www.thesun.co.uk/archives/news/1114074/terror-cells-leicestershire-jail-is-no-go-zone-due-to-muslim-extremists/

"Suspect shouts 'hail Islamic state' before attacking Kolkata jail warder." *Hindustan Times*, December 2, 2017. http://www.hindustantimes.com/india-news/is-suspect-shouts-hail-islamic-state-before-attacking-kolkata-jail-warder/story-

Sutter, John D. "Hackers take aim at prison locks and other real-world targets." *CNN*, August 8, 2011. http://www.cnn.com/2011/TECH/web/08/08/prison.hack.stuxnet/index.html

Swain, Elise. "It's still open: Will the Guantanamo Bay prison become a 2020 issue? *The Intercept*, March 3, 2019. https://theintercept.com/2019/03/03/guantanamo-bay-carol-rosenberg-intercepted/

"Taliban help nearly 500 escape from Afghan prison." *National Public Radio*, April 25, 2011. https://www.npr.org/2011/04/25/135693601/nearly-500-inmates-escape-from-afghan-prison

"Teen lone-wolf gets 20 years in prison for plot to shoot up Texas Mall." *Homeland Security Today*, April 19, 2019. https://www.hstoday.us/subject-matter-areas/counterterrorism/teen-lone-wolf-gets-20-years-in-prison-for-plot-to-shoot-up-texas-mall/

"'Terror' prisoner numbers jump by 63 percent since 2011." *Express*, September 22, 2016. http://www.express.co.uk/news/uk/713321/Terror-prisoner-numbers-increase-63-since-2011-prison-terroism

"Terrorism plotter Jose Padilla has prison sentence extended." *The Guardian*, September 9, 2014. https://www.theguardian.com/world/2014/sep/09/jose-padilla-al-qaida-new-prison-sentence

Thompson, Cara. "Myths & facts: Using risk and need assessments to enhance outcomes and reduce disparities in the criminal justice system." National Institute of Corrections and Community Corrections Collaborative Network, March 2017. https://s3.amazonaws.com/static.nicic.gov/Library/032859a.pdf

Thompson, Don. "Leaders of White supremacist prison gang charged in killings." *Associated Press,* June 6, 2019. https://apnews.com/e2f42249d8e3492592e69f1a5b6eea24

Times of Israel Staff. "Jailbreak probe said to find 11 Gilboa prisoners started tunnel dig in November." *Times of Israel.* September 14, 2021. https://www.timesofisrael.com/jailbreak-probe-said-to-find-11-gilboa-prisoners-started-tunnel-dig-in-november/

Travers, Russell E. "The terrorist threat is not finished." *Foreign Affairs,* August 21, 2020. https://www.foreignaffairs.com/articles/africa/2020-08-21/terrorist-threat-not-finished

Travis, Alan. "UK terror arrests rise 68% to record level during year of attacks." *Guardian,* September 14, 2017. https://www.theguardian.com/uk-news/2017/sep/14/uk-terror-arrests-rise-68-record-level-during-year-attacks

"Treating offenders with drug problems: Integrating public health and public safety." *NIDA Topics in Brief,* National Institute of Drug Abuse, 2011. https://dhhr.wv.gov/bhhf/sections/programs/ProgramsPartnerships/AlcoholismandDrugAbuse

Tully, Andrew. "U.S. panel cites lack of imagination in failure to prevent 9/11 Attacks." *Radio Free Europe/Radio Liberty,* July 22, 2004. https://www.rferl.org/a/1053987.html

Turner, Nicholas, & John Wetzel. "Treating prisoners with dignity can reduce crime." *The Atlantic,* May 22, 2014. https://www.theatlantic.com/politics/archive/2014/05/treating-prisoners-with-dignity-can-reduce-crime/430962/

Tzu, Sun. *The Art of War.* Samuel B. Griffith translator, May 1, 2012. London: Duncan Baird.

U.S. Congress, House, Committee on Homeland Security. "Terror threat snapshot, 2006–2010." https://www.hsdl.org/?view&did=795868

U.S. Department of Homeland Security. "Bomb threat stand-off chart." (n.d.). https://www.hsdl.org/?view&did=4506

U.S. Department of Homeland Security. "Soft targets and crowded places, security planning, 2018–05." https://www.hsdl.org/?abstract&did=812763

U.S. Department of Justice. Office of the Inspector General Evaluation and Inspections Division. "The Federal Bureau of Prisons' monitoring of mail for high-risk inmates." September 2006, Report 1-2006–007. https://oig.justice.gov/reports/BOP/e0609/final.pdf

"Use of religion as a justification for violence." *Understanding World Religions,* October 1, 2014. https://uwreligions.wordpress.com/2014/10/01/the-use-of-religion-as-a-justification-for-violence/

Van Duyn, Donald. "Testimony." *Senate Committee on Homeland Security and Governmental Affairs and Related Agencies,* 109th Cong., September 19, 2006, https://archives.fbi.gov/archives/news/testimony/prison-radicalization-the-environment-the-threat-and-the-response.

"VERA 2R: Measuring the likelihood of violent extremist action in prison." Retrieved July 30, 2017, http://www.cep-probation.org/vera-2r-measuring-the-likelihood-of-violent-extremist-action-in-prison/

Vinograd, Cassandra, Alastair Jamieson, Florence Viola, & Alexander Smith. "Charlie Hebdo shooting: 12 killed at Muhammad Cartoon Magazine in Paris." *NBC News* Online, January 7, 2015. https://www.13danger news.com/storyline/paris-magazine-attack/charlie-hebdo-shooting-12-killed-muhammad-cartoons-magazine-paris-n281266

Vinopal, Courtney. "Should thousands of ISIS families be allowed to return home?" *PBS News Hour*, April 5, 2019. https://www.pbs.org/newshour/world/should-thousands-of-isis-fighters-and-their-families-be-allowed-to-return-home

Westrop, Samuel. "UK: Extremist chaplains and prison radicalization." *Gatestone Institute International Policy Council*, June 16, 2014. https://www.gatestoneinstitute.org/4357/uk-muslim-prison-chaplains

"White supremacist," definition. https://www.bing.com/search?q=google+dictionary

"White supremacy extremism: The transnational rise of the violent White supremacist movement." *Soufan Center*, September 2019. https://thesoufancenter.org/research/white-supremacy-extremism-the-transnational-rise-of-the-violent-white-supremacist-movement/

Williams, R. "Approaches to violent extremist offenders and countering radicalisation in prisons and probation." 2016. https://efus.eu/files/2017/04/RAN-paper-PP-group-EN.pdf

Willsher, Kim. "Charlie Hebdo survivor tells of being forced to unlock door by Gunmen." *The Guardian*, September 8, 2020. https://www.theguardian.com/world/2020/sep/08/charlie-hebdo-survivor-tells-of-being-forced-to-unlock-door-by-paris-gunmen

Wilson, Jason. "White nationalist hate organizations have grown 55% in Trump Era, report finds." *The Guardian*, March 18, 2020. https://www.theguardian.com/world/2020/mar/18/white-nationalist-hate-organizations-southern-poverty-law-center

Wilson, Jason. "How US police failed to stop the rise of the far right and the Capitol attack." *The Guardian*, January 17, 2021.

Wilson, Mark. "Prisons are breeding ground for terrorists?" *Prison Legal News*, October 15, 2011. https://www.prisonlegalnews.org/news/2011/oct/15/prisons-are-breeding-ground-for-terrorists/

Worth, Robert F. "Second attack on Iraq prison in 48 hours wounds 5 Iraqis." *New York Times*, April 5, 2005. https://www.nytimes.com/2005/04/05/world/middleeast/second-attack-on-iraq-prison-in-48-hours-wounds-5-iraqis.html

Zalman, Amy. "Jihadi or jihadist defined." *ThoughtCo*, October 16, 2019. https://www.thoughtco.com/jihadi-or-jihadist-3209289

INDEX